AAT

FOUNDATION (NVQ)

COMBINED **COMPANION** Units 21, 22, 23

Office Skills

Unit 21 Working with computers
Unit 22 Health and safety
Unit 23 Achieving personal effectiveness

BPP

PROFESSIONAL EDUCATION

Second edition May 2006
First edition 2004

ISBN 0 7517 2607 9 (previous edition 0 7517 1724 X)

British Library Cataloguing-in-Publication Data
A catalogue record for this book is available from the British Library

Published by

BPP Professional Education
Aldine House,
Aldine Place,
London, W12 8AW

Printed in Great Britain by WM Print
Frederick Street
Walsall
West Midlands, WS2 9NE

CONTENTS

INTRODUCTION

This is the second edition of BPP's Combined Companion for AAT Unit 21: Working with computers, Unit 22: Contribute to a healthy, safe and productive working environment and Unit 23: Achieving personal effectiveness. It has been carefully designed to enable students to practise all aspects of the requirements of the Standards of Competence and performance criteria, and ultimately be successful in their assessments.

We deal first with Units 22 and 23. These units have a Course Companion section (chapters 1 to 6) containing these key features:

- clear, step by step explanation of the topic

- logical progression and linking from one chapter to the next

- numerous illustration and practical examples

- interactive activities within the text itself, with answers supplied

- a bank of questions of varying complexity again with answers supplied.

The Revision Companion section contains:

- graded activities corresponding to each chapter of the Course Companion, with answers

- a practice skills based assessment for each Unit with answers.

Unit 21 is dealt with in a Combined Companion section at the end of the book. There are three chapters (chapters 7 to 9). They fully cover the Standards of competence and are highly interactive, containing numerous chapter activities and end of chapter questions, all with answers. There is also a skills based assessment for Unit 21, with answers supplied. The Unit 21 material is also designed to cover the computerised accounting requirements of NVQ Foundation Units 1 to 4.

Accounting packages

The chapters covering Unit 21 recommend that you have access to a Sage accounting package while studying the Unit. Most of the activities assume that you are doing this and can practise the tasks described as you go along. BPP can also supply additional material free of charge to lecturers, and students, for use in practical exercises. Visit http://www.bpp.com/aat/companions and follow the links.

THE STRUCTURE OF THE STANDARDS FOR UNITS 21, 22 AND 23

Each unit commences with a statement of the **knowledge and understanding** which underpin competence in the Unit's elements.

The Unit of Competence is then divided into **elements of competence** describing activities which the individual should be able to perform.

Each element includes:

(a) A set of **performance criteria**. This defines what constitutes competent performance.

(b) A **range statement**. This defines the situations, contexts, methods etc in which competence should be displayed.

(c) **Evidence requirements**. These state that competence must be demonstrated consistently, over an appropriate time scale with evidence of performance being provided from the appropriate sources.

(d) **Sources of evidence**. These are suggestions of ways in which you can find evidence to demonstrate that competence. These fall under the headings: 'observed performance; work produced by the candidate; authenticated testimonies from relevant witnesses; personal account of competence; other sources of evidence.'

The elements of competence for each of Units 21,22 and 23 are set out below. Knowledge and understanding required for the unit as a whole are listed first, followed by the performance criteria and range statements for each element. Performance criteria are cross-referenced below to chapters in this Companion.

UNIT 21 STANDARDS OF COMPETENCE

Unit 21: Working with computers

What is the unit about?

This unit is about your ability to use a computer system safely and effectively. For the first element, you will need to demonstrate that you are fully aware of your responsibilities when using a computer system and the software packages you will need.

For the second element you will be required to show an understanding of the need to keep data confidential and secure.

Knowledge and understanding

General information technology

■ The importance of carrying out simple visual safety checks on hardware and correct powering up and shutting down procedures (Element 21.1)

■ The purpose of passwords (Element 21.2)

■ How to save, transfer and print documents (Element 21.2)

■ How to take back up copies (Element 21.1)

■ Causes of difficulties, necessary files which have been damaged or deleted, printer problems, hardware problems (Element 21.1)

■ Different types of risk, viruses, confidentiality (Element 21.2)

■ Relevant security and legal regulations, data protection legislation, copyright, VDU legislation, health and safety regulations, retention of documents (Element 21.2)

The organisation

■ Location of hardware, software and back up copies (Elements 21.1 & 21.2)

■ Location of information sources (Element 21.1)

■ The organisation's procedures for changing passwords, and making back-ups (Element 21.1)

■ House style for presentation of documents (Element 21.1)

■ Organisational security policies (Element 21.2)

Element 21.1: Use computer systems and software

Performance criteria Chapter

- Perform **initial visual safety checks** and power up the **computer system** 7

- Use **passwords** to gain access to the **computer system** where limitations on 7
access to data is required

- Access, save and print data files and exit from relevant software 7,9

- Use appropriate file names and save work 7,9

- Back up work carried out on a **computer system** to suitable storage media 7,9
at regular intervals

- Close down the computer without damaging the **computer system** 7

- Seek immediate assistance when **difficulties** occur Throughout

Range statement

- **Visual safety checks**: hardware components; plugs; cables; interfaces

- **Computer system**: stand alone PC; networked system

- **Passwords**: system; software

- **Difficulties**: hardware failure; software failure; corruption of data

Element 21.2: Maintain the security of data

Performance criteria Chapter

- Ensure passwords are kept secret and changed at **appropriate times** 8

- Ensure computer program and hardware disks are kept securely located 8

- Identify **potential risks** to data from different **sources** and take steps to 8
resolve or minimise them

- Maintain **security** and **confidentiality** of data at all times 8

- Understand and implement relevant **legal regulations** 8

Range statement

- **Appropriate times** (changing passwords): on a regular basis; if disclosure is suspected

- **Potential risks**: corruption; loss; illegal copying

- **Sources (of risks)**: internal; external; viruses; poor storage facilities; theft

- **Security**: back-up copies; secure storage

- **Confidentiality**: passwords

- **Legal regulations**: data protection legislation; VDU regulations; health and safety; document retention

UNIT 22 STANDARDS OF COMPETENCE

Unit 22: Contribute to the maintenance of a healthy, safe and productive working environment

What is the unit about?

This unit is about monitoring your working environment and making sure it meets requirements for health, safety, security and effective working conditions. **You must show that you can achieve this standard of health, safety and security in all areas of your work.**

Knowledge and understanding

Health, safety and security at work

■ The importance of health, safety and security in your workplace (Element 22.1)

■ The basic requirements of the health and safety and other legislation and regulations that apply to your workplace (Element 2.1)

■ The person(s) responsible for health, safety and security in your workplace (Element 22.1)

■ The relevant up-to-date information on health, safety and security that applies to your workplace (Element 22.1)

■ The importance of being alert to health and safety hazards that affect people working in an administrative role and how to identify these (Element 22.1)

■ The common health, safety and security hazards that affect people working in an administrative role and how to identify these (Element 22.1)

■ Hazards you can put right yourself and hazards you must report (Element 22.1)

■ The importance of warning others about hazards and how to do so until the hazard is dealt with (Element 22.1)

■ Your organisation's emergency procedures (Element 22.1)

■ How to follow your organisation's emergency procedures and your responsibilities in relation to these (Element 2.1)

■ How to recommend improvements to health and safety (Element 22.1)

■ Health and safety records you may have to complete and how to do so (Element 22.1)

Effectiveness and efficiency at work

■ How the conditions under which you work can affect your effectiveness and efficiency and the effectiveness and efficiency of those around you (Element 22.2)

■ How to organise your own work area so that you and others can work efficiently (Element 22.2)

- Your organisation's requirements on how you organise your working area (Element 22.2)

- The importance of organising your work area so that it makes a positive impression on other people and examples of how to do so (Element 22.2)

- The importance of working in a way that shows respect for other people and examples of how to do this (Element 22.2)

- Conditions you can put right yourself and conditions you would have to report (Element 22.2)

- Manufacturer's instructions and your organisation's procedures for the equipment you use as part of your job (Element 22.2)

Element 22.1: Monitor and maintain a safe, healthy and secure working environment

Performance criteria	Chapter
Make sure you read, comply with and have up-to-date information on the health, safety and security requirements and procedures for your workplace	1
Make sure that the procedures are being followed and report any that are not to the relevant person	1
Identify and correct any hazards that you can deal with safely, competently and within the limits of your authority	1
Promptly and accurately report any hazards that you are not allowed to deal with to the relevant person and warn other people who may be affected	1
Follow your organisation's **emergency procedures** promptly, calmly and efficiently	2
Identify and recommend opportunities for improving health, safety and security to the responsible person	1
Complete any health and safety records legibly and accurately	2

Range statement

Emergency procedures

- Illness

- Accidents

- Fires

- Other reasons to evacuate the premises

- Breaches of security

Element 22.2: Monitor and maintain an effective and efficient working environment

Performance criteria	Chapter
■ Organise the work area you are responsible for, so that you and others can work efficiently	3
■ Organise the work area you are responsible for, so that it meets your organisation's requirements and presents a positive image of yourself and your team	3
■ Identify conditions around you that interfere with effective working	3
■ Put right any conditions that you can deal with safely, competently, within the limits of your authority and with the agreement of other relevant people	3
■ Promptly and accurately report any other conditions to the relevant person	3
■ Use and maintain equipment in accordance with manufacturer's instructions and your organisation's procedures	3

Range statement

There are no additional contextual requirements for this element.

UNIT 23 STANDARDS OF COMPETENCE

Unit 23: Achieving personal effectiveness

What is the unit about?

This unit is concerned with the personal and organisational aspects of your role. In the first element you need to show that you plan and organise your work effectively and also demonstrate that you prioritise your activities. The second element requires you to demonstrate that you work effectively with others by offering assistance, resolving difficulties, meeting deadlines, etc. In the final element in this unit you need to show that you develop yourself through leaning and acquiring new skills and knowledge.

Knowledge and understanding

Business environment

- Relevant legislation

- Sources of legal requirements

- Where to access information about new developments relating to your job role

- Employee responsibilities in complying with the relevant legislation

Methods

- Work methods and practices in your organisation

- Handling confidential information

- Establishing constructive relationships

- Why it is important to integrate your work with other people's

- Ways of identifying development needs

- Setting self-development objectives

- Development opportunities and their resource implications

- Ways of assessing own performance and progress

- Maintaining good working relationships, even when disagreeing with others

- The scope and limit of your own authority for taking corrective actions

- Use of different styles of approach in different circumstances

- Target setting, prioritising and organising work

- Work planning and scheduling techniques and aids

- Time management

- Team working

- Seeking and exchanging information, advice and support

- Handling disagreements and conflicts

- Showing commitment and motivation towards your work

- Deadlines and timescales

- Dealing with changed priorities and unforeseen situations

- Information and consulting with others about work methods

- Negotiating the assistance of others

- Co-ordinating resources and tasks

The organisation

- The organisational and department structure

- Own work role and responsibilities

- Colleagues' work roles and responsibilities

- Reporting procedures

- Procedures to deal with conflict and poor working relationships

- Where to access information that will help you learn including formal training courses

- The people who may help you plan and implement learning you may require

Element 23.1: Plan and organise your own work

Performance criteria	Chapter
■ Identify and prioritise **tasks** according to organisational procedures and regulatory requirements	4
■ Recognise changes in priorities and adapt resources allocations and work plans accordingly	4
■ Use appropriate **planning aids** to plan and monitor work progress	4
■ Identify, negotiate and co-ordinate relevant assistance to meet specific demands and deadlines	4
■ Report anticipated difficulties in meeting deadlines to the **appropriate person**	4
■ Check that work methods and activities conform to legal and regulatory requirements and organisational procedures	4

Range statement

- **Tasks**

  Routine
  Unexpected

- **Appropriate person**

  Line manager
  Project manager
  Colleague(s) relying on the completion of your work

- **Planning aids**

  Diaries
  Schedules
  Action plans

Element 23.2: Maintain good working relationships

Performance criteria	Chapter
Communicate with other people clearly and effectively, using your organisation's procedures	5
Discuss and agree realistic objectives, resources, working methods and schedules and in a way that promotes good working relationships	5
Meet commitments to colleagues within agreed timescales	5
Offer **assistance and support** where colleagues cannot meet deadlines, within your own work constraints and other commitments	5
Find workable solutions for any conflicts and dissatisfaction which reduce personal and team effectiveness	5
Follow organisational procedures if there are **difficulties in working relationships** that are beyond your authority or ability to resolve, and promptly refer them to the appropriate person	5
Treat others courteously and work in a way that shows respect for other people	5
Ensure data protection requirements are followed strictly and also maintain confidentiality of information relating to colleagues	5

Range statement

- **Communicate**

  Face-to-face
  By telephone
  By fax
  By e-mail
  By creating word-processed documents

- **Difficulties in working relationships**

  Personality
  Working style
  Status
  Work demands

- **Other people**

  Those familiar with the subject matter
  Those not familiar with subject matter

- **Assistance and support**

  Personal
  Practical

Element 23.3: Improve your own performance

Performance criteria	Chapter
Identify your own development needs by taking into consideration your current work activities and also your own career goals	6
Define your own development objectives and, where necessary, agree them with the appropriate person	6
Research appropriate **ways of acquiring new skills and knowledge**	6
Ensure that development opportunities are realistic and achievable in terms of resources and support from relevant persons	6
Review and evaluate your performance and progress and also to agreed timescales	6
Monitor your own understanding of developments relating to your job role	6
Maintain and develop your own specialist **knowledge** relevant to your own working environment	6
Undertake learning that will help you improve your performance	6

Range statement

- **Identify your own development needs**

  Through training
  Through discussions
  Self-study of relevant materials

- **Ways of acquiring skills and knowledge**

  Courses
  Internet
  Journals/trade publications
  Books
  Through colleagues
  Observation

- **Performance and progress are reviewed and evaluated**

  By self
  In conjunction with others

COURSE COMPANION
UNITS 22 & 23

chapter 1:
HEALTH, SAFETY AND SECURITY

chapter coverage 📖

In this initial chapter we consider the health, safety and security issues that you are likely to come across in your workplace and the respective responsibilities of employers and employees in these areas. The topics we shall cover are:

✍ introduction to health, safety and security issues

✍ legislation for health and safety

✍ health and safety regulations

✍ other regulations which are of relevance

✍ risk assessment by employers

✍ health and safety in your own workplace

✍ dealing with hazards in the workplace

✍ suggesting improvements to health, safety and security

Unit 22

knowledge and understanding – health, safety and security at work

- the importance of health, safety and security in your workplace

- the basic requirements of the health and safety and other legislation and regulations that apply to your workplace

- the person(s) responsible for health, safety and security in your workplace

- the relevant up-to-date information on health, safety and security that applies to your workplace

- the importance of being alert to health, safety and security hazards

- the common health, safety and security hazards that affect people working in an administrative role and how to identify these

- hazards that you can put right yourself and hazards you must report

- the importance of warning others about hazards and how to do so until the hazard is dealt with

- how to recommend improvements to health and safety

Performance criteria – element 22.1

- make sure you read, comply with and have up-to-date information on the health, safety and security requirements and procedures for your workplace

- make sure that the procedures are being followed and report any that are not to the relevant person

- identify and correct any hazards that you can deal with safely, competently and within the limits of your authority

- promptly and accurately report any hazards that you are not allowed to deal with to the relevant person and warn other people who may be affected

- identify and recommend opportunities for improving health, safety and security to the responsible person

HEALTH, SAFETY AND SECURITY

Unit 22 is about monitoring your working environment and making sure that it meets the requirements for health, safety, security and effective working conditions. The first element of the Unit concerns monitoring and maintaining a healthy, safe and secure working environment.

Feeling healthy, feeling safe and feeling secure are probably not factors that you necessarily think about at work as you are more likely to be concerned about your ability to carry out your day to day tasks, so we will start by considering the importance of these three factors in the working environment:

- health
- safety
- security

Health

How many days off work have you had this year? How many days have you gone into work feeling under the weather?

We all have days when we are not well but it is in the interests of an employer to do whatever he can to keep his employees healthy and to minimise the number of sick days. If someone is off sick then their duties have to be covered by someone else or alternatively jobs will be left unfinished until the employee returns to work. If an employee comes into work not feeling well they will generally not perform to the best of their ability.

So what can an employer do to try to keep his employees healthy? We will look at the employer's legal responsibilities later but many answers to this are common sense.

- offices are well ventilated

- offices and working areas are a reasonable temperature – not too hot or too cold

- employees are allowed regular breaks particularly if using a computer screen

- employees are provided with suitable seating and desk height

Safety

There will of course be times when employees become sick and the employer can do little about ensuring that this never happens. However an employer can attempt to ensure that his employees are safe when they are at work. Accidents will happen but a little forethought can minimise the risk of such accidents. Obviously in sectors such as the building trade or highly mechanical manufacturing, accidents are more likely to happen than in the average office. However there are again many common sense things that an employer can do to guard against accidents in an office, retail or light industrial sector.

Let us consider the types of accidents that were reported in the service sector during 2004/2005.

Types of accident	Reported numbers
Lifting or carrying objects	Almost 32,000
Slips, trips or falls	Almost 27,000
Struck by falling object	Over 10,000
Strike against fixed object	Over 4,000
Exposure to harmful substance	Over 2,000
Contact with electricity	Over 200

So even in the comparative safety of an office accidents can and will happen.

What can the employer and yourself as employee do?

- keep drawers and filing cabinets closed
- provide good lighting on stairs
- ensure there are no loose wires to trip over
- ensure there is no loose or badly fitting carpet to trip over
- wipe up any floor spillages immediately

There are many other answers but these are just a few of the common sense factors that we will be considering in this chapter.

Activity 1

Can you think of any other ways to try to ensure that accidents do not happen in an office environment?

Security

Security in a working environment has a number of aspects.

- physical security of assets such as computers or petty cash
- physical security of employees' valuables and belongings
- personal security of employees
- security of information

Security measures in an office environment can range from simple tasks to more complex procedures. Again lets think of some common sense security procedures:

- locking windows when everyone goes home
- locking away petty cash
- locking filing cabinets
- using passwords to gain access to computers
- wearing security passes at all times
- questioning and reporting any strangers in the office.

HOW IT WORKS

So now that we have considered generally the aspects of health, safety and security, lets consider a typical office scenario.

You have just started work as an accounts assistant at Southfield Electrical, a supplier of a wide range of electrical appliances to high street electrical stores. You know that your job description states that you will be dealing with invoicing, receipts and payments and other general accounting matters. It is Monday morning on the your first day at work and your supervisor has shown you to your desk and asked you to wait for a few moments before being taken to be introduced to the accountant.

You use this time to have a look around at the office and people around you. What do you notice?

- a colleague has left a desk draw open at about knee height

- a cup of coffee has been perched precariously on top of a printer

- a colleague has a post it note on his computer screen saying 'PASSWORD – FREDBLOGGS123'

- spare packs of printer paper appear to be stored on a high shelf that a normal height person could not reach

- there is about six feet of electrical cable connected to a laptop computer running across the middle of the floor

- most people appear to be wearing security passes but not everyone

What problems, from a health, safety and security perspective, could there be from the things that you have noticed?

- someone might walk into the desk draw and injure themselves or spill or drop what they are carrying

- the cup of coffee may get knocked over damaging the printer and making the floor surface slippery

- anyone could access the computer using the password on the post it note

- in order to reach the spare printer paper someone would have to stand on a chair

- someone might trip over the wire running across the floor and injure themselves

- if security passes are not generally worn, un-authorised people could get into the accounts department.

Activity 2

What types of equipment would typically be used in an office which may have a safety issue?

LEGISLATION

As we are starting to see, much of health, safety and security is about common sense; however as it is so important that workers are healthy, safe and secure in their workplace there is much legislation in this area. For the purposes of Unit 22 you only need to know 'the basic requirements of the health and safety and other legislation that apply to your workplace.' So we will now consider the requirements of this legislation. We will start by briefly describing the bodies which deal with the legislation for and policing of health and safety issues.

The Health and Safety Commission and the Health and Safety Executive are responsible for the regulation of almost all the risks to health and safety arising from work activity in the UK. Their aim is to ensure that risks to people's health and safety from changing work activities are properly controlled.

Health and Safety Commission

The HEALTH AND SAFETY COMMISSION is a government body with overall responsibility for health and safety. The job of the Commission is to protect everyone in Great Britain against risks to health or safety arising out of work activities, to sponsor research, to promote training, to provide information and an advisory service and to submit proposals for new or revised regulations and approved codes of practice.

Health and Safety Executive

The role of the HEALTH AND SAFETY EXECUTIVE is to help the Health and Safety Commission ensure that risks to people's health and safety from work activities are properly controlled. The Executive is staffed by people from a range of different backgrounds including administrators, lawyers, inspectors, scientists, engineers, technologists and medical professionals.

Legislation and Regulations

Health and safety legislation in the UK is made under the power of various Acts of Parliament. The Health and Safety at Work etc Act 1974 is the main Act which allows the Health and Safety Commission to bring in new legislation as appropriate. Some pieces of legislation are initiated by European Directives which have been agreed by all European Union Member States.

The Workplace (Health, Safety and Welfare) Regulations 1992 complete a series of six sets of health and safety regulations implementing these EC Directives and replacing a number of old laws.

Activity 3

What is the main aim of the Health and Safety Commission?

HEALTH AND SAFETY REGULATIONS

Under the Health and Safety at Work etc Act 1974 employers have a general duty to ensure, as far as is reasonably practicable, the health, safety and welfare of their employees at work. There is also a duty to non-employees who use the premises such as contractors, cleaners and visitors.

We will now summarise the main regulations that employers must follow.

Health

Ventilation   the workplace must be adequately ventilated with fresh, clean air – either natural air or a ventilation system

Temperature   in a workplace where employees are largely sitting, such as an office the temperature should be at least 16 degrees Celsius (13 degrees if the work involves physical effort)

Lighting   sufficient to enable people to work and move about safely

Cleanliness   the workplace and furniture, furnishings and fittings should be kept clean as well as floors, walls and ceilings

Waste   waste should be stored in suitable receptacles and removed as necessary

Personal space   each employee in a room should have a minimum of 11 cubic metres of free space to allow them to move about with ease

Workstations	must be suitable for the people using them and for the work – employees should be able to leave them swiftly in an emergency
Seating	should give adequate support for the lower back and footrests should be provided for workers who cannot place their feet flat on the floor

Safety

Maintenance	equipment should be maintained in efficient working order
Floor surfaces	should not have holes or be uneven or slippery
Entry/exit routes	all entry and exit routes and routes of passage must be safe
Staircases	a handrail should be provided on at least one side of every staircase
High places	if there is a danger of employees falling from a height then safety rails or other guards must be installed
Falling objects	materials and objects need to be stored and stacked in such a way that they are not likely to fall and cause injury
Glass	where necessary should be made of safety material or protected against breakage
Windows	openable windows should be capable of being opened, closed and adjusted safely and when open should not be dangerous
Doors/gates	doors and gates should be suitably constructed and fitted with safety devices if necessary
Escalators	escalators and moving walkways should function safely, be equipped with necessary safety devices and one or more emergency stop controls
Fire	fire fighting equipment must be available and escape routes must be adequately signposted

Welfare

Toilets	toilets and washing facilities should be kept clean and adequately lit and should have hot and cold or warm water, soap and clean towels or other means of drying

Water	an adequate supply of wholesome drinking water should be provided	student notes 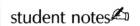
Clothes	space should be provided for workers' own clothes and as far as is reasonably practical a facility for drying clothes	
Rest areas	rest areas should be suitable and sufficient and should have enough seats with backrests and tables for the number of workers likely to use them at any one time	
Eating	there must be facilities for employees to eat in the workplace although food need not necessarily be provided	
First aid	first aid must be available normally in the form of a trained first aider and a first aid box	

OTHER REGULATIONS

There are also a number of other regulations that are relevant to this Unit which you need to be aware of.

Control of Substances Hazardous to Health 1999

This regulation, known as COSHH, requires that hazardous substances must be identified and stored in a safe manner. If necessary employees dealing with such hazardous substances must be supplied with, and must wear, suitable protective clothing.

Display Screen Equipment Regulations 1992

These are regulations for employees who use computers and VDU screens. The main regulations are:

- employees must have regular breaks
- equipment and furniture must comply with standards of safety and comfort
- employees must be offered eye tests

Reporting of Injuries, Diseases and Dangerous Occurrences Regulations 1995

These regulations are generally abbreviated to RIDDOR and require that the Health and Safety Executive must be informed on official RIDDOR forms (see Chapter 2 for more detail) of any fatal or serious injuries, dangerous occurrences or serious diseases in the workplace.

student notes✑

Activity 4

What does COSHH stand for?

So these are the main areas of legislation which apply to employers. We will now consider how an employer will take steps to ensure that he is meeting the requirements of the legislation.

RISK ASSESSMENT

If an employer is to ensure that he is satisfying the legal health and safety requirements then an assessment of the hazards and risks present in the workplace should be carried out. A RISK ASSESSMENT is nothing more than a careful examination of what could cause harm to people so that the employer can weigh up whether enough precautions have been taken or whether more needs to be done to prevent harm.

The aim is to make sure that no one gets hurt or becomes ill. A risk assessment involves identifying the hazards present and then evaluating the risks involved, taking into account existing precautions.

We must be clear here about the distinction between hazards and risks. A HAZARD is a condition that exists that could potentially cause harm, for example, electrical cable trailing across a floor to a computer. A RISK is the likelihood of this hazard causing harm, therefore with the electrical cable the likelihood that someone might trip over it.

The Health and Safety Executive have issued practical guidance on risk assessment in the work place and have set out a five step plan for carrying out such an assessment.

Five step plan

Step 1   Look for the hazards

- walk around the workplace and look afresh at what could reasonably be expected to cause harm

- ask the employees if they have noticed anything which is not immediately obvious

- examples of hazards as a guide:

  - slipping/tripping on poorly maintained floors or stairs
  - fire from flammable materials
  - chemicals
  - moving parts of machinery

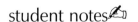

- working at height
- vehicles
- electricity and poor wiring
- dust/fumes
- noise
- poor lighting
- low temperature

Step 2   Decide who might be harmed and how

- employees in general but bear in mind in particular young workers, trainees, pregnant women and staff with disabilities

- cleaners, visitors, contractors, maintenance workers etc who may not be in the workplace all of the time

- members of the public if there is a chance that they could be hurt by the organisation's activities

Step 3   Evaluate the risks and decide whether existing precautions are adequate or more should be done

- for each significant hazard decide whether the risk is high, medium or low

- the aim is to make all risks small by adding to precautions

- ask two questions
  - 'can I get rid of the hazard altogether?'
  - 'if not, how can I control the risks so that harm is unlikely?'

- for the hazards listed do the precautions already taken meet legal requirements, recognised industry standards, good practice standards and is the risk reduced.as far as is reasonably practical?

Step 4   Record the findings

- if an employer employs more than five people then any significant findings of the risk assessment must be recorded

- write down the significant hazards and the conclusions

- the employer must tell his employees of his findings

Step 5   Review the assessment and revise it if necessary

- if a new significant hazard appears due to new machines, substances or processes add this to the assessment

- review the assessment from time to time to make sure that the precautions are still working effectively

HEALTH AND SAFETY IN YOUR WORKPLACE

Employees also have responsibilities under the Health and Safety at Work etc Act:

- to take reasonable care of their own health and safety

- to take reasonable care of the health and safety of others who might be affected by their actions

- to co-operate with the employer in order to meet health and safety requirements

Health and Safety Policy Statement

For organisations with five or more employees a written HEALTH AND SAFETY POLICY STATEMENT must exist and must be continually updated and circulated to all employees.

As an employee you have a duty to study this document and normally you will be asked to sign a form stating that you have read the Statement.

Health and Safety poster

A further responsibility of employers is to display a poster that is produced by the Health and Safety Executive or alternatively to provide a leaflet to employees. Either of these will summarise the employer's obligations under the Health and Safety Act.

Health and Safety Officer

In larger organisations there is normally a designated HEALTH AND SAFETY OFFICER whose name will normally be displayed on the Health and Safety poster. As an employee you should ensure that you know who this person is as this may be important if you need to report any health or safety issues.

DEALING WITH HAZARDS IN THE WORKPLACE

In this part of the chapter we will consider the various types of hazard that you might come across in the workplace and what you should do about them.

Procedures not being followed

We have seen that employer's have a duty to assess hazards and the risks involved with those hazards and to put in place precautions to reduce the risks of danger from these hazards. Often such precautions will take the form of procedures that employees should follow. For example, it will often be normal practice for the petty cash to be the responsibility of an individual within the accounting department and a procedure that the petty cash box should always be locked when unattended by that individual. If you notice that this procedure is not happening and that the petty cash box is being left unattended and unlocked then you should report this to your supervisor or to the accountant as this is obviously a security risk.

Hazards you can put right yourself

With some hazards you may simply be able to put them right yourself. However you must first consider whether you are safe, competent and authorised to take such action. As an example if a telephone wire has become dislodged and is now on the floor where it could be tripped over then it would be quite acceptable for you to carefully put it back into a safe place such as behind a desk.

Hazards you must report

In other cases however it will be necessary to report the hazard to the appropriate person in your organisation as you are not able or allowed to deal with the hazard directly. Having reported such a hazard it may then be necessary to warn other employees of this hazard until such time as it has been dealt with. For example, if you notice that an electric cable to one of the computers is frayed then you should report this immediately to the maintenance department or your supervisor rather than attempting to patch it up yourself. You would also warn the person whose computer it was of the situation and suggest that they used another terminal until the problem had been dealt with.

student notes✍

Warning others of potential hazards

If you discover a potential hazard that you cannot safely and immediately deal with then it is your responsibility to make sure that any other employees that are likely to come across the hazard are warned of it. If the hazard only involves an individual or a small number of people then you can warn then either verbally or by sending a memo or an e-mail. However if the hazard is of a more general nature which could affect any employee then the warning will need to be more general. For example, if the photocopier cable is frayed and the machine is not to be used until the maintenance department have dealt with it then a notice on the photocopier saying 'OUT OF ORDER – DO NOT USE' would be appropriate.

Examples of typical potential hazards

Health and safety

- open drawers and filing cabinets
- items on high shelves which may fall
- jammed photocopier
- photocopier overheating
- boxes or other obstacles in traffic routes
- boxes or other obstacles blocking emergency exits
- fire doors wedged open
- trailing wires or telephone cables
- frayed carpet
- liquid spillage on floor
- step up/down not marked
- standing on a chair to reach a high object
- lifting items which are too heavy or not bending properly when lifting
- unlabelled substance
- using harmful substance without wearing protective clothing
- rubbish not removed
- inaccessability of safety or emergency equipment

Security

- unescorted stranger on the premises
- unlocked window/exterior door
- broken lock on window/exterior door
- petty cash left unattended
- confidential files left unattended
- public knowledge of computer password
- computer program not exited but computer left unattended

HOW IT WORKS

You are again the new accounts assistant at Southfield Electrical. You have been working there for a couple of weeks and have now settled into a routine. On Tuesday of your third week you notice or are involved in the following incidents and in each case we will consider the best way of dealing with the incident.

Incident 1

You were using the photocopier when it became jammed. No one has yet explained to you how to deal with a paper jam in this machine.

As you have not been shown how to deal with a paper jam it is probably best not to have a go on your own. Instead you should try to find someone else in the office who can show you how to deal with this. If there is going to be a delay before the paper is removed then it would be worth putting a notice on the photocopier saying 'PAPER JAM – TEMPORARILY OUT OF ORDER'.

Incident 2

You notice that some new office computers have been delivered since yesterday and the boxes containing them have been piled up in front of a fire exit door.

This is potentially a serious hazard as in the case of emergency this fire exit could not be used so the boxes do need to be moved promptly. The boxes are likely to be heavy, containing computers, therefore it would not be wise to pick them up yourself. Instead you should inform your supervisor immediately.

Incident 3

You notice someone that you do not recognise, and without a security pass, packing away one of the laptop computers in the office.

In this instance the person you would probably initially approach the person and enquire what their business is in the department. This may be a member of the maintenance department who is not wearing his security pass but does then show it to you. Alternatively it could be a stranger in which case you should inform your supervisor or security immediately.

Incident 4

You notice that the lights on one of the stairwells are no longer working.

You should inform the maintenance department of this fact and also put a notice on the entrance to the stairwell saying 'LIGHT NOT WORKING – PLEASE USE OTHER STAIRS" in order to warn your colleagues of the danger.

Incident 5

You notice that an empty cup has been put dangerously close to the edge of a high shelf.

The cup could possibly be dislodged and fall on someone and therefore must be removed. Provided that you can reach the cup without endangering yourself by climbing on a chair then you should simply remove the cup and return it to the kitchen area.

Incident 6

You work late that night and are the last person to leave the accounts department and notice that one of the windows has been left open.

This is a security hazard but one that you should be able to deal with simply by shutting and locking the window.

Activity 5

If you noticed that the electrical cable to the photocopier was worn in one place and you thought that you saw a spark from the wiring what should you do?

IMPROVEMENTS TO HEALTH, SAFETY AND SECURITY

If you are aware of the types of health, safety and security issues that have been discussed in this chapter then you may notice that there are areas within the procedures of the business which could be improved in order to increase the health, safety and security of the employees and the business assets. If you do consider that there are areas which could be improved then you should discuss this with, or send a memo to, the organisation's health and safety officer.

CHAPTER OVERVIEW

- for Unit 22 there are three separate issues to consider – health, safety and security in the workplace

- it is in the employer's interest to take whatever measures he can to ensure the health and safety of his employees and the security of the organisation's and the employees' assets and of the employees themselves

- the government bodies that deal with health and safety issues are the Health and Safety Commission and the Health and Safety Executive

- the main Act of Parliament which covers health and safety is the Health and Safety at Work etc Act 1974 but under this act there are also many regulations which cover health and safety

- the employer has a general duty to ensure as far as is reasonably practicable the health, safety and welfare of his employees at work

- the employee also has a duty to take reasonable care of their own health and safety and that of others

KEY WORDS

Health and Safety Commission a government body with overall responsibility for health and safety

Health and Safety Executive body which helps the Health and Safety Commission to ensure that risks in the workplace are properly controlled

Risk assessment an employer's assessment of the hazards and risks in the workplace

Hazard a condition that could potentially cause harm

Risk the likelihood of the hazard causing harm

Health and Safety Policy Statement a statement of the policy of the organisation regarding health and safety issues

Health and Safety Officer the person within the organisation with overall responsibility for health and safety issues

- in forming a health and safety policy an employer should carry out a risk assessment which considers any hazards that exist in the workplace, the risk that such hazards will cause harm and the extent of any precautions that should be taken against these hazards

- any employer with more than five employees must produce a health and safety policy statement which must be circulated to all employees

- if an employee notices a hazard within the workplace then they must either put it right if they are capable of doing so and authorised to do so or if not report the hazard to the appropriate person

- once a hazard has been reported it will normally be necessary to warn other employees of the existence of the hazard until it has been dealt with

- all employees should be alert to potential hazards in the workplace and should make any suggestions for improvements to health and safety to the relevant person

HOW MUCH HAVE YOU LEARNED?

1   Give examples of why security within the workplace is so important.

2   What is the main Act of Parliament which governs health and safety issues?

3   Under the health and safety regulations what are the answers to each of the following questions?

    i)   In an office what is the minimum air temperature?

    ii)   What is the minimum allowed amount of space per employee in the workplace?

    iii)   If employees work largely seated what are the requirements regarding their seats and posture?

    iv)   What are the requirements regarding rest areas?

4   What does RIDDOR stand for?

5   Distinguish between a hazard and a risk.

6   What are the five steps in the Health and Safety Executive's guidance on employers carrying out a risk assessment?

7   Explain how you would deal with each of the following potential hazards in your workplace.

    i)   An open drawer which you have just tripped up over but have not really hurt yourself.

    ii)   A small step up from one area of the office to another which you have noticed a number of colleagues have stumbled and tripped on.

    iii)   A colleague who deals with the payroll regularly leaves his computer screen active when he leaves the office for his lunch break.

chapter 2:
DEALING WITH ACCIDENTS AND EMERGENCIES

— chapter coverage 📖 —

This chapter deals with the general procedures for dealing with various types of emergency in the workplace and any health and safety records that might have to be completed. The topics we shall cover are:

✎ dealing with accidents

✎ Reporting of Injuries, Diseases and Dangerous Occurrences Regulations 1995

✎ evacuation procedures

✎ dealing with a fire

✎ dealing with a breach of security

KNOWLEDGE AND UNDERSTANDING AND PERFORMANCE CRITERIA COVERAGE

knowledge and understanding – health, safety and security at work

- your organisation's emergency procedures

- how to follow your organisation's emergency procedures and your responsibilities in relation to these

- health and safety records you may have to complete and how to do so

Performance criteria – element 22.1

- follow your organisation's emergency procedures promptly, calmly and efficiently
- complete any health and safety records legibly and accurately

DEALING WITH ACCIDENTS

Unfortunately, however careful an employer and his employees are and however good the health and safety precautions are, there is always the chance that an employee will have an accident at work. If you are that employee, or if you have witnessed such an accident it is important that you are aware of the procedures that must be followed.

Legal requirements

As far as accidents at work are concerned the law requires that any major accidents, dangerous occurrences (such as near misses) and any diseases in the workplace must be reported. This aspect will be considered later in the chapter.

Health and safety policy statement

In the Health and Safety Policy Statement the following should normally be covered and of course communicated to all employees:

- the names of qualified first aiders
- where the first aid box is
- where the ACCIDENT BOOK is and how to fill it in
- guidance on manual handling and lifting items.

Accident book

If the employer has more than ten employees then by law the employer must keep an accident book where the details of all accidents must be reported.

It is important that all injuries are recorded accurately in the accident book. This is to protect both the employee and the employer. If the accident was due to some form of negligence by the employer then the employee may be able to take legal action against the employer. However, if the accident was the fault of the employee if the details have been recorded the employer will be better protected against any such claim.

Minor accidents

As an employee you have a duty to take reasonable care of your own health and safety and that of others. However, if a minor accident does happen in the workplace it is important to know as an employee, whether you are the injured party or not, the procedures to be followed.

If you are witness to an accident that takes place it is important to stay calm and to follow identified procedures.

Firstly find a qualified first aider and the first aid box. Offer any assistance that you can but do not carry out first aid unless you are qualified to do so. Try to remember as much about the incident as possible as these details must be recorded in the accident book. Finally report the accident to someone in authority in your office.

HOW IT WORKS

One morning you are at work in the accounts department at Southfield Electrical when one of your colleagues, Janis Jones, stumbles in her new high heeled shoes whilst carrying a tray of hot cups of coffee. Some of the coffee spills onto her arm and she is clearly in some considerable pain having dropped the tray and the other cups. You are at the desk nearest to where the accident took place and you immediately go to her assistance.

You sit Janis down in the nearest chair and ask around for a first aider. Fortunately Kelly McDonald has just arrived at work and she is the first aider so you call her over immediately. She takes Janis to the bathroom to run the wound under cold water and asks you to fetch the first aid box which is kept in a cupboard in the office kitchen. Kelly then dresses the wound and decides that hospital treatment is not necessary.

You then make an entry in the accident book and inform the office supervisor of the incident in a memo. Your name is Sean Taylor and you were the only witness to the accident. Today's date is 20 October 2006 and the accident happened at 9.35 am.

Accident Book

Date	Name of injured person	Details of accident (time, place, description and witnesses)	First aid treatment	Further action required
20/10	Janis Jones	9.35 am Accounts department Slipped in shoes carrying tray of coffees Witness – Sean Taylor	Minor burn dressed	Kelly McDonald to redress wound in two days

student notes✎

Activity 1

Why is it important for both the employer and the employee that an accident is reported correctly in the accident book.

REPORTING OF INJURIES, DISEASES AND DANGEROUS OCCURRENCES REGULATIONS 1995

In the previous chapter we considered the requirements of the Reporting of Injuries, Diseases and Dangerous Occurrences Regulations known as RIDDOR. Any such instances must be reported to the Health and Safety Executive on the appropriate RIDDOR form.

The instances that must be reported are:

- death or major injury – this includes any major fractures, amputations, dislocations, loss of sight, burns, electrocution and chemical poisoning. This relates to an employee, self-employed person or member of public on the premises

- OVER THREE DAY INJURIES – injuries that require being off work for three days or more

- work related diseases – examples might include Repetitive Strain Injury (RSI), skin diseases, lung diseases and infections such as legionnaires disease

- DANGEROUS OCCURRENCES – incidents which could have resulted in injury eg. explosions, collapses, radiation, vehicle collisions.

HOW IT WORKS

Southfield Electrical supplies a wide range of electrical appliances and as such there is a large amount of moving of appliances in the stores department. The Health and Safety Policy Statement provides detailed guidance on the lifting and handling of equipment and the procedures are that mechanical lifting equipment should be used on all occasions for loading appliances into lorries for delivery.

Pete Thomas has worked in the stores department for a year now and upon his employment he read and signed the Health and Safety Policy Statement. However on 4 October 2006 at about 5.15pm he persuaded a colleague, Len Watts, to help him to load a tumble dryer by hand as all of the mechanical devices were in use at the time and it was near the end of the day.

The tumble dryer slipped from their grasp and landed on Pete's lower leg and foot. The first aider, Kelly McDonald, was called immediately and arrived on the scene. Pete was in a great deal of pain and could not possibly walk. He was carried to Len Watts' car and taken straight to the local Accident and Emergency department. Here he was discovered to have broken his left ankle and will be in hospital overnight with at least four weeks' recovery time at home.

How is this dealt with?

Obviously an entry must be made in the accident book. This will probably include, as further recommendations, a proviso that the recommended safety precautions are stressed to all employees in the stores department.

A further issue here is that Southfield Electrical will have to comply with RIDDOR (see above). As this is an injury resulting in more than three days off work then Southfield must telephone the local Health and Safety Authority, which will be the local authority, to inform them of the nature of the accident, the person involved and the nature of their business.

Southfield must also complete the RIDDOR accident report form within ten days. A copy of the completed form is given below. The form has been completed by Kay Farrow, the Human Resources Manager, at Southfield Electrical.

student notes

Health and Safety at Work etc Act 1974
The Reporting of Injuries, Diseases and Dangerous Occurrences Regulations 1995

HSE
Health & Safety
Executive

Report of an injury or dangerous occurrence

Filling in this form
This form must be filled in by an employer or other responsible person.

Part A

About you
1 What is your full name?

KAY FARROW

2 What is your job title?

HUMAN RESOURCES MANAGER

3 What is your telephone number?

030 3379

About your organisation
4 What is the name of your organisation?

SOUTHFIELD ELECTRICAL

5 What is its address and postcode?

INDUSTRIAL ESTATE
BENHAM
DR6 2FF

6 What type of work does your organisation do?

ELECTRICAL APPLIANCE SUPPLIER

Part B

About the incident
1 On what date did the incident happen?

04 / 10 / 06

2 At what time did the incident happen?
(Please use the 24-hour clock eg 0600)

17.15

3 Did the incident happen at the above address?

Yes ✓ Go to question 4

No ☐ Where did the incident happen?

☐ elsewhere in your organisation - give the name, address and postcode

☐ at someone else's premises - give the name, address and postcode

☐ in a public place - give the details of where it happened

If you do not know the postcode, what is the name of the local authority?

4 In which department, or where on the premises, did the incident happen?

STORES DEPARTMENT

Part C

About the injured person
If you are reporting a dangerous occurrence, go to Part F.
If more than one person was injured in the same incident, please attach the details asked for in Part C and Part D for each injured person.

1 What is their full name?

PETER THOMAS

2 What is their home address and postcode?

14 SOUTH STREET
BENHAM
DR6 7PQ

3 What is their home phone number?

030 2142

4 How old are they?

26

5 Are they
✓ male?
☐ female?

6 What is their job title?

STORE KEEPER

7 Was the injured person (tick only one box)
✓ one of your employees?
☐ on a training scheme? Give details:

☐ on work experience?
☐ employed by someone else? Give details of the employer:

☐ self-employed and at work?
☐ a member of the public?

Part D

About the injury
1 What was the injury? (eg fracture, laceration)

FRACTURE

2 What part of the body was injured?

LEFT ANKLE

3 Was the injury (tick the one box that applies)

☐ a fatality?

☐ a major injury or condition? (see accompanying notes)

☑ an injury to an employee or self-employed person which prevented them doing their normal work for more than 3 days?

☐ an injury to a member of the public which meant they had to be taken from the scene of the accident to a hospital for treatment?

4 Did the injured person (tick all the boxes that apply)

☐ became unconscious?

☐ need resuscitation?

☐ remain in hospital for more than 24 hours?

☑ none of the above?

Part E

About the kind of accident

Please tick the one box that best describes what happened, then go to part G.

☐ Contact with moving machinery or material being machined

☐ Hit by a moving, flying or falling object

☐ Hit by a moving vehicle

☐ Hit by something fixed or stationary

☑ Injured while handling, lifting or carrying

☐ Slipped, tripped or fell on the same level

☐ Fell from a height
How high was the fall?

☐ _____ metres

☐ Trapped by something collapsing

☐ Drowned or asphyxiated

☐ Exposed to, or in contact with, a harmful substance

☐ Exposed to fire

☐ Exposed to an explosion

☐ Contact with electricity or an electrical discharge

☐ Injured by an animal

☐ Physically assaulted by a person

☐ Another kind of accident (describe it in part G)

Part F

Dangerous occurrences

Enter the number of the dangerous occurrence you are reporting. (The numbers are given in the Regulations and in the notes which accompany this form.)

Part G

Describing what happened

Give as much detail as you can. For instance
- the name of any substance involved
- the name and type of any machinery involved
- the events that led to the incident
- the part played by any people.

If it was a personal injury, give details of what the person was doing. Describe any action that has since been taken to prevent a similar incident. Use a separate piece of paper if you need to.

> Mr Thomas and a colleague, Mr L Watson, were manually loading a tumble dryer onto a lorry when it slipped from their grasp and landed on Mr Thomas's left leg and foot resulting in a broken ankle.
>
> It is our policy that mechanical equipment should always be used for loading appliances and this has been stressed to all employees in the stores department.

Part H

Your signature

K Farrow

Date

09 / 10 / 06

Where to send the form

Please send it to the Enforcing Authority for the place where it happened. If you do not know the Enforcing Authority, send it to the nearest HSE office.

For official use
Client number   Location number   Event number

☐ INV   REP ☐ Y ☐ N

EVACUATION PROCEDURES

In certain circumstances it may become necessary to evacuate the building in which you work. For example:

- on the discovery of a fire
- after receiving a bomb threat
- a suspected gas leak
- suspected anthrax discovered in the post

Your organisation should have clear procedures as to how the building should be evacuated and these should be communicated to each employee and clearly displayed in the building. As an employee you should ensure that you are aware of the EVACUATION PROCEDURES, the route you should take and where you should go.

The employer should also ensure that there are regular evacuation drills so that every employee is familiar with the procedure.

When an evacuation takes place either as a drill or in response to a real emergency there are a number of basic procedures that each employee should follow:

- leave the building by the designated route as quickly as possible but staying calm at all times (remember that in a fire the lifts should not be used)

- go immediately to the designated assembly point and ensure that any visitors or others on the premises who do not know where to go are directed

- pay particular attention to any people being evacuated with special needs for example wheelchairs or those with other disabilities

- respond when your name is called by your supervisor or the Safety Officer who will have a list of all employees who were in the building

- do not return to the building until instructed to do so by a senior official or the Safety Officer.

Activity 2

On hearing the fire alarm go off in your office what procedures should you follow?

DEALING WITH A FIRE

In most working environments it is possible that a fire could start. The main potential causes of a fire in the workplace are:

- electrical fires from equipment, appliances or faulty wiring

- smoking

- flammable materials coming into contact with heaters, sparks or cigarettes

- flammable substances overheating

Regulations

In the UK employers are subject to the Fire Precautions Act 1971 and the Fire Precautions (Workplace) Regulations 1997 (amended 1999). Under these regulations employers must:

- provide an appropriate number of suitable fire extinguishers

- install fire detectors and fire alarms where appropriate

- train employees how to deal with fighting a fire – ie explaining which type of fire extinguisher to use

- provide adequate and well signed emergency routes and exits

- communicate evacuation procedures to employees

- ensure that all fire fighting equipment is regularly maintained.

Fire extinguishers

The employer has a duty to instruct employees in how to use fire fighting equipment. Fire extinguishers should be provided but it is also important that employees are aware that different types of extinguishers are only suitable for some types of fire.

Water extinguisher	Use for wood, paper, textiles Do not use for flammable liquids or electrical fires
Carbon dioxide extinguisher	Use for flammable liquids or electrical fires Do not use for wood, paper, textiles
Powder extinguisher	Use for all types of fire Do not use on computers as these will be ruined

Activity 3

A small fire has started in a waste paper bin that is full of paper. What type of fire extinguisher could be used to put out this fire?

Fire prevention

Employees have a responsibility to help in the initial prevention of fires. Much of this is common sense but there are some basic principles of fire prevention that should be considered:

- keep the workplace clear of combustible materials or waste

- keep rubbish away from smoking areas or machinery that is likely to get hot

- never obstruct a fire escape route

- never prop open Fire Doors – these are fire resistant and are designed to stay shut unless escaping through them

- make sure that all Fire Exit signs can be seen

- only smoke in designated smoking areas

- ensure that any flammable materials or substances are properly stored.

Activity 4

Why should a fire door never be propped open?

DEALING WITH A BREACH OF SECURITY

We considered security in the previous chapter and saw that in a working environment it has a number of aspects:

- physical security of assets such as computers or petty cash
- physical security of employees' valuables and belongings
- personal security of employees
- security of information

Employees have a duty to be alert to breaches of security such as:

- doors or windows being left unlocked

- sensitive information being left unattended

- strangers being allowed in the workplace

- individuals in the workplace under false pretences – such as bogus computer engineers

In the case of an unrecognised person in the workplace it is an employee's duty to try to discover what their purpose is. If there is any suspicion that this person is not in the workplace for a valid reason then you should either contact your supervisor immediately or in extreme cases call for the Security department of the organisation in order to have the intruder escorted off the premises.

CHAPTER OVERVIEW

- the organisation's Health and Safety Policy Statement should state the names of qualified first aiders, where the first aid box is, where the accident book is and how to fill it in and guidance on manual and lifting techniques

- if an employer has more than ten employees then an accident book must be kept in which details of all accidents are recorded

- if there is a death or major injury, an injury which keeps an employee off work for more than three days, a work related disease or a dangerous occurrence then this must be recorded on a RIDDOR form and reported to the Health and Safety Executive

- any organisation should have clear procedures, which are communicated to the employees, on how to safely evacuate the building in the event of an emergency

- employers have a number of regulations regarding fire precautions which must be adhered to

- fire extinguishers must be provided and employees should be informed regarding the types of fire extinguisher which should be used on different types of fire

- employees have a general responsibility to help in the initial prevention of fires

- employees should be vigilant with regard to any breaches of security which may have consequences for the security of the assets of the organisation, the assets of the employees, the safety of the employees or the security of information.

KEY WORDS

Accident book a book in which details of any accident in the workplace should be recorded

Over three day injury an injury to an employee that requires them to be off work for three days or more

Dangerous occurrence an incident which could have resulted in injury

Evacuation procedures an organisation's procedures for ensuring that all employees safely leave the building in case of an emergency

HOW MUCH HAVE YOU LEARNED?

1   What must normally appear in an organisation's Health and Safety Policy Statement regarding accidents in the workplace?

2   If an employer has more than ten employees what must be kept by that employer in the case of an accident in the workplace?

3   If you are a witness to an accident in the workplace what procedures should you follow?

4   One morning in your office a colleague, Gwen Franks, trips up a small step between two offices whilst carrying some empty coffee cups. She falls over, dropping the coffee cups which break. Gwen has a small gash in her arm which is bleeding from a broken piece of china. Ken Jones, the office first aider, comes to her assistance and tends to the wound and dresses it. The wound does not require further medical attention at this time but Ken says that he will check it in two days' time and redress it if necessary.

Your name is Paul Fish and you witnessed the accident and have been asked to complete an entry in the accident book. Today's date is 22 November and the time of the accident was 9.20am.

Complete your entry in the accident book given below.

Date	Name of injured person	Details of accident (time, place, description and witnesses)	First aid treatment	Further action required

5   According to the Reporting of Injuries, Diseases and Dangerous Occurrences Regulations 1995:

i)   what is a dangerous occurrence?

ii)   what is an over three day injury?

iii)   what might be classified as a work related disease?

6   What procedures should be followed if your office manager announces that the building must be evacuated immediately as there has been a telephone bomb threat made against your organisation?

chapter 3:
EFFECTIVENESS AND EFFICIENCY

chapter coverage 📖

This chapter covers Element 22.2 which deals with the monitoring and maintenance of an effective and efficient working environment. The topics we shall cover are:

✍ effectiveness and efficiency in the workplace

✍ organisation of your own work area

✍ maintaining an effective and efficient working environment

✍ dealing with office equipment

KNOWLEDGE AND UNDERSTANDING AND PERFORMANCE CRITERIA COVERAGE

knowledge and understanding – effectiveness and efficiency at work

- how the conditions under which you work can affect your effectiveness and efficiency and the effectiveness and efficiency of those around you

- how to organise your own work area so that you and others can work efficiently

- your organisation's requirements on how you organise your working area

- the importance of organising your work area so that it makes a positive impression on other people and examples of how to do so

- the importance of working in a way that shows respect for other people and examples of how to do this

- conditions you can put right yourself and conditions you would have to report

- manufacturers' instructions and your organisation's procedures for the equipment you use as part of your job

Performance criteria – element 22.2

- organise the work area you are responsible for, so that you and others can work efficiently

- organise the work area you are responsible for, so that it meets your organisation's requirements and presents a positive image of yourself and your team

- identify conditions around you that interfere with effective working

- put right any conditions that you can deal with safely, competently, within the limits of your authority and with the agreement of other relevant people

- promptly and accurately report any other conditions to the relevant person

- use and maintain equipment in accordance with manufacturer's instructions and your organisation's procedures

EFFECTIVENESS AND EFFICIENCY IN THE WORKPLACE

Element 2 of Unit 22 is all about maintaining an effective and efficient working environment. Therefore, we need to start with consideration of what is meant by effectiveness and efficiency in the workplace.

EFFECTIVENESS is all about getting the job done. You will be effective at work if you can carry out the tasks that are assigned to you. In terms of the organisation as a whole this will be viewed to be effective if it achieves its objectives such as profit targets, sales targets and a motivated workforce.

EFFICIENCY is about getting the job done with the minimum amount of resources. This means ensuring that the tasks that are undertaken are done in the quickest manner and with the minimum possible use of resources.

HOW IT WORKS

Let's take an example. You are Sean Taylor and you are the new accounts assistant at Southfield Electrical. One of your tasks is to write to potential suppliers asking for quotations regarding price, delivery terms, discounts etc.

You will be able to do this effectively if you know who you are writing to, exactly why and you have your computer terminal switched on. You can do it efficiently if you check the letter thoroughly before printing it out. If you printed it before checking for errors then you would have to print it out a second time once the errors had been spotted – not efficient in terms of either time or printer paper!

Activity 1

Your task this morning is to prepare a batch of sales invoices on the computer. Give two examples of how you would carry out this task effectively and efficiently.

Effectiveness versus efficiency

In some cases it is perhaps necessary to find a balance between effectiveness and efficiency. A manager may be very efficient and cut costs and save time but if this leads to demotivation of his team and a fall in their productivity then his behaviour is not necessarily effective. It is important to strike a balance between efficiency and effectiveness.

Effectiveness, efficiency and other employees

It is also important to appreciate that your own effectiveness and efficiency, or lack of it, may well affect your colleagues. Often within an organisation one employee will carry out a task which will then be passed on to another employee in order to process it further. If the first employee does not carry out the tasks effectively and efficiently then this may mean that the next employee in line has to wait for the task to be finished before they can do their element of the process.

HOW IT WORKS

One of your tasks at Southfield Electrical is to list any cheques received in the post each morning. This listing is then passed on to the cashier Ron Howard for entry into the cash receipts book and updating of the debtors ledger. He can only do his daily task once you have finished yours.

Therefore if you do not finish the cheque listing early on in the morning or if you mislay the cheque listing for the day this will have an affect on Ron's work for the day as well.

Activity 2

When one of your colleagues was out of the office on his lunch break you answered his telephone and took down details of an urgent message from a customer. When your colleague returns from lunch what should you do?

ORGANISATION OF YOUR OWN WORK AREA

What is your WORK AREA?

- your desk and chair and probably your computer terminal

- shelving units above your desk

- the surrounding area, for example, waste bin, filing cabinets etc

- any work flow routes that you frequently use such as to cross the office to a centralised filing system

- the space around your desk and filing cabinets.

The aim is to organise this work area not only so that you can work effectively and efficiently but also so that those around you can work effectively and efficiently.

Lets start with the furniture. Your desk and chair should be the right height for each other to ensure that you have a comfortable working position. Your computer screen, keyboard and mouse should be positioned in such a way that you do not have to twist your body to use it and the screen should be in a position where there is no glare from the screen caused by lighting or sunlight.

You should ensure that any equipment that you regularly use, such as a calculator or your telephone, are readily to hand and not buried under piles of papers. Any files that you require on a frequent basis should ideally be in a filing cabinet that is close to your desk.

In order to ensure effectiveness and efficiency your work area should be organised and neat and tidy. You must be able to find equipment and papers that you need to carry out your work with the minimum amount of effort. You should be able to find any forms or stationery that you regularly use quickly. Ideally they should be available from a draw near your desk.

Activity 3

Have a look around the area that you are working in at the moment. Is there any ways in which you could organise it better?

Organisational requirements

On the whole the organisation of an employee's work area will be the responsibility of the individual employee. However, care should be taken to ensure that any organisational requirements are met.

For example, the organisation may have rules regarding the amount of personal trivia that is displayed in the work area such as photographs of family and friends, posters or postcards. This will often depend upon the type of work environment in which you work. In a large open plan office which rarely receives visits from external parties such as customers, suppliers, the public etc then it might be quite acceptable to have family photographs or amusing postcards displayed providing of course that they are also acceptable to those working around you.

However, in an office that is regularly visited by customers an air of efficiency and organisation is required and this may lead to organisational restrictions on the type or amount of personal possessions allowed in the workplace.

There may not be any formal 'rules' regarding personal items in your work area but there may be informal understandings. You can discover the employer's views of personalising your work area by asking colleagues or your line manager or simply by observing the work areas of your colleagues to find out what is appropriate.

Clearly an employee will be expected to tidy away any documents being used, particularly any sensitive documents, at the end of the day. However in some organisations there may be a CLEAR DESK POLICY which requires that everything must be cleared from your desk top at the end of the day. This is one way of attempting to ensure organised working practices that is popular within some organisations.

Positive impression

Your work area, will to some degree, define you to your colleagues and any customers etc that visit you. If your desk is tidy and documents are filed away this gives an impression of a tidy mind and efficient employee. Conversely an untidy desk with documents strewn around your desk gives the definite impression of someone who is not effective and efficient at work. If you have taken a telephone message for a colleague then you must be able to find it on your desk when your colleague returns – it should not be buried under piles of paper and files.

MAINTAINING AN EFFECTIVE AND EFFICIENT WORKING ENVIRONMENT

There are many factors that will contribute to an effective and efficient working environment and if any of these factors or conditions are not right then it will be necessary to either put them right yourself or report any that you cannot put right. In determining whether or not you can put a condition right you must consider whether you can deal with it safely and competently and whether it is within your authority to put it right.

Examples of conditions in the workplace that may not be contributing to effectiveness and efficiency include the following:

- temperature in the office – too hot or too cold
- lighting – natural or artificial
- sunlight and reflection
- noise
- not enough space
- queues for services such as using the photocopier or fax
- flickering computer screens

When attempting to deal with factors such as these it is also important to consider the effect of putting something right on other employees in the environment. What suits you may not necessarily suit your colleagues. For example, if you think that the office is too warm and you are beginning to feel drowsy perhaps the answer is to open a window. However, if this leaves a colleague in a draft or blows a colleague's papers off their desk then it was not necessarily the right way to deal with the situation.

HOW IT WORKS

You are Sean Taylor and you are the new accounts assistant at Southfield Electrical. You work in an open plan office with seven other accounting staff and you report to the accountant, Jenny Faulkner.

You have noticed the following problems and are considering how to deal with them.

Problem 1

One of your colleagues, Amy Bartlett, constantly has Radio 1 playing on a small portable radio. You sometimes find it hard to concentrate with the background noise and also feel that customers and suppliers may be able to hear the music when they are on the telephone to you.

The first approach here is to talk to Amy and explain that you find it hard to concentrate with the radio playing and ask if she could turn it off or at least down. If you get no positive response from this and it continues to be a problem you will need to explain the problem to Jenny Faulkner the accountant.

Problem 2

In the afternoons you find that the sun shines directly onto your computer screen making it very hard to read.

You may find that by changing the positioning or angle of your computer screen that you can deal with this matter yourself. However, if not, then you should explain the problem to Jenny who may be able to authorise an anti glare device for your screen or a blind for the window.

Problem 3

As the day wears on, with computers on all day, you find that the office gets very warm in the afternoons and you feel a little drowsy. You have seen that the airconditioning system controls, which are near your desk, are set for 22 degrees.

Clearly you can simply turn the temperature on the airconditioning system down. However, this should not be done without consulting your colleagues first. Only if they are in agreement that it is too hot in the afternoons should you alter the temperature.

Problem 4

You find that a lot of documents that you need to refer to on a regular basis are filed in a large centralised filing cabinet at the furthest end of the office to your desk and you spend a lot of time walking up and down the office. Most of your other colleagues appear to have to use this filing cabinet as well but you think it would be much more efficient to move it nearer to your desk.

It is unlikely that you would have the authority to move a large filing cabinet and although it is inconvenient for you, it may be the best place for the office as a whole. Therefore you should not do anything yourself; instead explain the problem and your suggested solution to Jenny and she will take the decision whether it is to be moved or not.

Activity 4

You are working in your office one afternoon and the sun shining through the window is directly in your eyes. There is a blind on the window but you have never seen it shut.

What should you do?

DEALING WITH OFFICE EQUIPMENT

During the course of your work it is likely that you will find yourself needing to use a variety of office equipment. Typically this might include:

- your computer
- photocopier
- fax machine
- binding machine
- guillotine
- calculators

Obviously the use of a calculator is fairly straightforward but for the more complex machines you must make sure that when using them you follow your organisation's instructions and any manufacturer's instructions. This is not only for your own safety and efficiency but also in order to safeguard the machinery which should not be misused.

HOW IT WORKS

The photocopier in Southfield Electrical's accounts department is clearly new and very high-tech! You have been shown how to make basic photocopies and the instructions on the top of the photocopier for other functions such as double sided photocopying, clearing a paper jam and making enlargements have been pointed out to you. You have also spotted a notice on the wall behind the photocopier – 'TONER MUST ONLY BE CHANGED BY RON HOWARD'.

One day you find that you are doing a lot of photocopying of sales invoice documentation. The following instances occur:

- the 'paper jam' symbol starts to flash
- the 'toner needs replacing' symbol starts to flash

What should you do?

Paper jam

Carefully read the instructions on the top of the photocopier on how to deal with a paper jam. If you think that you understand them then follow them through and remove the jammed paper. However, if you have any doubts about how to deal with this or you get stuck in the process then ask for help from one of your colleagues. Once you have been shown how to do this safely and without damaging the machine you should be able to do it on occasions in the future.

Toner

There is clearly an organisational requirement that only Ron Howard should change the toner in the machine therefore you should find Ron and ask him politely if he could do this for you.

Activity 5

You are in the process of printing out a number of letters that you have drafted to suppliers. In the course of the printing the 'out of ink' symbol flashes on the printer.

What should you do?

CHAPTER OVERVIEW

- effectiveness in the workplace is the ability to do the tasks that are set

- efficiency in the workplace is carrying out the tasks using the minimum possible time and other resources

- not only should employees work effectively and efficiently but they should ensure that their actions also allow other employees to work efficiently and effectively

- it is the employee's responsibility to organise his work area in order to be able to work effectively and efficiently. The work area is generally a desk, chair, shelving, filing, computer, stationary and the surrounding area

- some organisations will often have either a formal or informal policy concerning the degree of personalisation that employees can have in their work area. It is important to follow any organisational policies regarding the work area as a professional impression is required.

- some factors or conditions affecting the ability to work effectively and efficiently can be put right by individual employees with the agreement of colleagues. However other conditions may need to be reported rather than dealt with directly by employees.

- employees may often be required to use various types of office equipment. For their own safety and in order to safeguard the equipment it is important that manufacturers' instructions and any organisational policies regarding the equipment are followed.

KEY WORDS

Effectiveness The ability to get the job done

Efficiency getting the job done with the minimum amount of resources

Work area your desk, chair, surrounding furniture and space and any work flow routes

Clear desk policy an organisational policy that all desks must be left clear at the end of each working day

HOW MUCH HAVE YOU LEARNED?

1   Explain what is meant by:

    i)   effectiveness in the workplace
    ii)   efficiency in the workplace

2   Explain how your effectiveness and efficiency, or lack of it, could affect other employees. Give an example of how this could happen.

3   i)   Give examples of what might make up your work area
    ii)   Explain the importance of organisation of your work area

4   Most employees like to personalise their work area with personal objects. Explain how appropriate this may or may not be in:

    i)   an accounts department where there are rarely any visits from non-employees

    ii)   in an office which is open to the public as it is behind the reception area

5   Explain how you would deal with each of the following situations:

    i)   You come into the office in the morning and notice that the temperature gauge states that the office temperature is only 14 degrees. You do not have access to the thermostat.

    ii)   A fluorescent light bulb is flickering over your desk making it hard to see and concentrate.

    iii) Overnight the cleaners have moved your computer screen to a different part of your desk where the light reflects on the screen making if difficult to read.

    iv) The office becomes stuffy and you want to open the window however the office is on a major road and with the window open there is a great deal of traffic noise.

    v)   You have run out of filing space in your filing cabinet and notice that a new filing cabinet has been delivered and is sitting outside the accountant's office unused.

6   If you are using the fax machine in your office for the first time explain why it is important to either read any written instructions on how to send a fax or to seek help.

chapter 4:
PLANNING AND ORGANISING WORK

chapter coverage 📖

This is the first chapter which deals with Unit 23 which is concerned with the personal and organisational aspects of a student's role in the workplace. This chapter deals with Element 23.1 which requires students to show that they can plan and organise their work effectively and prioritise their activities. The topics we shall cover are:

✍ what is involved in a job

✍ routine tasks and unexpected tasks

✍ setting priorities

✍ dealing with changes in priorities

✍ planning aids

✍ time management

✍ seeking assistance

✍ external legal constraints on working practices

✍ handling confidential information

KNOWLEDGE AND UNDERSTANDING AND PERFORMANCE CRITERIA COVERAGE

knowledge and understanding – the business environment

- relevant legislation
  - copyright
  - data protection
  - equal opportunities
- sources of legal requirements
  - data protection
  - companies acts
- employee responsibilities in complying with relevant legislation

knowledge and understanding – methods

- work methods and practices in your organisation
- handling confidential information
- target setting, prioritising and organising work
- work planning and scheduling techniques and aids
- time management
- team working
- showing commitment and motivation towards your work
- deadlines and timescales
- dealing with changed priorities and unforeseen situations
- informing and consulting with others about work methods
- negotiating the assistance of others
- co-ordinating resources and tasks

knowledge and understanding – the organisation

- the organisational and departmental structure
- own work role and responsibilities
- reporting procedures

Performance criteria – element 23.1

- identify and prioritise tasks according to organisational procedures and regulatory requirements

- recognise changes in priorities and adapt resources, allocations and work plans accordingly

- use appropriate planning aids to plan and monitor work progress

- identify, negotiate and co-ordinate relevant assistance to meet specific demands and deadlines

- report anticipated difficulties in meeting deadlines to the appropriate person

- check that work methods and activities conform to legal and regulatory requirements and organisational procedures

YOUR JOB

When you are at work you will have a job to do which is more than likely to be made up of a variety of different tasks. However, within an organisation it is not necessarily as simple as just performing those tasks.

If you worked on your own, for example as a self-employed decorator, then the constraints on you would be fairly limited. You could choose which jobs you wanted to take on, decide when to do each job and turn down other jobs if you felt you did not have the time for them. However, you still might not be totally free to 'do your own thing'! Suppose that a client calls you to complain about a painting job that you did yesterday now that the paint has dried. The client says that she will not pay you until you have painted over areas where the colour beneath is showing through. You will probably have to break off from the job you are doing today in order to rectify yesterday's job in order to be paid.

Within an organisation there are likely to be many more constraints and pressures which you will have to deal with as part of carrying out the tasks that form part of your job.

Job description

A basic but important element of being able to work effectively is knowing exactly what is required of you and what you are not necessarily expected to do. In most cases an employee will be given a JOB DESCRIPTION when they first join the organisation. This should include a job title and an outline of the tasks that are required of the employee in the daily carrying out of the job. This job description will have been produced by management within the context of the objectives of the organisation and the roles of other employees within the organisation.

Reporting procedure

When you work within an organisation you are not working in isolation. You will have colleagues, managers of varying levels of seniority and possibly employees to whom you can delegate tasks. As part of an employee's job description it is common for the REPORTING PROCEDURE for that role to also be detailed. Who are you doing tasks for? Who needs the data or documents next? Who are you providing information for?

The precise reporting procedure will differ from organisation to organisation depending upon the organisational structure of the business. In a very small business all employees may report directly to the owner of the business. In a large multi-national company there could be various organisational structures covering the entire organisation, each country, each site or each department.

However, in the types of organisation that most students are likely to work there are likely to be one or a number of managers to whom the employee is due to report. Most commonly most work is done for your LINE MANAGER. This is normally the head of your particular department or team. In an accounts department this is likely to the accountant or financial controller or it could be the general office manager.

If you were working on a particular project, for example preparing costings for a major new product launch, then you may find that you are reporting to the particular PROJECT MANAGER.

You may also find that on occasions you are required to do a one-off job for a particular manager to whom you do not normally report. For example, the sales manager might have requested a break down of sales by geographical area in which case you would be reporting directly to the sales manager.

It is important for you to know who you are reporting to particularly as the Performance Criteria for this element require you to report any difficulties to the appropriate person.

HOW IT WORKS

We will continue with the case study of Sean Taylor at Southfield Electrical. He is the new accounts assistant and when he started work he was given the following job description.

JOB DESCRIPTION

Job title: Accounts assistant

Job summary: General financial and management accounting duties

Job content: Opening post
Preparing daily cheque listing
Obtaining quotes from suppliers
Preparing sales invoices from despatch notes
Prepare credit notes from goods returned notes
Prepare monthly sales summary
Checking purchase invoices to goods received notes

Reporting structure: Accountant – Jenny Faulkner

Accounts supervisor/cashier – Ron Howard

Accounts assistant – Sean Taylor

Hours: 9.00am to 5.30pm Monday to Friday

1 hour for lunch

Training: Necessary training to be provided

Prepared by: Head of personnel

ROUTINE TASKS AND UNEXPECTED TASKS

Much of a day at work will revolve around the carrying out of the ROUTINE TASKS that will have been detailed in the employee's job description. Some of these will be daily tasks, such as opening the post and dealing with incoming e-mails. Other tasks may be weekly tasks such as paying suppliers' invoices. Other tasks may be monthly tasks such as preparing the bank reconciliation statement.

HOW IT WORKS

We will return to Sean Taylor and expand upon his duties that were listed in his job description.

Every day Sean is required to open the post in the morning. Any cheques that are received from customers must be listed by him and the cheque listing given to Ron Howard. If any purchase invoices are received from suppliers these must be kept by Sean as he is required to check them against goods received documentation during the week and once checked hand them over to Ron Howard each Friday morning for payment.

Sean must put any other post received into the in-tray of the relevant person each morning.

During the course of each day Sean will receive despatch notes from the stores department for goods which have been sent out to customers. Each day Sean is required to prepare sales invoices for these despatch notes which are then sent to Jenny Faulker, the accountant, for checking by the end of each day in order for them to be sent out to the customers the next day.

Sean will also receive goods returned notes from the stores department and by the end of each week must have produced, and sent to Jenny Faulkner, a credit note for each goods returned note.

At the end of each month Jenny Faulkner requires a listing of all of the invoices and credit notes sent out during the month.

A number of times a week Sean will receive purchase requisitions which have been authorised by Jenny Faulkner and his task is to write to any suppliers listed requesting quotations regarding price, delivery terms, discounts etc.

All copy invoices, credit notes, purchase invoices and purchase requisitions should be filed each day.

As office junior Sean is also required to ensure that there is always tea, coffee, milk, biscuits etc in the office kitchen.

We can therefore summarise the routine tasks that Sean must carry out each week.

Daily	Open post
	Prepare cheque listing
	Distribute other post
	Check e-mails and respond
	Prepare sales invoices
	Filing

During the week	Check purchase orders – ready for Friday morning
	Send out purchase quotation request letters
	Prepare credit notes

Monthly	Prepare sales invoice/credit note listing

Unexpected tasks

As well as the general, routine tasks that are part of your everyday job you may well also be asked to perform other unexpected tasks. These may be one-off jobs for a more senior staff member, cover for an employee who is off sick or being instructed by a manager to help a colleague with a task in order to meet a deadline.

Such UNEXPECTED TASKS are part of general working life and although they may appear to make a mess of your day or your week you will need to fit them into your work schedule.

Activity 1

Distinguish between routine tasks and unexpected tasks and give two examples of each.

Urgent tasks and important tasks

Some of both your routine tasks and the unexpected tasks will be URGENT TASKS. This means that the task needs to be done for a deadline in the very near future. For example, perhaps the marketing director needs a breakdown of sales by product for a meeting first thing tomorrow morning.

Other tasks might be classified as IMPORTANT TASKS. These are tasks that are your responsibility to complete but they may not necessarily be urgent tasks.

Activity 2

Distinguish between urgent tasks and important tasks and give two examples of each.

SETTING PRIORITIES

Even with routine tasks it will be necessary to determine in what order those tasks must be carried out but when unexpected tasks are introduced as well then it becomes even more important. This process of determining the order in which tasks should be carried out is known as PRIORITISING. So how do you go about determining the order in which to carry out your allotted tasks?

Clearly urgent tasks are more important than non-urgent tasks. Equally important tasks are more important than unimportant tasks. Therefore, the tasks that are to be carried out can be split into four categories in order of priority:

Urgent and important

These are tasks that must be done in the very near future and which are important to yourself and to other people in the organisation. For example, if you are asked to produce a report for a manager for a meeting tomorrow morning.

Urgent but not important

These are tasks which if not done will not be a major problem but they are necessary and are required to be done in the near future. If there is no milk in the kitchen then no one can have tea or coffee – not the end of the world but also not good for employee morale!

Not urgent but important

These are tasks which are important and must be done but they do not necessarily have to be started immediately as there is a little time before they are due. For example, if today is Monday and you have been asked for some product costings for the production director for Friday.

Not urgent and not important

These are tasks that are not required to be done for any particular timescale. They must be done but can be done at any time when perhaps you are less busy. For example, routine tasks such as packing up out of date files to be stored in the archives.

HOW IT WORKS

As well as Sean's routine tasks that were detailed earlier in the chapter he has discovered a number of other tasks that are required of him today, Thursday, when he came into work this morning:

- there is only about half an inch of milk in the fridge and it is his responsibility to replace it

- Jenny Faulkner has left a note on his desk saying that she needs the November sales figures by lunchtime for a meeting with the managing director

- Kelly McDonald requires the copies of the cheque listings for the last two weeks by Friday lunchtime

Remember that Sean also has his routine duties to carry out. How should he plan his day?

To start with Sean should prioritise both his routine and unexpected tasks according to their urgency and importance.

Urgent and important

Unexpected task   November sales figures for Jenny Faulkner

Routine tasks   Opening the post
                        Producing the daily cheque listing
                        Distributing post
                        Checking e-mails

Although these routine tasks as not as important as the job for Jenny they are still important as Sean's colleagues rely on him performing these tasks – Ron Howard needs the cheque listing, his colleagues need their post and Sean needs to check that there are no urgent and important e-mails to attend to.

Urgent but not important

Unexpected task – the milk needs replacing – this should be just a quick trip to the shop but certainly ranks behind the urgent and important jobs. Your colleagues may disagree therefore you may be able to persuade one of them to do you a favour and go to the shop for the milk!

Not urgent but important

Unexpected task   photocopy the cheque listings for the last two weeks for Kelly McDonald

Routine tasks   Prepare sales invoices

Check that purchase invoices will be ready for Friday morning

Check that all credit notes have been prepared

Sean's day is now organised with the tasks undertaken in the order given above.

Activity 3

It is 4.00 pm on Friday afternoon and you are in the process of printing off the sales invoices for the day that are to be checked by the accountant and must be sent out this evening. Your supervisor approaches you and asks you to print out a confidential report that she requires for a meeting on Monday at 12.00 noon. There is only one printer in the accounts department and you estimate that there is still another 30 minutes of sales invoice printing and that the report will take about two and half hours to print.

What should you do?

CHANGES IN PRIORITIES

Just because you have planned your tasks for a day or a week does not mean that they are fixed in stone. As other unexpected tasks come along then you may well need to change your priorities and therefore the order in which you carry out your tasks.

HOW IT WORKS

Sean Taylor has been working hard in the accounts department at Southfield Electrical this Thursday morning and by 11.30 am he has produced the November sales figures for Jenny, opened the post, prepared the cheque listing and distributed the post. He also managed to persuade Kelly McDonald to go and buy the milk. However, he was just about to check his e-mails when Jenny Faulkner comes over to his desk.

She tells Sean that Sam Piper, another accounts assistant, has had to be sent home after feeling very ill. One of Sam's most urgent tasks today had been to prepare statements for two large customers who are querying the amount that they owe. As Sean has done this before Jenny asks him if he will do this for Sam and get them to her by 4.00 pm for checking and sending out in the post tonight.

Sean now has to change his priorities as this task is both urgent and important.

His day will now look like this:

- prepare customer statements by 4.00 pm at the latest

- check e-mails – deal with any that are urgent

- photocopy the cheque listings for the last two weeks for Kelly McDonald

- prepare sales invoices for the day

- check that purchase invoices will be ready for Friday morning

- check that all credit notes have been prepared

A pretty full day!

Activity 4

An accounts assistant has the following routine daily duties:

- enter sales invoices/credit notes in computer in batches
- enter purchase invoices/credit notes in computer in batches
- enter cash receipts in computer
- enter cheque payments in computer
- print daily cheque run
- deal with customer queries
- file all sales and purchases invoices and credit notes

Today is Thursday and there are three notes on the accounts assistant's desk when she arrives for work:

- from the accountant asking for a statement to be sent to a large customer today – all post must be in the mail out tray by 4.00pm

- from a colleague asking for the balances on the accounts of eight customers which he requires for a meeting at 10.00am tomorrow

- from the personnel manager asking you to attend a meeting in her office at 3.00pm.

How would the accounts assistant prioritise her tasks for the day?

PLANNING AIDS

So far we have been looking at how to prioritise the tasks that are required of you for the day. However good your memory it is far better to write down your prioritised tasks than simply to keep them in your head as you run the risk of forgetting something. There are a variety of PLANNING AIDS ranging from very simple to more complex that can help you to ensure that all of your tasks are completed and are completed on time.

To do list

The simplest form of planning aid is a TO DO LIST or tick list. Here you simply write down each task that is required of you for the day, preferably in prioritised order. Then as each task is completed tick it off from the list – the satisfying part!

At the end of the day if there is anything left unticked on the to do list then it must be carried over to tomorrow's to do list and fitted into tomorrow's tasks and priorities.

Diaries

Keeping a DIARY is useful way of ensuring that events or meetings are not missed. Diaries can be paper-based or electronic and can be used in combination with to do lists. The purpose of the diary is to make a note of any scheduled event or meeting as soon as you know about it and then to refer to the diary on a regular basis to ensure that you do not miss the event or meeting. For example, if you have a scheduled performance evaluation with the personnel director next Wednesday at 2.00 pm then this would be entered into your diary and your tasks organised around this meeting.

Planning schedules

PLANNING SCHEDULES are used for more complex tasks or projects. They tend to be used when the project involves a number of separate tasks and some of those tasks must be completed before others can be started. As a simple example if you want your car serviced by the end of the month then you must make an appointment for the service probably two weeks or so earlier. Therefore the telephone call making the appointment must take place by the middle of the month.

HOW IT WORKS

Jenny Faulkner has to produce the quarterly cost accounts for the quarter ending 30 November for the managing director by Monday 13 December. From experience she knows the following:

- once she has all of the information to hand it will take her two full days, around her other tasks to produce the accounts

- she will need a variety of information from the accounts assistants and this will take them two days to prepare

- the typing of the accounts can be done in half a day and then there will be another half day of proofing and checking

- the accounts must then be sent to the general office for binding which will take a further day.

If Jenny is to have the accounts on the managing director's desk by the morning of Monday 13 December she will have to start work on this project some time in advance of this. So she draws up a planning schedule by working backwards through the process based upon the assumption that the cost accounts are to be fully completed and bound up by the end of Friday 10 December.

Friday 10 December – binding
Thursday 9 December – typing and proofing
Tuesday 7 and Wednesday 8 December – preparation time
Friday 3 December – request information from accounts assistants

However, having drawn up this draft planning schedule Jenny then realises that she is out of the office all day on Tuesday 7 December at meetings. Therefore she will need to be working on the accounts by Monday 6 December and therefore must request the information from the accounts assistants on Thursday 2 December.

The final schedule for the preparation of the cost accounts will therefore be:

	December						
	Thur	Fri	Mon	Tues	Wed	Thurs	Fri
	2	3	6	7	8	9	10
Request information	X						
Receive information			X				
Preparation of accounts				X	X		
Typing and proofing						X	
Binding							X

From this Jenny will also be able to warn the typist that the cost accounts will need typing on Thursday 9 December and warn the general office that the accounts will be sent for binding on Friday 10 December.

Activity 5

You have been asked to prepare a report for your manager which must be with him on Wednesday 22 August. You will need to requisition some files for this which will take a day to arrive. You estimate that the research will take you three days and the analysis required another two days. The report will be with the typist for a further day and then you will need one final day for checking and proofing.

Prepare a planning schedule for preparation of this report.

Action plans

An ACTION PLAN is an even more detailed planning tool which can be used for complex and usually longer term projects. It will contain a lot of detail and will be monitored on a regular basis to ensure that things are going to plan or, if they are not, how the situation can be rectified. An action plan will normally contain the following:

- details of each task which is part of the project
- start date of each task
- completion date for each task
- person responsible for each task
- in some cases the expected and actual costs

HOW IT WORKS

Each year Southfield Electrical publish an updated glossy brochure and price list. This involves a number of activities and the action plan devised by the marketing director, whose responsibility this is, has been reproduced below:

Activity	Date to be started	Date completed	Responsibility	Budgeted cost	Actual cost
Book printer	1 Nov	1 Nov	KM		
Book photographer	1 Nov	1 Nov	KM		
Draft text	15 Nov		JG		
Photo shoot	20 Nov	20 Nov	JG	£2,800	£3,000
Proof photos	6 Dec		HD		
Proof text	8 Dec		HD		
Send to printer	10 Dec		HD	£22,000	
Proof printer's copy	15 Dec		HD		
Receive from printer	2 Jan		JG		
Mail to customers	3 Jan		JG	£1,800	

Monitoring plans

Plans are all well and good but the unexpected does happen and things do not always go to plan. Therefore, it is important that schedules and action plans are carefully monitored to ensure that everything is going to plan or to change the plan if necessary. For example, in the action plan above it is the responsibility of JG to draft the text of the brochure which was due to be started on 15 November. This text is needed for proofing by 8 December and it is now 30 November. The marketing director is likely to check with JG that the draft is well underway and ensure that it will be ready for 8 December or if there are problems find JG help with this task.

TIME MANAGEMENT

In this chapter so far we have talked about planning and scheduling your tasks in order to make sure that the tasks are completed as and when they should be. This is a matter of TIME MANAGEMENT.

You only have a certain number of hours at work and in that time you have to achieve a number of set tasks. By working efficiently and effectively and by planning your tasks, as we have seen, then you should be able to produce the work that is required of you. However, there will be occasions when this may not be possible.

A DEADLINE is a set time when a task must be completed. It is important to realise that a deadline will be set for a reason. Some are obvious reasons. The sales director has a meeting with a large customer this afternoon and needs a printout of the sales to this customer for the last six months. Obviously he must have the figures before he goes into the meeting.

Other reasons for deadlines may not appear to be so obvious. Your line manager has asked for some figures for Wednesday. The reason she has asked for the figures on Wednesday is that she has to write a report based upon those figures for the production director which must be on his desk by Monday morning. Your line manager knows that it will take her at least two days to complete the report.

Missing deadlines

As deadlines are set for a reason then if you fail to complete the task by the deadline then this is going to have an affect on the person who has asked you to complete the task. If you missed the deadline in the two examples above the sales director will not have the information required for the meeting and your line manager will in turn most likely miss her deadline of producing the report by Monday morning.

There will, of course, be occasions when it will become apparent to you that you are not going to meet a deadline. This could be for a number of reasons:

- your other deadlines mean that your workload is too much to finish everything on time

- colleagues who are providing you with information have failed to meet their deadlines to you

- you simply have not worked hard enough.

Reporting problems in meeting deadlines

Whatever the reason – if you think that you cannot meet a deadline then you must report this immediately to the appropriate person. The appropriate person may be your line manager, a particular project manager or a colleague who is relying on you completing your work on time.

It is never easy to admit to someone that you are not able to complete a task on time but it is important that you do as soon as you anticipate difficulties for two main reasons:

- the manager or colleague expecting the work may find that if the deadline is missed then they in turn will miss a deadline set for them which they must report immediately

- a manager may be able to ensure that factors are changed in order that you can meet the deadline.

This second point is particularly important. Provided that you report any anticipated difficulties in meeting a deadline early enough there are things that can be done to help:

- the manager can put pressure on any other employees that are holding you up by not producing the information

- the manager can lighten your existing workload in order to free up time to meet the deadline

- the manager can provide you with additional resources, such as extra computer time or another colleague's time.

Activity 6

If you think that you will not be able to meet a deadline, why is it important to report this to the appropriate person immediately?

SEEKING ASSISTANCE

In some instances you may realise that it is going to be extremely difficult or impossible to meet a deadline but that it would be possible if additional resources were made available to you. What is important here is that you can:

- recognise that assistance is required
- identify the assistance required
- negotiate for that assistance
- co-ordinate the assistance given

Recognising assistance is required

The first stage is to recognise that you are not going to be able to complete the assignment without some additional help. It may be that you have too many tasks with similar deadlines or you do not have the available resources to achieve the deadline or the deadline is simply too close and there are not enough hours available. Be prepared to admit to yourself that the deadline is not possible.

Identify the assistance required

If you are to get the assistance required in order to meet a deadline then you must be aware of the resources that you need. This may be extra time to get the task done yourself, additional computer time or help from a colleague or someone who works for you.

Negotiate the assistance

If there are other employees in the organisation that report to you and that you routinely delegate work to then these employees are the obvious choice if more man hours are required. However, in most cases it is likely that you will have to approach the line manager or project manager with a clear idea of the assistance that you require and attempt to negotiate that assistance. You will need to explain specifically why you need the assistance and precisely what is required. The manager may well then be able to free up computer time or allow another employee to help you with the task.

Co-ordinate the assistance

Once you have been granted the assistance that you require it is important that this does help you not hinder you. It is also important to ensure that the fact that you are being assisted does not disrupt the performance and tasks of the person providing the assistance.

EXTERNAL LEGAL CONSTRAINTS ON WORKING PRACTICES

In this chapter so far we have been considering some of the internal constraints which will lead to problems with completing the tasks that are required for you to perform your job effectively. However, you must also be aware of external constraints on how you carry out the tasks involved in your job in the form of legal requirements.

For Unit 23 you need to be aware of legal requirements relating to:

- copyright
- data protection
- equal opportunities
- Companies Acts

Copyright

This is a complex area of law covered by the Copyright, Designs and Patents Act 1988. The basic principle of the law is that written and electronic materials must not be copied for either business or personal use. There are of course exceptions but the general rule is that if material is marked with the international copyright symbol © then this material cannot be copied for widespread distribution without written permission from the copyright owner. This applies to written material as well as computer software.

Data Protection

The Data Protection Act 1998 is concerned with protection of individuals and PERSONAL DATA that is held about them in either manual or electronic form. If an organisation processes such personal data, such as information about customers – name, address, telephone number, credit ratings etc, then it must register with the Data Protection Commission.

The Data Protection Act sets out eight guiding principles to ensure that personal data is handled correctly. These principles state that personal data should be:

1   obtained and processed fairly and lawfully

2   held only for specified purposes

3   adequate, relevant and not excessive for those purposes

4   accurate and kept up to date

5   not be kept for longer than is necessary

6   available to the individual whose data is being held

7   kept securely

8   not be exported to countries outside the European Union unless it will be adequately protected in that country

Equal opportunities

As an employee you have a responsibility under equal opportunities legislation not to discriminate or show any prejudice against people due to their sex, race, religion, age or any disability.

Companies Acts

The Companies Acts provide much legislation regarding the manner in which external financial statements are produced and when annual financial statements must be produced by companies.

There are also legal rules regarding the retention of business records which must normally be kept for at least six years. For accounting records this is so that they can be inspected if required by HM Revenue and Customs.

HANDLING CONFIDENTIAL INFORMATION

In the course of your work you will come across a variety of confidential information. You must be extremely careful how you deal with this information.

Details of customers and suppliers must not be disclosed to anyone outside the organisation. Any personal details, for example payroll details, about employees must be kept strictly confidential.

Activity 7

How would you deal with each of the following requests and why:

   i)   a customer asks for the address and telephone number of another customer

   ii)   a colleague asks you for the home address of two other employees as you work in the personnel department

   iii) a colleague asks what personal data is held about her on the company's computer records

CHAPTER OVERVIEW

- an employee's job will usually consist of a variety of tasks which will normally be detailed in a job description which will include who the employee reports to for the various tasks

- on a daily basis employees will normally report to their line manager but for specific projects reporting may be to a project manager or some other specific manager

- an employee's job will be made up of a number of daily, weekly, monthly routine tasks but also other unexpected tasks which they are required to perform

- tasks can be categorised as urgent or non-urgent and important or unimportant when setting priorities as to which order the tasks should be carried out

- employees must be able to deal with changes in priorities and therefore changes to their planned work schedule

- there are a variety of planning aids that can be used in order to ensure that all tasks are completed on time – these include to do lists, diaries, planning schedules and action plans

- completing all tasks on time within the available working hours is a matter of good time management

- if deadlines are set then they are set for a reason and should be met – however if an employee considers that they will not be able to meet a particular deadline then this should be reported to the relevant manager immediately

- if an employee feels that a deadline cannot be met then it is important to recognise that assistance is required, identify the assistance required, negotiate for that assistance and co-ordinate the assistance given

KEY WORDS

Job description a written summary of the main duties and tasks required as part of a particular job

Reporting procedure who an employee reports to in their job

Line manager the head of department or person most directly responsible for your work

Project manager the manager running a particular project

Routine tasks the general daily, weekly, monthly tasks which make up a job

Unexpected tasks other non-routine tasks that an employee will be expected to perform as part of their job

Urgent tasks tasks for which there is a deadline in the near future

Important tasks tasks which affect others and the organisation, for which you are responsible

Prioritising ordering tasks according to their degree of urgency and importance

Planning aids written methods of organising tasks and projects

To do list list of tasks to be done where each task is ticked off when completed

Diary a written record of the date and time of events and meetings

Planning schedules written records of plans for more complex tasks or projects

Action plan detailed record of all of the tasks involved in a complex project – normally includes start and finish dates and responsibility for each task

Time management ensuring that work is carried out efficiently and effectively so that all tasks are completed on time and within the time available

Deadline a set time when a task must be completed

Personal data data held in manual or electronic form about an individual

CHAPTER OVERVIEW cont.

- there are some external constraints on employees' working practices provided by the law

- under copyright law any copyrighted written or electronic material should not be copied for either business or personal use

- under the Data Protection Act 1998 there is considerable protection for individuals regarding any personal data that is held about them in either manual or electronic form

- under equal opportunities laws an employee has a responsibility not to discriminate against people due to sex, race, religion, age or disability

- employees should take great care when handling or being in possession of confidential information.

HOW MUCH HAVE YOU LEARNED?

1 What is meant by the term 'reporting procedure'?

2 What is a line manager?

3 If each task that an employee is required to perform is classified as urgent or not urgent and important or not important in what order would the employee carry out the tasks?

4 An accounts assistant has the following routine duties:

- open the morning post

- pass any cheques received to the cashier

- deal with e-mails

- deal with any employee petty cash claims

- enter sales invoices/credit notes daily in batches into computer system

- match purchase invoices to goods received notes daily and pass to the accountant for authorisation

- file sales invoices/credit notes daily

- file paid purchase invoices weekly every Friday

Today is Friday 27 September and having opened the post and passed the cheques to the cashier you get a telephone call from the accountant to say that one of your colleagues is not coming in today due to sickness and you need to enter the weekly purchase invoices into the computer before the end of the day. You also have a pile of about 20 purchase invoices that need to be matched to GRNs before the end of the day.

It is now 10.30am. What would be the order in which you would carry out the tasks for the day (assume that no employees need to have petty cash claims dealt with yet).

5 Continuing from the previous task. By the time you have taken your lunch break you return to your desk at 1.30pm. You have already entered the sales invoices, credit notes and purchase invoices into the computer system and therefore you are fairly relaxed about the rest of your day. However there are two notes on your desk when you return from lunch.

Please can I have a summary of the petty cash book for the last month for a meeting first thing on Monday morning

Thanks

Accountant

Please call Harry Featherstone, salesman. He has an urgent petty cash claim that he needs to make.

You call Harry Featherstone and arrange for him to come in to see you at 2.30 pm. You estimate that the petty cash summary will take an hour and a half and you must leave the office at 5.30pm this evening.

How would you schedule your afternoon?

6   Discuss the purpose of three different types of planning aid.

7   You have been asked to prepare a report on the payment patterns of 12 of your organisation's largest customers. The information for the current month will not be available until Tuesday 5 April. However, the information for earlier months is to be collated by a colleague and she thinks that this will take her two days. The report should take you about four days to prepare on your computer around your other tasks. You should be able to work for two days without the current month information. Six copies of the report are required for a Board meeting on Friday 8 March at 2.00pm. You estimate that it will take three hours to print and collate the copies of the report.

Prepare a planning schedule for production of this report.

8   You have been asked to prepare a report on materials costs over the last six month period. This is required for the production manager for a meeting at 10.00am on Wednesday 14 May. The basic information is to be collated by an accounts assistant who has said that the information will be ready for you by the end of Thursday 8 May. You know that you are out of the office on Monday 12 May on a training course and your estimate is that the report will take you two working days to complete.

i)   Prepare a planning schedule for production of this report.

ii)   On Wednesday 7 May you check with the accounts assistant that the information will be ready for tomorrow but he has apologised and said that due to being off sick on Monday and Tuesday the earliest that he can get the required information to you is Friday lunchtime. What should you do?

9   What are the eight guiding principles of the Data Protection Act 1998?

chapter 5:
MAINTAINING GOOD WORKING RELATIONSHIPS

chapter coverage

In this chapter we shall consider the benefits and the problems of working as part of a team with a number of other people either as part of a department or section or as part of a special project team.

We will also consider methods and styles of communication with other members of your team and other employees and managers.

Finally we will consider the problem of disagreements or conflicts within the workplace or within teams and how such conflicts can be resolved.

The topics we shall cover are:

✍ team working in general

✍ working as a team

✍ communication methods

✍ communication and content

✍ styles of communication

✍ dealing with conflicts

✍ grievance procedures

knowledge and understanding – methods

- establishing constructive relationships
- why it is important to integrate your work with other people's
- maintaining good working relationships, even when disagreeing with others
- the scope and limit of your own authority for taking corrective actions
- use of different styles of approach in different circumstances
- team working
- seeking and exchanging information, advice and support
- handling disagreements and conflicts
- deadlines and timescales

knowledge and understanding – the organisation

- the organisational and department structure
- colleagues' work roles and responsibilities
- procedures to deal with conflict and poor working relationships

Performance criteria – element 23.2

- communicate with other people clearly and effectively, using your organisation's procedures

- discuss and agree realistic objectives, resources, working methods and schedules and in a way that promotes good working relationships

- meet commitments to colleagues within agreed timescales

- offer assistance and support where colleagues cannot meet deadlines, within your own work constraints and other commitments

- find workable solutions for any conflicts and dissatisfaction which reduce personal and team effectiveness

- follow organisational procedures if there are difficulties in working relationships that are beyond your authority or ability to resolve, and promptly refer them to the appropriate person

- treat others courteously and work in a way that shows respect for other people

- ensure data protection requirements are followed strictly and also maintain confidentiality of information relating to colleagues

TEAM WORKING

In most working situations an employee will find that they are not working in isolation but instead as part of a TEAM. This team might be a department such as the accounts department, a section of a department such as the payroll section or a special project for which a team has been set up, for example for costing and sales projections for a new project.

Whatever type of team that you are part of as an employee then your tasks will be not only be concerned with completing your own job but also with meeting the OBJECTIVE of the team. For example, the accounts department objective may be to complete the monthly management accounts, the payroll section objective will be to complete the weekly payroll and the objective of any special project team will be to complete that project in the time allocated.

Advantages of team working

There are a number of advantages of working as part of a team rather than on an individual basis:

- **additional resources** – within a team there are likely to be individuals with different types of skills and techniques which can be used by the whole team

- **inspiration** – it is often the case that if a number of people are involved in a task or project then they each inspire each other and this may encourage individuals to be more creative and hard working

- **motivation** – the overall goal of the team and the help and support of individuals within the team can often provide additional motivation to team members in their work.

The down side of team working

Team working however is often not easy. When you are at work you will find yourself working with a variety of different types of people. We are all very different with different skills, personalities and working styles and although this can often be a help to a team it can also cause frictions and conflicts within the team.

Typical types of team member that you may come across include the following:

- the **team leader** – this may be the actual leader of the team due to seniority or another employee who effectively leads the group due to personality traits

- the **hard worker** who gets the job done

- the **ideas person** who provides the creativity and inspiration for the team

- the **sensitive person** who provides help and support to others

- the **complaints person** for whom nothing is ever right

- the **lazy worker** who rarely completes tasks on time

You may recognise yourself as any one of these! The important point when working as part of a team is that you must attempt to establish constructive relationships with each and every member of the team in order to achieve the team objective.

WORKING AS A TEAM

As we have seen working as part of a team rather than as an individual will mean that there are not only additional opportunities for individual employees but also additional potential problems. Not only must individual tasks be completed but the overall objective of the team must be met.

Therefore it is important from the outset to:

- set and be aware of the objectives of the team
- recognise the resources that are available to the team
- agree working methods, timescales and schedules

Agreeing objectives

In some cases the objectives of the team will be self explanatory. For example, the accounts department must prepare monthly cost accounts annual financial accounts, invoice and receive money from customers and pay suppliers and other expenses. The objectives, resources, working methods and time scales will be well known and familiar although possibly refined over time.

However, in other cases, for example where a team has been set up for a specific purpose, then it will be necessary to discuss and agree realistic objectives for the team.

Resources

It is important that all members of the team are aware of the resources that are available to them. This may be resources such as secretarial time o computer time or physical resources such as the files and information available to help in the completion of the objectives of the team.

Working methods and schedules

As part of a team it is highly likely that the tasks that you perform will have an affect on other team members. Information that you provide will be used by other members of the team and they cannot complete their tasks until you have provided that information or completed your tasks. Therefore schedules and working methods must be set by the team leader to ensure that there is full integration of the work of all members of the team. As we saw in the previous chapter it is always important to meet deadlines as they will have been set for a purpose. Similarly within a team it is important that each individual meets their commitments according to the schedules set in order for the team to achieve its objectives.

HOW IT WORKS

A few months after starting work as an accounts assistant at Southfield Electrical, Sean Taylor is asked by Jenny Faulkner, the accountant, to form a small project team with Amy Bartlett, accounts assistant, Sam Piper, accounts assistant and Ron Howard, accounts supervisor.

This morning, Friday 3 March, Sean, Amy, Sam and Ron had a meeting with Jenny to discuss the purpose of the project team and the work that is to be done.

Jenny explained that the company was looking into changing its credit terms to credit customers and in particular was reviewing its policy of offering prompt payment discounts to some customers. This will require a wide ranging analysis of credit sales in general and the payment patterns of all credit customers. She hands out the following briefing notes:

CREDIT SALES PROJECT

BRIEFING NOTES

OBJECTIVE

Analysis of credit limits and payment patterns of all credit customers – to be produced by Ron Howard by Friday 31 March.

TASKS

Accounts assistants to analyse each credit customer's account for the last year. Analysis to be prepared as follows:

- credit limit

- number of times credit limit exceeded

- average amount by which credit limit exceeded

- total credit sales for the year

- ■ if prompt payment discount offered percentage of total credit sales on which discount is taken

- ■ monthly average of outstanding amount which has been due for more than 60 days and more than 90 days

Sean Taylor – credit customers from A to G
Amy Bartlett – credit customers from H to N
Sam Piper – credit customers from O to Z

Sean Taylor is also to set up a computer spreadsheet in order to input the analysed data. Amy Bartlett and Sam Piper are to input the data to the spreadsheet. Ron Howard to write final report summarising the findings regarding credit limits and payment patterns.

RESOURCES

Computerised sales ledger
Monthly aged debtor listing
Manual customer data file

TIMETABLE

Computer spreadsheet to be completed by Friday 10 March
Accounts assistants' analysis to be completed by Monday 20 March
Completed spreadsheet to Ron Howard by Friday 24 March

Sean realises that, given his other workload, he cannot possibly set up the spreadsheet and analyse all of his assigned credit customers by the due dates and voices this concern to Jenny. Sean also explains that he will need test data to be input into the spreadsheet.

Jenny agrees that perhaps this is asking too much and assigns customers beginning with E and F to Amy and customers beginning with G to Sam leaving Sean with a more manageable workload. Jenny also decides that Sam should have the analysis for 30 credit customers ready for Sean to input as test data on 13 March.

Ron agrees to supervise the analysis and sets up a weekly meeting every Friday morning at 10.00 am in order to assess the progress that is being made.

Integration of work with others

As can be seen from the case study above when working as a team it will often be the case that the work that you do impacts upon the work of another person. For example, in the project above Sean must finish the spreadsheet in time for Amy and Sam to input the data and equally Sam must provide the test data in time for Sean to input it into the spreadsheet. If just one person in the group fails to keep to the schedule then this can have an affect on the work of the others in the team and might even result in the final objective not being achieved within its deadline.

Providing assistance

There will undoubtably be occasions when a member of the team realises that they cannot fulfil their commitments to the team, maybe through lack of time or lack of resources. On such occasions other members of the team should be prepared to provide assistance or support. For example, if one team member is running out of time to carry out their task which is required for another team member then one of the team could offer to help in order to get the task finished or could allow the person struggling to have first option on printer time.

HOW IT WORKS

Let's return to the Southfield Electrical credit sales project. On 10 March the first project progress meeting is held at 10.00am. Sean reports that he has the spreadsheet set up and is ready for the test data to be input on Monday. Ron checks with Sam to ensure that the test data will be ready by Monday morning. Unfortunately Sam has to admit that he is struggling with the analysis so far and has only analysed data for 18 customers. Ron asks Sean and Amy about their workload.

Sean feels that he has to get on with his analysis of credit customers as his time has been taken up by the spreadsheet. Amy also feels that in order to meet the deadline of 26 March for her analysis she has no spare time. However Amy does suggest that as she has already completed analysis of 29 customers that the remaining 12 analyses required for the test data are taken from her customers. Ron agrees and it is further agreed that Sean will input the test data on Monday as originally planned.

Activity 1

What three elements of working in a team are particularly important if the team is to operate successfully?

COMMUNICATION

The key to good working relationships is COMMUNICATION Communication is about putting across your message and ensuring that that message is fully understood.

Communication can take many forms but in a workplace context the following are the most common forms:

- face to face
- telephone
- fax
- informal notes

- memos
- e-mail
- word-processed documents

We will now consider how to use each form of communication effectively.

Face to face

Obviously this is the most common method of communication in a working environment. This may take place in formal meetings, when handing out instructions, when appraising work, whilst discussing work informally etc.

There has been a vast amount written about effective communication face to face and we will only scratch the surface here. Most of it is common sense.

- **body language** – you should be aware that when talking to another person the vast majority of our meaning is conveyed by body language and tone of voice rather than what we actually say. So take care to avoid behaviour like crossing your arms, yawning or talking with an angry tone of voice.

- **clarity** – think clearly about what it is that you are going to say before you say it. Then say it clearly and distinctly – there is nothing worse than being asked to repeat yourself constantly.

- **eye contact** – although it is sometimes difficult try to ensure that you look at the person that you are talking to and make eye contact. Try to make sure that you look and sound positive so that they realise that you mean what it is you are saying.

- **understanding** – communication will only be effective if the person that you are talking to understands what you are saying. Therefore it is important to make sure that you have been understood by your audience.

- **listening** – an important part of communication is not just getting over what you are trying to say but also listening to any feedback from your audience. Listen carefully to the replies that you get and react where necessary.

Telephone

It has been shown that over half of our meaning of what we are trying to convey in communication is done by body language. Of course this element is lost in a telephone conversation. Therefore it is necessary to be even clearer with the other elements of communication when on the telephone.

- make sure that you are speaking to the right person and that they know exactly who you are.

- if you have made the telephone call make sure that you know precisely what you want to talk about – jot down notes if necessary.

- make sure that you speak clearly and confirm that the recipient understands your meaning fully – without the benefit of visual contact it is often easy to have a misunderstanding on the telephone.

- concentrate on your tone of voice – remember that the other person cannot see you so your voice must convey the positive message that you are sending.

Fax

Fax is a convenient method of sending documents to another person. This can be done either using a computer or a fax machine. Using a fax machine the sheet of paper is fed into the machine (sometimes with a header document first), dial the telephone number of the person to whom you are sending the document and the recipient's fax machine will print out an exact copy of the document.

Some care needs to be taken with confidential documents as anybody could pick up the document at the recipient's end. When you have sent it you will not necessarily know that it has been received by the person to whom you were meant to be sending it.

Informal notes

Much communication in the workplace will take place via informal notes from one person to another. This might be a request for a document if the person is not at their desk or passing on a telephone message that has been taken for that person whilst they were out of the office.

There is no set format for an informal note but a few details will always be necessary:

- the name of the person the note is for
- the name of the person the note is from
- the message itself
- date and time that the message was left

Memo

A MEMO or memorandum is a slightly more formal note from one person to another which could also be copied to a number of other people. In many organisations there will be pre-printed memo forms to complete showing:

- person to whom the memo is addressed
- person the memo is from
- date
- subject
- persons to whom a copy of the memo has been sent
- space for the message

The use of memos however is declining as the use of e-mail in the workplace increases.

E-mail

E-MAIL is the sending of messages from one computer to another, either internally within the workplace or to an external party. E-mail is easy to use and relatively cheap. Simply log onto the e-mail software, the most common being Microsoft Outlook, and press 'Create mail' or 'New mail'. Then type in the e-mail address of the person the message is to, the address of anyone else who is to be copied into the message, a subject title and then the body of the message itself. When you have finished the message always check it through thoroughly as once it has been sent there is no retrieving it. Finally press send and your message will be received next time the recipient logs onto their e-mail software.

A further use of e-mail is that computer files or spreadsheets can be sent via e-mail as attachments.

HOW IT WORKS

Back at Southfield Electrical Sean Taylor is working on his analysis of the customers that have been allocated to him. Just to check that he is doing it correctly he would like a copy of an analysis which Amy has already completed and so sends her an e-mail.

Amy

Please could you forward a copy of an analysis of a customer that you have already completed so that I can check that I am doing it right.

Thanks

Sean

Word-processed documents

These days only short, informal notes tend to be hand-written. With the advent of computers and word-processing packages most documents, be they letters, memos, notes etc, are typed into the computer and then either printed out and sent in hard copy or sent via e-mail. It is important to realise that each organisation will have its own 'house style' particularly for letters sent out externally and standard documents can easily be produced from template files on the computer.

Activity 2

Which form of communication would be most appropriate for an urgent order from a supplier?

Communication and content

Whichever method of communication is chosen it is necessary to ensure that the message being sent is understood. Take care with the language and terminology which you use and tailor it to the person with whom you are communicating. In some cases you will be communicating with others in the accounting department who are, like you, au fait with accounting terminology. However on other occasions you may be communicating with someone in your organisation who is not familiar with accountancy and accountancy jargon.

Try to tailor the language that you use and the way that you explain matters to the person that you are communicating with – some people you communicate with will be familiar with the subject matter whereas others will not.

HOW IT WORKS

Kelly McDonald is one of the accounts assistants at Southfield Electrical. She has received a request for a summary of the comparison of the monthly sales per product type to budget for last month from Ron Howard, accounts supervisor, and Taylor Smith the new marketing manager. Both Ron and Taylor have requested the information to be sent in a memo.

Although Kelly is sending the same information to both people she may well word the memos slightly differently. Ron is an accountant with detailed knowledge of accounting terminology whereas it is unlikely that the new marketing manager would have such detailed knowledge of the subject. The two memos might look like this.

MEMO

To: Ron Howard, accounts supervisor
From: Kelly McDonald
Date: 8 December 2006
Subject: Sales variances – November

The following sales variances by product type were incurred in November:

Product	Variance
Washing machines	£14,300 adverse
Dishwashers	£ 2,700 favourable
Cookers	£21,600 adverse
Fridges/freezers	£18,600 favourable

MEMO

To: Taylor Smith, marketing manager
From: Kelly McDonald
Date: 8 December 2006
Subject: Comparison of actual sales to budgeted sales – November

I have compared the actual sales per product type for November to the budgeted sales for that product with the following results:

Washing machines	– sales were £14,300 less than budget
Dishwashers	– sales were £2,700 more than budget
Cookers	– sales were £21,600 less than budget
Fridges/freezers	– sales were £18,600 more than budget

Choice of communication method

As we have seen there are a variety of possible methods of communicating within the workplace and you must therefore make choices as to which is the most appropriate method for the circumstances and for the message that is to be relayed.

Face to face verbal communication is frequently the most effective as you can express yourself fully and gain immediate feedback. However this is often not possible due to time constraints or physical location. It is also often the case that, particularly with a complex subject, it is better to communicate the details in writing whereby the recipient has time to consider the details and complexities before replying.

If immediate feedback is required but face to face communication is not an option then the next best option is a telephone call.

Notes and memos are good methods of passing on information if the person with whom you are communicating is not around and such written communication also serves as a reminder if the note/memo was asking someone to carry out a task. E-mails serve basically the same purpose a notes or memos but even though they are delivered immediately there is no guarantee of when the recipient will log on to receive it.

Styles of communication

Whether communicating in writing or verbally there are many different styles of communication ranging from formal through to extremely informal. It is important that the right style of approach is used for different circumstances.

As we are talking about communication within the workplace then one basic point is that your communication style must of course always be polite and professional. However, within these boundaries there are a variety of different styles of communication and the appropriate one may reflect, in part, the culture of your organisation. If you work in an organisation where all levels of employees and managers are on first name terms then the style of communication will tend to be less formal than in an organisation where all managers are addressed by their title and surname, eg Mr Jones.

The style that you adopt should also reflect the purpose of the communication – whether you are informing, influencing, questioning, requesting help or negotiating.

Informing if you are providing information then you must be aware of who you are talking to, how much they already know and how much they need to know. Keep the information as clear, simple and precise as possible.

Influencing if you are trying to influence someone, for example if you disagree with their solution to a problem and are putting forward your own solution, then you will need to be assertive without being aggressive and put forward your views clearly. Also be seen to be listening to the other party's arguments as nothing is more difficult to deal with than someone who will not accept that other people have ideas as well!

Questioning if you are seeking information then you must be quite clear about exactly what it is you need to know and try to be as succinct as possible. When asking someone for information you are taking up their valuable time; therefore be organised about what it is you need to know and also be prepared to explain why you need the information.

Requesting help the temptation when requesting help might be to grovel. However, it is probably more constructive to be direct and honest explaining the problem, the help that is required and how the other party or the team in general would benefit from the help that is sought.

Negotiating negotiating and requesting help are very similar. The aim is to reach an agreement which both parties can live with. Again an assertive, direct and honest approach is best. Make sure that you are positive in your approach but appreciate any sacrifices that you are asking the other party to make.

CONFLICTS

In any working relationships there are bound to be conflicts on occasion. Such conflicts may be due to any of the following:

- personality
- working style
- status
- work demands

Your aim in the workplace is to be able to handle disagreements and conflicts and to maintain good working relations even when disagreeing with others. In some cases this may simply not be possible due to the gravity of the situation in which case you may need to take the matter further and we will consider grievance procedures later in the chapter. For now however we will concentrate on trying to handle disagreements effectively.

Causes of conflict

Disagreements and conflicts within a team can be caused by all sorts of factors – a few examples are given below but you will probably be able to think of many more.

- someone within the team is inefficient or lazy which means that others have more work to do to compensate

- a team member is consistently rude, insulting or offensive

- a manager persists in making sexist comments

- a team member has too much work to do in the hours available but the manager will not accept the fact

Disagreement

Some causes of conflict are simply a matter of disagreement and it is important that you are able to disagree with someone but still maintain good working relations and not bear a grudge. For example, suppose that your supervisor believes that one method of dealing with purchase invoices is the most efficient but you have a different view. Once you have tried to persuade your supervisor that your method is more efficient and failed then accept the superior authority, forget the argument and continue with your tasks. Agree to disagree!

More serious conflicts

Other disagreements or conflicts may be more serious and you need to be aware of the scope you have to deal with the problem and the limits of your own authority for taking any corrective action. You may be able to sort the problem out yourself but in some instances you may need to take it to a higher authority.

HOW IT WORKS

Returning to the credit sales project at Southfield Electrical, it is now 19 March and the accounts assistants' analysis is due to be completed tomorrow. Sean has a couple of problems.

Sam has been spending a lot time this week on the phone to his new girlfriend and has now admitted to Sean that he cannot possibly get his analysis completed by tomorrow. Sam has a strong personality and has told Sean that as Sean is the 'new boy' in the office then he will have to help him today and tomorrow in order to get the job finished otherwise the whole team will be in trouble. Sean already has plenty of work of his own to do over the next two days.

Last night the accounts department all went down to the local pub. Whilst Sean was at the bar to buy a round of drinks he overheard Ron Howard talking to someone he did not recognise as an employee in a loud voice about one customer of Southfield Electrical. Ron appeared to be telling the stranger about this customer's poor payment record.

What should Sean do?

Sam   Sean could go to Ron or Jenny and complain that Sam is bullying him into doing his work as Sam has been wasting time all week. However, it might well be better for Sean to try to sort this out himself. He could ask other colleagues how they find Sam and see if they have the same problems. He could then approach Sam directly and explain that he will help him for the next two days if he can but that he also has his own work to complete. Sean might suggest that Sam tells Ron about the problem to see if his deadline can be extended a little.

Ron   Ron should not be talking about customers with someone outside Southfield Electrical and certainly not in a public place. As Ron is effectively Sean's line manager on this project then Sean will need to go to a higher authority and should talk to Jenny Faulkner, the accountant, about what he heard and then leave it for her to deal with.

GRIEVANCE PROCEDURES

In many cases any conflicts can be dealt with amongst the individuals involved. In other cases it may be necessary to report the incident or conflict to a more senior level of management.

However in some cases the matter or incident is so serious that a more formal approach needs to be adopted. All employers should have a written GRIEVANCE PROCEDURE which is available to all employees. A GRIEVANCE is a complaint against the employer where the individual feels that he/she is being wrongly treated by colleagues or managers. Such complaints might include:

- a serious case of harassment

- examples of unfair treatment by managers such as an employees not being promoted due to race, gender or disability

- an employee being given an unfair workload

- an employee being blocked for promotion

- unfair pay, for example a male employee being paid more for the same work than a female employee.

The grievance procedure policy should state who an employee should go to with a grievance, probably initially a line manager, and then if the grievance cannot be sorted out at that level the more senior manager that should be consulted. If the grievance has to be taken to a higher level of management than the line manager then it is normal for the personnel department to become involved.

If the grievance cannot be sorted out internally then the employee may have to take the problem before an EMPLOYMENT TRIBUNAL which works as an independent informal court.

CHAPTER OVERVIEW

- in many workplace situations employees will find that rather than working individually they are working as part of a team

- team working as opposed to working individually can provide additional resources, inspiration and motivation

- teams will tend to have a number of different types of members with different personalities and work styles

- if a team is set up for a specific project then it is important that objectives are set for the team, the resources available are made known to the team and the working methods, time scales and schedules are made known

- as part of a team it may become necessary to provide assistance or support to other team members in order to achieve the objectives of the team

- in the workplace communication methods will tend to include face to face communication, telephone calls, fax, informal notes, memos, e-mails and word-processed documents

- when communicating in any form the content of the communication must be tailored to the recipient – some will be familiar with the subject matter that is being communicated whereas others will not be

- the style of communication as well as the method are important as this will be dependent upon the culture of the organisation and the reason for the communication

- there may often be conflicts within working relationships which may be caused by personality, working style, status or work demands

- in general disagreements or conflicts should be dealt with whilst still maintaining good working relations with the employee with whom there is the disagreement

- in some cases conflicts or disagreements can be satisfactorily dealt with between the individual employees whereas in other more serious cases an employee may have to report a matter to the line manager or other more senior manager

- employers should have a written grievance procedure policy which employees can follow if the grievance is more serious and needs to be dealt with by senior management or an external employment tribunal

---

KEY WORDS

Team a group of employees working together to meet the group objective

Objective the final outcome that the team wishes to achieve

Communication a method of putting across a message and ensuring that the message is understood

Memo a formalised note sent from one person to another

E-mail an electronic method of sending a note or other information via computer

Grievance a complaint against an employer where the employee feels wrongly treated by colleagues or managers

Grievance procedure an employer's formalised procedure for an employee with a grievance

Employment tribunal an informal, independent court that can deal with employee grievances if they cannot be dealt with internally

---

HOW MUCH HAVE YOU LEARNED?

1   Give three examples of teams that might operate within an accounting function.

2   Give six examples of the type of team member that you might come across.

3   If a team is working to complete a particular project why is it important that all schedules and timetables are met?

4   Give seven examples of ways of communication within the workplace.

5   For each of the following situations which would be the most appropriate method of communication?

   i)   leaving a telephone message for a colleague

   ii)   informing an employee that his work has not been up to standard recently

   iii)   requesting a customer's sales ledger account balance from the credit controller

   iv)   requesting production details for the last month from the factory manager where the factory is situated 5 miles away

   v)   sending monthly variances to the sales manager

6   Write a memo to a non-accountant explaining why the balance on a supplier's purchase ledger account might not agree to the balance on the statement sent by the supplier.

7   You have recently joined the accounting department of a company and have found one of your fellow accounts assistants to be extremely rude to you and constantly demanding that you fetch the coffee, clean up the kitchen etc.

   What action could you take to deal with this?

8   You are an accounts assistant for a company and on one occasion whilst having lunch in the canteen you overhear the payroll clerk passing on to another accounts assistant how much the accounts supervisor earns.

   What action should you take?

chapter 6:
IMPROVING YOUR OWN PERFORMANCE

chapter coverage 📖

In this chapter we are going to consider how each individual within an organisation should develop themselves through learning and acquiring new skills and knowledge. The topics we shall cover are:

✍ career goals and development needs

✍ defining personal development objectives

✍ new skills and knowledge

✍ evaluating your progress

✍ maintaining knowledge and skills

KNOWLEDGE AND UNDERSTANDING AND PERFORMANCE CRITERIA COVERAGE

knowledge and understanding – the business environment

- where to access information about new developments relating to your job role

knowledge and understanding – methods

- ways of identifying development needs
- setting self-development objectives
- development opportunities and their resource implications
- ways of assessing own performance and progress

knowledge and understanding – the organisation

- where to access information that will help you learn including formal training courses
- the people who may help you plan and implement learning you may require

Performance criteria – element 23.3

- identify your own development needs by taking into consideration your current work activities and also your own career goals

- define your own development objectives and, where necessary, agree them with the appropriate person

- research appropriate ways of acquiring new skills and knowledge

- ensure that development opportunities are realistic and achievable in terms of resources and support from relevant persons

- review and evaluate your performance and progress and also to agreed timescales

- monitor your own understanding of developments relating to your job role

- maintain and develop your own specialist knowledge relevant to your own working environment

- undertake learning that will help you improve your performance

CAREER GOALS AND DEVELOPMENT NEEDS

This chapter considers areas which are individual to each student reading this Course Companion. We are concerned with each individual's personal development in the workplace and therefore the chapter will be fairly generalised. The aim of the chapter is to give you guidance on the thought processes that you should consider regarding your working life and some ideas as to how to develop those thought processes in practical terms.

Current job

When considering your working life and CAREER DEVELOPMENT it is probably best to initially start with a consideration of your current job. You may wish to refer back to your original job specification or simply consider what it is that you do on a day to day basis.

Ask yourself some questions:

Am I doing my job as well as I possibly can?
Do I have all of the knowledge necessary to carry out my tasks effectively?
Do I have the skills necessary to perform my job well?
Do I carry out all of the duties stated in my job specification?

If the answer to any of these questions is 'no' then there is certainly scope for personal and professional development in your current role. For example, when answering the questions above you might have come up with the following answers:

Am I doing my job as well as I possibly can?

On the whole yes but I still struggle with the monthly sales ledger control account reconciliation which I know takes me longer than it should do.

Do I have all of the knowledge necessary to carry out my tasks effectively?

Going back to the sales ledger control account reconciliation my problems with it are not helped by the fact that I have always struggled with double entry bookkeeping.

Do I have the skills necessary to perform my job well?

Again on the whole but whenever I have to prepare a computer spreadsheet I have to ask one of the other accounts assistants for help as I don't know how to do it on my own.

Do I carry out all of the duties stated in my job specification?

Mostly, but it is stated that I should be responsible for petty cash when the cashier is absent or on holiday but I have never been asked to do this nor do I know how to.

The answers to these questions indicate that there is some need for personal development within your current job:

- you could benefit from help from a senior colleague who will show you how to perform the sales ledger reconciliation more efficiently

- you could benefit from either a short bookkeeping course or from studying a textbook on double entry bookkeeping

- you might wish to attend a computer spreadsheet course or have formal tuition on how to prepare a spreadsheet from a colleague

- you should perhaps spend some time with the cashier being shown how she deals with petty cash claims in case you are called upon to carry out the role whilst she is on holiday.

Activity 1

Consider your own current job and ask yourself the questions raised above. Are there any areas of your own development that are necessary in order to perform your current job better?

Where next?

Although you may be happy with your current job and role in the workplace most employees do have ambitions to develop their career. This can be for many reasons but two of the most common are for personal satisfaction and monetary gain. Before you can recognise any development needs that you have you will need to consider where it is that you are aiming for whether within your current organisation or at some future date with another organisation. What are your CAREER GOALS?

Realism

Ambition is good but take care to be realistic in this exercise. As a first year accounts assistant it is probably realistic to aspire to become an accounts supervisor but perhaps not to aspire to be Finance Director within two years.

It may help to talk informally to colleagues and to those in positions above yours as to how they achieved their posts. It may also be useful to have a more formal conversation with your line manager or the human resources function in order to determine what are realistic career goals for you as an individual.

How do you get there?

Once you have decided either from the experience of others or from more formal discussions what your future aims in the workplace are then you need to consider how you get from your current position to the job that you aspire to.

Firstly of course you will need to ensure that you are carrying out your current role efficiently and effectively which hopefully the earlier chapters of this Learning Pack will have helped you with. Then you must consider the job that you wish to have and the requirements for that job.

You may well need to talk to your line manager or human resources manager in order to find out the details of the knowledge, skills and any qualifications that are required for this job. Once you are armed with this information then you can consider setting yourself PERSONAL DEVELOPMENT OBJECTIVES.

DEFINING PERSONAL DEVELOPMENT OBJECTIVES

Although there may be a fairly structured career route within your organisation it is important that you define your own personal development objectives. You should do this within the context of your career goals and within the context of your own abilities. It has been suggested by some theorists that development objectives should be, what is known as, SMARTER:

S	Specific
M	Measurable
A	Agreed
R	Realistic
T	Time-bounded
E	Evaluated
R	Reviewed

We will now consider each of these elements in turn to help you to develop SMARTER personal development objectives.

Specific

This is key to the setting of development objectives. 'I hope to be promoted soon' is far too vague – 'I hope to pass my first year AAT exams and be promoted to accounts assistant (senior)' – this is much better.

Try to be exact about what you hope to achieve and break it down into small, manageable steps.

Measurable

One of the factors involved in personal development is being able to review your progress and determine how you are progressing towards your goals. One way of doing this is to be able to measure how you are moving towards your objectives. Did you pass the last set of exams that you sat? Have you successfully completed the computer course you were booked onto?

Agreed

Despite the fact that you might be setting your personal development objectives yourself in many cases the achievement of these objectives will require the commitment of resources from your employer. This may be simply the loss of your time while you study or go on a training course but will also encompass the direct costs of your development. Therefore, it is important that, where necessary, any personal development objectives are agreed with the appropriate person which will often be your line manager or human resources manager.

Realistic

We touched on the subject of realism in an earlier paragraph. When setting personal development objectives you must ensure that you are able to achieve these objectives within the various constraints under which you operate – time, resources, ability and current commitments.

Time-bounded

This element is tied in with realism but it is essential when setting personal development objectives to include a time scale in which the objective is to be achieved. 'To be promoted to accounts supervisor' is the start of an objective but is this within a two year time scale or a ten year time scale – 'to be promoted to accounts supervisor within two years' is a much better development objective.

Evaluated

This will be part of the process of agreeing your personal development objectives with the appropriate manager. There will need to be an evaluation process as to whether the objective is worth pursuing given the time, cost and other resources that it will require.

Reviewed

This is an important aspect of setting personal development objectives. When and how will your progress towards meeting the objective be reviewed?

Activity 2

What does SMARTER stand for in the context of setting personal development objectives?

NEW SKILLS AND KNOWLEDGE

The aim of your personal development objectives will in most cases be to acquire new SKILLS and KNOWLEDGE which will help you to meet those personal development objectives. However, where will you find ways of acquiring new skills and knowledge? This will require research on your own part and in this section we will consider some of the ways in which you may be able to find such skills and knowledge.

Courses

One of the most obvious ways of enhancing your skills and knowledge is by attending courses. These may be training courses that are run internally by your organisation which you may find advertised on the office notice board or via e-mail, or external courses. You may need to research to find external courses, for example by contacting a local college of further education or by using the Internet.

Internet

The Internet can not only be used to find details of local course providers but also to find information on areas of development that are important to you. For example, you could use a search engine such as Yahoo! or Google to find articles on assertiveness or managing conflict in the workplace.

Journals

In most industries and professions there are a number of journals or trade publications which will invariably include articles that might be useful to your personal development. It might be worth subscribing to such a publication in order to keep up to date with developments within your industry or service sector and also for any technical material that is published.

Books

Go into any major high street book store and you will find books on any and every subject. For example, if you have some doubts about your double entry bookkeeping skills then it might be worth investing in a textbook and spending a few hours a week working through this in your own time.

Colleagues

One of the most obvious sources of information and potential personal development is that of your colleagues. Other employees may be able to give you advice on training courses to attend or books or journals to read and you may also be able to learn new skills from colleagues.

Observation

During your work time you may find that you can watch more experienced colleagues at work to learn from their methods, procedures, techniques and behaviour. This observation may take place informally as you work with colleagues or on a more formal 'shadowing' basis.

Activity 3

You are due to start a new element of your accounts assistant role by working in the credit control department. What new skills or knowledge do you think that you might require for this additional role?

EVALUATING YOUR PROGRESS

The evaluation and review process was touched upon when we considered the SMARTER method of setting personal development objectives. There is no point in setting an objective if you are not prepared to evaluate how you are achieving that objective and review your progress on a regular basis. It is also important to ensure that any objectives that were set are being reached within the timescale that has been set or agreed.

Obviously on a fairly regular basis you can review your own progress. For example, have you kept up to date with reading the monthly technical journal that will keep you up to date with technical changes that affect your job? Have you booked yourself onto the internal training course on assertiveness that you decided would be a necessary part of your personal development?

However, in many cases there will be more formal methods of evaluation and review. In most organisations there will be a regular, normally annual, assessment procedure for all employees. This may be with your line manager or with the human resources department. This is usually known as the APPRAISAL PROCESS. This will normally consist of a review of your work in the last period together with an evaluation and review of any personal development objectives that were set at your previous assessment. How successful have you been in achieving those objectives?

MAINTAINING KNOWLEDGE AND SKILLS

In most of this chapter so far we have considered your aims in terms of progressing your career and setting personal development objectives that will further your career goals.

However, it is also important to consider your current role in the workplace and to ensure that you monitor any developments in your own job role and maintain any specialist knowledge that is required for your current job role. For example, if there are any relevant changes in legislation or in accounting standards that affect the job that you perform then it is your responsibility to remain up to date with such developments.

This updating procedure may be helped by your organisation which may run courses to keep you up to date with any relevant changes. Keep a regular eye on the office noticeboard or organisation's newsletter or website to discover whether any courses are on offer.

Alternatively it may be your own responsibility to keep up to date by the regular reading of relevant journals or newspapers.

Continuous process

Just to finish this chapter it should be noted that the setting of personal development objectives, their review, appraisal and updating will be a continuous process throughout your working career rather than simply a one off exercise.

CHAPTER OVERVIEW

- when considering your own development needs the best starting point is the current job that you perform. Are there any additional skills or knowledge that you require to carry out your role effectively and efficiently?

- most employees will have a degree of ambition to succeed and be promoted within the organisation and must consider what additional skills and knowledge are required in order to be successful in their career development

- at this stage you should consider setting your own personal development objectives – in order to be meaningful and useful such objectives should be specific, measurable, agreed, realistic and time-bounded and they should be evaluated and reviewed by the appropriate person

- your personal development objectives may include the need to acquire new skills and knowledge and for this you might need to carry out research into ways of acquiring these new skills and knowledge including courses, the Internet, journals and trade publications, books, colleagues and observation of others

- once personal development objectives have been set then they must be reviewed and evaluated in order to assess your performance and progress – this may be personal review and evaluation or a formal appraisal process

- even in your current role in the organisation there may be development, for example legal or accounting changes, which means that you must maintain and update your knowledge and skills

- the process of setting personal development objectives and reviewing progress in meeting these objectives is a continuous process which should take place throughout your working career.

KEY WORDS

Career development the way in which you intend to move on from job to job in the workplace

Career goals your aims in terms of the job you aspire to in the workplace

Personal development objectives your individual aims as far as personal and professional development are concerned

SMARTER the process of setting specific, measurable, agreed, realistic, time-bounded objectives which are evaluated and reviewed

Skills the core expertise and techniques required to carry out a job

Knowledge the background understanding necessary to carry out a job

Appraisal process the formal, organisational process of regular review of each individual employee's performance, progress and objectives

HOW MUCH HAVE YOU LEARNED?

1   In the context of setting personal development objectives, what is meant by each element of setting SMARTER objectives?

2   Briefly explain four methods of finding new skills and knowledge in the workplace.

3   What factors do you think would be discussed in a typical appraisal process with your human resources manager?

CHAPTER 1 Health, safety and security

1
- responsible behaviour by employees
- no smoking policies
- no alcohol or drugs
- employee alertness to danger
- common sense
- consideration for others
- following procedures
- good maintenance procedures

2
- photocopier   – electrical parts
                 – moving parts may get hot ie when unjamming paper
- guillotine
- staplers
- letter openers
- staple removers
- fax machine
- computer equipment (electricity, working practices)

3   The main aim of the Health and Safety Commission is to protect everyone against risks to health or safety arising out of work activities.

4   Control of substances hazardous to health

5   Report the problem immediately to the maintenance department, unplug the photocopier and place a notice on it saying that it is temporarily out of order until dealt with by maintenance.

CHAPTER 2 Dealing with accidents and emergencies

1   An accident should be correctly recorded in the accident book. From the employer's perspective this is important as if any legal claim is made at a later date against the employer for the results of the accident then the details in the accident book may help the employer to fight the claim. From the employee's viewpoint if the employer, and/or health and safety factors, were contributory to the accident then this record may help in any subsequent legal claim.

2   On hearing the fire alarm you would do the following:

- leave the building quickly but calmly by the designated route
- do not stop to gather personal belongings
- go immediately to the designated assembly point
- help any visitors to the building who do not know where to go
- help any other employees with special needs
- respond when your name is called in order to confirm that you are out of the building
- do not return to the building until the all clear has been given by a responsible official

3   Either a water extinguisher or a powder extinguisher.

4   The purpose of a Fire Door is that it is fire resistant and is therefore should be kept shut in order to try to limit the spread of any fire. Therefore it is important that Fire Doors are not propped open as they cannot serve their purpose if open.

CHAPTER 3   Effectiveness and efficiency

1   - ensure that you had all of the information to hand that is required eg. price lists, customer details, master files, customer orders

    - check the invoice thoroughly before printing it out

2   You should give the message to your colleague immediately on his return and explain that the customer said it was an urgent matter.

3   Think about the equipment you are using, the space on your desk, where and how you file any notes etc

4   Firstly ask your colleagues in the office whether they mind you shutting the blind explaining the problem you have. Provided that they are happy then shut the blind as long as you can do this safely.

5   If you have not replaced the ink in the printer before then find the instructions to do so. Often these are printed inside the top of the printer. Provided that you understand the instructions and know where the correct spare ink is then go ahead and change the ink cartridge. If you are at all unsure then ask for help.

CHAPTER 4   Planning and organising work

1   Routine tasks are the general everyday tasks that form the basis of an employee's job. Examples in an accounts department might be producing sales invoices each day and preparing a sales ledger control account reconciliation each month.

Unexpected tasks are other tasks that an employee is required to perform other than the routine tasks. Examples might include preparing figures for a special project or performing the tasks of another employee who is on holiday.

2 Urgent tasks are tasks for which there is a fairly imminent deadline. For example, producing a schedule of product costings for the production manager for a meeting this afternoon or completing a report which is required for the chief accountant tomorrow morning.

Important tasks are tasks for which the employee is responsible and which will have an effect on other employees or the organisation. For example, the checking of purchase invoices to goods received notes and the opening of the morning post.

3 Clearly without staying in the office until about 7.00 pm it will not be possible to print both sales invoices and the report. You might consider completing the sales invoice print run and then setting up the report print and leaving the office until Monday morning. However, as the report is confidential it would not be advisable to leave it unattended.

Both tasks are urgent but the sales invoices are more urgent as they must be sent out today. The report however is not needed until 12.00 noon on Monday so provided that you start the print run by say 9.00am on Monday and agree this with your supervisor this is probably the best plan of action.

4 Clearly the urgent task of producing the statement must be carried out first of all in the day as, given the meeting at 3.00pm, the accounts assistant cannot run the risk of missing the post deadline. It would probably also be advisable to produce the list of account balances for your colleague early in the day so that it is definitely done and not forgotten. Thereafter the routine tasks should be carried out with the meeting at 3.00pm scheduled in.

5 On the assumption that you will want the report completed by Tuesday 21 August the planning schedule would be as follows:

	Fri 10	Mon 13	Tues 14	August Wed 15	Thurs 16	Fri 17	Mon 20	Tues 21
Requisition files	X							
Research			X	X	X			
Analysis					X	X		
Typing							X	
Proofing								X

6 If you think that you will not be able to meet a deadline then you must inform the person that you are reporting to immediately for two main reasons:

■ the manager involved may be able to access resources which will mean that you can meet the deadline

■ if you are unable to meet your deadline this may mean that the person you are providing the information for will also miss a deadline.

7 i) Under the Data Protection Act such information cannot be supplied

ii) This is confidential information and should not be given to your colleague

iii) An individual has the right under the Data Protection Act to be informed of any personal data that the organisation holds on her.

CHAPTER 5 Maintaining good working relationships

1   Agreeing objectives
    Agreeing resources
    Setting working methods and schedules

2   Fax or e-mail

CHAPTER 6 Improving your own performance

1   The answer to this activity will be personal to each student

2   **S**   Specific
    M   Measurable
    A   Agreed
    R   Realistic
    T   Time-bounded
    E   Evaluated
    R   Reviewed

3   ■ procedures regarding credit limits
    ■ procedures regarding credit control
    ■ how to produce and interpret an aged debtor listing
    ■ how to produce a debtors statement
    ■ format of standard letters to debtors

CHAPTER 1 Health, safety and security

1   Security in the workplace is important as it covers a number of different aspects:

- security of the organisation's assets and information
- security of employees' valuables and belongings
- personal security of employees from external harassment

2   Health and Safety at Work etc Act 1974

3   i)   16 degrees celsius

   ii) 11 cubic metres

   iii) seats must give adequate support for the lower back and a footrest must be provided if employees cannot put their feet flat on the floor

   iv) there must be adequate seating and tables for the number of people expected to use the facilities at any one time

4   Reporting of Injuries, Diseases and Dangerous Occurrences Regulations 1995

5   A hazard is a condition which may be a threat to health, safety or security. Risk is the likelihood that the hazard will cause a problem for health, safety and security.

6   <u>Step 1</u>   Look for the hazards

   <u>Step 2</u>   Decide who might be harmed

   <u>Step 3</u>   Evaluate the risks and decide whether existing precautions are adequate or more should be done

   <u>Step 4</u>   Record the findings

   <u>Step 5</u>   Review the assessment and revise it if necessary

7   i)   Close the drawer and draw it to the attention of the person who uses that draw

   ii) Report the potential to the health and safety officer but in the interim period put up a temporary notice saying mind the step

   iii) This is a security risk as unauthorised employees could discover personal information about other employees so it should probably be brought to the attention of your supervisor.

CHAPTER 2 Dealing with accidents and emergencies

1
- the names of the qualified first aiders
- where the first aid box is
- where the accident book is
- how to fill in the accident book
- guidance on safe lifting and manual handling

2   An accident book

3
- stay calm
- find a qualified first aider
- find the first aid box
- offer any assistance that you can
- try to remember as much about the accident as possible
- report the accident to someone in authority in the office
- complete the accident book

4

Date	Name of injured person	Details of accident (time, place, description and witnesses)	First aid treatment	Further action required
22 Nov	Gwen Franks	Tripped up small step between offices Small cut on arm from broken cups 9.20 am Witness – Paul Fish	Wound dressed by Ken Jones	Wound to be checked by Ken Jones in 2 days Warning notice to be put by step

5   i) A dangerous occurrence is an incident which could have resulted in injury such as an explosion collapsed structure, radiation or a vehicle collision.

ii) An over three day injury is one which requires the injured person to be off work for three days or more.

iii) A work related disease might include Repetitive Strain Injury (RSI), skin or lung diseases or an infection such as legionnaires disease.

6
- leave your desk immediately without waiting to gather your belongings
- stay calm
- leave the building by the designated route as quickly as possible
- be aware of anyone who is not an employee or does not know the emergency procedures
- be aware of anyone with special needs or who requires help
- go to the designated assembly point
- respond when your name is called by the person in charge of the evacuation
- do not return to the building until the all clear has been given by the person in charge of the evacuation.

Chapter 3 Effectiveness and efficiency

1   i)   Effectiveness in the workplace is the ability to perform the jobs that are required of an employee and achievement of the organisation's overall objectives.

    ii) Efficiency is achievement of the tasks required to be performed with the minimum usage of resources, in particular time and material resources.

2   In many office situations the work of one employee is dependent upon that of another or alternatively the resources used by one employee are also used by others. As an example one employee has been using the sales ledger master file for invoicing but it is now required by another employee to answer a customer query. The first employee has mislaid the file and therefore the second employee is unable to carry out his task of answering the customer query.

3   i)   Desk and chair
         Computer screen, keyboard and mouse
         Shelving
         Filing cabinets
         Surrounding area
         Work routes frequently taken

    ii) If you are to work effectively and efficiently then this can only be done if the work area is organised. You must be able to obtain equipment, files, stationary etc that you need quickly and easily.

4   i)   In an accounts department where there are rarely any visits from non-employees the employer may be happy for a degree of personalisation of work areas to take place by the use of personal affects such as photographs etc. However, these must of course be acceptable to the other employees in the office.

    ii) In an office which is open to the public as it is behind the reception area it will be important the office area gives the right impression of the organisation. Therefore, in order to appear professional and efficient there may be limits on the amount of personalisation of work areas that is allowed by the employer.

5   i)   In this case the temperature is less than the Health and Safety requirements of 16 degrees, therefore it is important that the office manager or line manager is informed. Even if the thermostat had been accessible it would also have been necessary to inform the relevant manager to ensure that the situation did not happen again.

    ii) This is obviously a problem for effectiveness at work and the office manager should be informed immediately to ensure that the situation is rectified and the bulb changed.

    iii) This is a simple situation that you can deal with by moving your computer screen back to a position where there is no reflection.

    iv) In this situation you will have to consult with your colleagues. Although the office may be stuffy it may also be the case that the other employees cannot work effectively with the traffic noise.

    v)   You are unlikely to have the authority simply to use the new filing cabinet therefore you should not attempt to. Instead inform your office manager or the accountant of your need for more filing space.

6   It is important that a fax is properly sent, according to the manufacturer's instructions, firstly to ensure that the fax is received by the person to whom it is being sent and secondly to ensure that the fax machine is not damaged in any way by incorrect use.

CHAPTER 4 Planning and organising work

1   The reporting procedure in an organisation details who reports to whom; as an employee who you prepare information for, who you provide information for and who needs any data or documents next.

2   A line manager is usually your head of department or the person most directly responsible for your work as an employee.

3   Urgent and important
     Urgent but not important
     Not urgent but important
     Not urgent and not important

4   Enter sales invoices/credit notes into computer system
     Enter weekly purchase invoices into the computer
     Match purchase invoices to goods received notes and pass to the accountant for authorisation
     Filing

5   1.30 to 2.30   Petty cash summary

     2.30 to 2.45 (say)   Deal with petty cash claim

     2.45 to 3.15   Complete petty cash summary

     3.15 to 5.30   Match purchase invoices to goods received   notes and pass to the accountant for authorisation
                                Filing

6   Any three of the following:

     A to do list is a list of tasks that you are required to do each day, normally in order of priority. As each task is completed it can be ticked off the list.

     A diary can either be manual or electronic. It is used to record the date, time and place of specific events or meetings.

     A planning schedule is a detailed timetable of tasks to be carried out in order to complete a more complex task or project.

     An action plan is a yet more detailed list of tasks, start and completion times, responsibilities and costs for completion of a complex project.

7   Thursday 31 March request information from colleague

Monday 4 April and Tuesday 5 April prepare report using historical information

Wednesday 6 April and Thursday 7 April prepare rest of report

Friday 8 April 9.00am to 12.00 print report

8   i)   Friday 9 May and Tuesday 13 May prepare report

    ii) If the information you require does not arrive until Friday lunchtime then you only have one and a half days in the office in order to produce a report that is due to take two days. You must inform the production manager immediately. He may be able to speed up the accounts assistant with providing you with the information you require by finding additional help or he may be able to postpone your training course thereby freeing up another day. Alternatively he may be able to reschedule his meeting until the next day when the report is complete.

9   The Data Protection Act sets out eight guiding principles to ensure that personal data is handled correctly. These principles state that personal data should be:

1   obtained and processed fairly and lawfully

2   held only for specified purposes

3   adequate, relevant and not excessive for those purposes

4   accurate and kept up to date

5   not be kept for longer than is necessary

6   available to the individual whose data is being held

7   kept securely

8   not be exported to countries outside the European Union unless it will be adequately protected in that country

CHAPTER 5 Maintaining good working relationships

1   Sales ledger team
     Payroll section
     Special project team

2   Team leader
     Hard worker
     Lazy worker
     Ideas member
     Supportive member
     Complainer

3   Schedules and timetables will have been set for a reason and will normally mean that work is required to be completed on a particular date or time because someone else requires the completed work at this time.

4   Face to face
Telephone
Fax
Informal notes
Memos
E-mail
Word-processed documents

5   i)   informal note
ii) face to face
iii) telephone, memo or e-mail
iv) E-mail or fax
v) E-mail or memo

6

MEMO

To: Non-accountant
From: Accounts assistant
Date: 25 November 2006
Subject: Purchase ledger account balance

The balance shown for a supplier on the account in the purchase ledger in our accounts department may not necessarily be the same as the balance shown on the statement sent from that supplier.

There are a number of reasons for this. The most obvious is that either our accounts department or the supplier's accounts department has made an error.

However, there are other reasons for any difference. It is entirely possible that just before sending out the statement the supplier sent us an invoice and recorded this on the statement. However, on the date we receive the statement the invoice has not yet been entered in our books. Equally we might have made a payment to the supplier but as it had not yet reached the supplier it would not be recorded on their statement but would have been recorded in our purchase ledger account.

7   The first most obvious course of action is to discuss the accounts assistant's behaviour with your colleagues as they may have the same problems themselves or may tell you that he always behaves like this with new employees for a few weeks but then it is over. At this point you may wish to talk to the accounts assistant himself and explain your concerns. If there is no solution drawn from these discussions then your only action would be to talk to your line manager about the problem.

8   This is a serious confidentiality matter and should be reported to the payroll clerk's line manager immediately.

CHAPTER 6 Improving your own performance

1	**Specific**	Development objectives must be specific rather than general
	Measurable	In order to be able to measure progress towards meeting objectives then the objectives themselves must be measurable
	Agreed	Personal development objectives will often require significant resources from the employer and therefore must be agreed with the appropriate manager
	Realistic	In order for personal development objectives to be motivating to an employee they must be realistic and potentially achievable
	Time-bounded	In order for personal development objectives to be motivational then they must be set within a time-scale
	Evaluated	Objectives that are set by individuals may require significant resources from the employer – time, costs etc and therefore will need to be evaluated in order to ensure that the benefit outweighs the cost
	Reviewed	Progress towards the achievement of personal development objectives must be reviewed on a regular basis

2 Any four of:

Courses	Internal or external educational courses
Internet	Information on external courses or research information on topics relating to skills and knowledge
Journals/trade publications	Technical and educational courses
Books	Technical and educational purposes
Colleagues	Learning skills, methods and techniques from colleagues on a formal or informal basis
Observation	A method of learning by observing how colleagues or superiors carry out their tasks

3
- review of work performance since last appraisal
- formal appraisal from managers that you work for
- review of progress towards meeting objectives set at last appraisal
- setting of new objectives for next period.

REVISION COMPANION UNITS 22 & 23

chapter 1:
HEALTH, SAFETY AND SECURITY

1 What are the respective roles of the Health and Safety Commission and the Health and Safety Executive?

2 List as many of the legal health and safety regulations as you can remember.

3 What does COSHH stand for?

4 Distinguish between a hazard and a risk in the workplace and give an example of both.

5 What are the five recommended steps in a risk assessment?

6 What are employee's responsibilities under the Health and Safety Act?

7 State how you would deal with each of the following health, safety and security issues:

i) You notice that a piece of frayed carpet has become raised up in the middle of the office floor.

ii) A colleague's computer has a frayed wire and you think that you have just seen a spark from it.

iii) Having just walked past the payroll office you noticed that the computer was logged onto the payroll details programme but no one is in the office.

iv) When you arrived this morning you noticed that a window had been left open the night before – when you tried to close it you realised that the lock was broken.

v) You are feeling a little cold during the day and notice that the air conditioning unit states that the temperature is 14 degrees celsius. You have never been instructed on how to alter the air conditioning temperature.

vi) On making coffee this morning the coffee machine spluttered and spilt out hot coffee all over the kitchen floor – it would appear that the coffee machine needs mending.

chapter 2:
DEALING WITH ACCIDENTS AND EMERGENCIES

1 Under what circumstances is an employer legally bound to keep an accident book?

2 One day whilst at work you witness an accident where a colleague, Jennifer Cage, walks into an open desk drawer whilst carrying a pile of files. She cuts her leg quite badly and says that she feels faint.

i) As the first person on hand at the incident what should you do if you are not a qualified first aider?

ii) Your name is Sasha Grimes and having witnessed the accident you must complete an entry in the accident book given below. Make up any details not provided in the activity.

Date	Name of injured person	Details of accident (time, place, description and witnesses)	First aid treatment	Further action required

3   Under the requirements of the Reporting of Injuries, Diseases and Dangerous Occurrences Regulations (RIDDOR) what types of incidents should be recorded and reported?

4   You are the human resources manager at J J Donald Engineering and your name is Penny Vincent. On Monday 21 May 2006 at about 9.30am one of the warehouse assistants, Patrick Spence, was hit in the warehouse by a forklift truck. His leg was broken and he spent two days in hospital with a recommendation that he should not return to work for at least three weeks and then only for desk duties until the plaster has been removed.

The accident has been investigated and it appears that the forklift truck was reversing at the time and the driver did not see Patrick step out in his way. The driver of the forklift has been cautioned and all forklift truck drivers have been warned to be vigilant. The warehouse assistants have also been warned to take special care when forklifts are around.

You are required to complete the following RIDDOR Form 2508 to report this incident. Make up any details such as addresses which are not included in this activity information.

Health and Safety at Work etc Act 1974
The Reporting of Injuries, Diseases and Dangerous Occurrences Regulations 1995

HSE
Health & Safety
Executive

Report of an injury or dangerous occurrence

Filling in this form
This form must be filled in by an employer or other responsible person.

Part A

About you
1 What is your full name?

2 What is your job title?

3 What is your telephone number?

About your organisation
4 What is the name of your organisation?

5 What is its address and postcode?

6 What type of work does your organisation do?

Part B

About the incident
1 On what date did the incident happen?

/ /

2 At what time did the incident happen?
(Please use the 24-hour clock eg 0600)

3 Did the incident happen at the above address?

Yes ☐ Go to question 4

No ☐ Where did the incident happen?

☐ elsewhere in your organisation - give the name, address and postcode

☐ at someone else's premises - give the name, address and postcode

☐ in a public place - give the details of where it happened

If you do not know the postcode, what is the name of the local authority?

4 In which department, or where on the premises, did the incident happen?

Part C

About the injured person
If you are reporting a dangerous occurrence, go to Part F.
If more than one person was injured in the same incident, please attach the details asked for in Part C and Part D for each injured person.

1 What is their full name?

2 What is their home address and postcode?

3 What is their home phone number?

4 How old are they?

5 Are they
☐ male?
☐ female?

6 What is their job title?

7 Was the injured person (tick only one box)
☐ one of your employees?

☐ on a training scheme? Give details:

☐ on work experience?

☐ employed by someone else? Give details of the employer:

☐ self-employed and at work?

☐ a member of the public?

Part D

About the injury
1 What was the injury? (eg fracture, laceration)

2 What part of the body was injured?

3 Was the injury (tick the one box that applies)

☐ a fatality?

☐ a major injury or condition? (see accompanying notes)

☐ an injury to an employee or self-employed person which prevented them doing their normal work for more than 3 days?

☐ an injury to a member of the public which meant they had to be taken from the scene of the accident to a hospital for treatment?

4 Did the injured person (tick all the boxes that apply)

☐ became unconscious?

☐ need resuscitation?

☐ remain in hospital for more than 24 hours?

☐ none of the above?

Part E

About the kind of accident

Please tick the one box that best describes what happened, then go to part G.

☐ Contact with moving machinery or material being machined

☐ Hit by a moving, flying or falling object

☐ Hit by a moving vehicle

☐ Hit by something fixed or stationary

☐ Injured while handling, lifting or carrying

☐ Slipped, tripped or fell on the same level

☐ Fell from a height
How high was the fall?

[   ] metres

☐ Trapped by something collapsing

☐ Drowned or asphyxiated

☐ Exposed to, or in contact with, a harmful substance

☐ Exposed to fire

☐ Exposed to an explosion

☐ Contact with electricity or an electrical discharge

☐ Injured by an animal

☐ Physically assaulted by a person

☐ Another kind of accident (describe it in part G)

Part F

Dangerous occurrences

Enter the number of the dangerous occurrence you are reporting. (The numbers are given in the Regulations and in the notes which accompany this form.)

[   ]

Part G

Describing what happened

Give as much detail as you can. For instance
- the name of any substance involved
- the name and type of any machinery involved
- the events that led to the incident
- the part played by any people.

If it was a personal injury, give details of what the person was doing. Describe any action that has since been taken to prevent a similar incident. Use a separate piece of paper if you need to.

[   ]

☐☐☐☐ [   ]

Part H

Your signature

[   ]

Date

[/   /   ]

Where to send the form
Please send it to the Enforcing Authority for the place where it happened. If you do not know the Enforcing Authority, send it to the nearest HSE office.

For official use
Client number   Location number   Event number

[   ] [   ] [   ]   ☐ INV REP ☐ Y ☐ N

5   You have recently been appointed as the Safety Officer for your Head Office building. You are required to prepare a presentation to be made to each department explaining the procedures to be followed if the building is to be evacuated.

6   What precautions against fire must employers take under the Fire Precautions Act and Fire Precautions (Workplace) Regulations?

7   Describe three different types of fire extinguisher and the uses to which each one should be put.

8   What practical measures should be taken in order to prevent a fire in an office building?

chapter 3:
EFFECTIVENESS AND EFFICIENCY

1 Distinguish between what is meant by effectiveness and efficiency.

2 Give examples of conditions that may not be contributing to the effectiveness and efficiency of your own work and that of other employees.

3 What are the main characteristics of an organised work area?

4 Why might an organisation have policies regarding the appearance of the work area of employees and why is it important to respect the organisational policies regarding the appearance of your work area?

5   You work in an open plan accounts office with six other accounts assistants. You have been working there for two months now and have noticed a number of problems:

i)   your desk is situated near to the photocopier. You find that people tend to congregate around the photocopier for a chat and this disturbs your work.

ii)   a colleague has complained to you that where she works is very dark and she struggles to see clearly enough to work at times. She has said that she has noticed a spot where her desk and filing cabinets could be moved nearer to the window and has asked you to help her move her work area this evening after every one else has gone home.

iii)   close to your desk is that of another colleague who spends a lot of time making personal telephone calls. He tends to talk in a very loud voice and this does not help your concentration.

iv)   at times in the afternoons you feel that the office temperature is so hot that you are finding it hard to work. You know where the thermostat for the air conditioning is and you are considering turning it down this afternoon.

v)   on a number of occasions now you have noticed that your waste paper bin has not been emptied for two or three days. It is also situated near to the photocopier.

Briefly explain how you would deal with each of these situations.

6 A new photocopier has arrived and the office manager has asked you to draft a notice to be placed on top of the photocopier outlining the internal regulations about how the photocopier is to be used. The photocopier should be switched on at the start of each day by the first person to arrive in the office and switched off at the end of each day by the last person to leave. The changing of the paper cassettes is shown in diagrams and is straightforward but the replacement of toner and clearing of paper jams is more complex and only the accounts supervisor has been trained to deal with these aspects. The overall responsibility for the maintenance of the photocopier, via the leasing company, is that of the Financial Controller.

Draft a set of internal regulations for use of the photocopier.

chapter 4:
PLANNING AND ORGANISING WORK

1 Distinguish between routine tasks and unexpected tasks.

2 In what circumstances might unexpected tasks arise?

3 Distinguish between urgent tasks and important tasks.

4 If you prioritise your tasks for a day on the basis of whether or not they are urgent and whether or not they are important there would be four categories of tasks.

What are these four categories of tasks and in what order should you carry them out? Give an example of a typical task that might fall into each of the categories.

5   You are an accounts assistant working in a busy accounts office. You have the following routine daily duties:

- produce sales invoices/credit notes from despatch notes and orders
- enter sales invoices/credit notes in computer in batches
- enter cash and cheque receipts in computer
- deal with customer queries
- file all sales invoices and credit notes

You also have to produce monthly statements for each customer on the last Thursday of each month which normally takes about three hours of your time.

Today is Thursday 29 May and when you arrive at work there are three notes on your desk:

- from the accountant asking for a breakdown of sales to a large customer which is required for a meeting at 12.00pm tomorrow (you estimate that this will take about 1 hour to produce)

- from the personnel manager asking you to attend a meeting in he office from 2.00pm to 2.30pm today

- from a colleague asking for the balances on the accounts of eight customers which he requires for a meeting at 11.00pm tomorrow (you estimate that this will take about 30 minutes to prepare)

You are required to prioritise your tasks for today and tomorrow morning. Briefly explain why you have prioritised the tasks in this way.

6 Briefly describe three planning aids that can be used in the workplace.

7 You are an accounts assistant and you have been asked to prepare a report for the accounts manager which must be with him on Thursday 15 February. It is currently the morning of Tuesday 6 February.

You will need to requisition some files for this report which will take a day to arrive. Your estimate is that the research will take you one day and the analysis required another two days. The report will be with the typist for half a day, but this must be booked at least two days in advance, and then you will need one final day for checking and proofing.

Prepare a planning schedule for preparation of this report.

8   What is an action plan?

9   Explain why it is important that you should meet any deadlines that are set for tasks that you are performing. If you believe that you cannot meet a specific deadline explain what you should do and why.

10   If you are carrying out a project for a line manager and feel that you need assistance in order to meet the deadline for the project explain how you should go about getting that assistance.

11   What are the eight guiding principles from the Data Protection Act 1998?

12   How would you deal with each of the following requests and why?

i)   a more senior accounts assistant asks you to photocopy a training manual from another company which you notice has the © symbol

ii)   a colleague asks you for the home telephone number of another employee as you work in the personnel department

iii)   a customer asks you for the address and telephone number of another customer

chapter 5:
MAINTAINING GOOD WORKING RELATIONSHIPS

1 What are the main advantages of working in a team rather than individually?

2 When working within a team why is it important to agree schedules and timetables?

3 What is meant by communication?

4 What would be the most appropriate method of communication in each of the following circumstances?

    i)   explaining to a customer that a cash discount that has been deducted was not valid as the invoice was not paid within the discount period.

    ii)   requesting customer balances from a colleague in the sales ledger department.

    iii) arranging your holiday period with the human resources manager

    iv) a complaint to a supplier regarding the delivery times of goods which are not as agreed

v)   information to be provided to the sales director regarding the breakdown of sales geographically for the last two years.

5   Write a brief memo to a non-accountant explaining the difference between a trade account and a cash discount account.

MEMO

To:

From:

Date:

Subject:

---

6   If you are trying to influence a decision as you disagree with the current decision how should you behave?

7   Give examples of possible grievances within the workplace.

8   Whilst out for lunch you find yourself sitting at a table behind one of the sales ledger staff from your organisation who is lunching with a friend. You overhear the sales ledger staff member telling her friend that one of your company's customers has not been paying regularly and speculating on whether or not the customer may be in financial difficulties.

What should you do?

chapter 6:
IMPROVING YOUR OWN PERFORMANCE

1   What does SMARTER stand for in the context of setting personal development objectives?

2   Why will it normally be necessary to agree any personal development objectives with your line manager or human resources manager?

3   i)   What is the AAT's website address?

     ii)   What is the website address of the AAT magazine?

UNIT 22
CONTRIBUTE TO THE
MAINTENANCE OF A HEALTHY,
SAFE AND PRODUCTIVE WORKING
ENVIRONMENT

The performance criteria tested in this practice simulation are:

Element 22.1

A   make sure you read, comply with and have up-to-date information on the health, safety and security requirements and procedures for your workplace

B   make sure that the procedures are being followed and report any that are not to the relevant person

C   identify and correct any hazards that you can deal with safely, competently and within the limits of your authority

D   promptly and accurately report any hazards that you are not allowed to deal with to the relevant person and warn other people who may be affected

E   follow your organisation's emergency procedures promptly, calmly and efficiently

F   identify and recommend opportunities for improving health, safety and security to the responsible person

G   complete any health and safety records legibly and accurately

Element 22.2

A   organise the work area you are responsible for, so that you and others can work efficiently

B   organise the work area you are responsible for, so that it meets your organisation's requirements and presents a positive image of yourself and your team

C   identify conditions around you that interfere with effective working

D   put right any conditions that you can deal with safely, competently, within the limits of your authority and with the agreement of other relevant people

E   promptly and accurately report any other conditions to the relevant person

F   use and maintain equipment in accordance with manufacturer's instructions and your organisation's procedures

You are allowed 3 hours to complete your work.

Correcting fluid may be used but should be used in moderation. Errors should be crossed out neatly and clearly. You should write in black ink not in pencil.

DATA

Your name is Leon Hutton and you have just started working as an accounts assistant for GD Enterprises Ltd, a wholesaler of novelty gifts and toys. You report to the accounts manager.

Task 1

During the first few days of your employment you have been on an induction course regarding all aspects of the business of GD Enterprises and the work which you will be expected to do. As part of this induction training you are due to attend a short presentation on health and safety.

What documents, information and equipment would you expect to be shown during the health and safety presentation?

Task 2

At the start of the health and safety presentation you are asked by the presenter if you know what an employee's responsibilities are as regards health and safety at work. What would be your answer to this question?

Task 3

In your first few days in the accounts office you have noticed the following:

)   One of your colleagues has a habit of leaving her filing cabinet drawer open which is at about knee height.

i)   Today when you went to the photocopier you found a document marked 'highly confidential' which had been left in the copier.

ii)   You have been given instructions to shred various documents after use; however, in all of the time that you have been in the office the shredder has been marked 'out of order'.

v)   Your computer has been set up so that there is a trailing wire across a walkway from the printer. This could be tucked away under the carpet.

√)   On the way to the canteen today you have noticed that the fire door is propped open.

Write brief notes detailing how you would deal with each of these situations and why.

Task 4

In your previous job you had some involvement in a health and safety risk assessment. You mentioned this at your interview and the personnel manager at GD Enterprises Ltd, Karen Jones, has just asked you to send her a memo setting out the five main steps involved in a health and safety risk assessment.

Use the blank memo given below. Today's date is 20 January 2006.

MEMO

To:

From:

Date:

Subject:

Task 5

Earlier today you were asked to go downstairs to the archive filing room. You noticed that the fluorescent light bulb on the staircase is not working making the stairs quite dark and dangerous.

How would you deal with this situation?

Task 6

At about 2.00 o'clock this afternoon you were waiting to use the guillotine to tidy up a report whilst a colleague Fran Davis was using it. Fran was talking to you whilst working and managed to slice a chunk of skin off two fingers. The wounds were bleeding quite profusely and Fran was clearly in a lot of pain. You sat her down in the nearest chair, asked someone else in the office to contact the First Aider, Charles Wells, and then fetched the first aid box from the kitchen together with some kitchen roll to wipe up the blood. Charles Wells arrived fairly promptly and cleaned and dressed the wounds. He did not think that Fran needed hospital treatment but as she was quite shaken it was agreed with the accounts manager that she would go home for the rest of the day and that Charles would redress the wounds in three days time.

As the only witness to the accident you are required to write up your entry in the accident book given below. Today's date is 20 January 2006.

Date	Name of injured person	Details of accident (time, place, description and witnesses)	First aid treatment	Further action required

Task 7

The next day at about 10.30am the fire alarm goes off in the building. At first everyone looked around discussing whether or not this was a real emergency or just a drill. Then the accounts staff started to leave their desks but there appeared to be no unanimous view of the escape route to use or where the meeting point was. Eventually the accounts staff left their desks and made their way out of the building; however, you noticed that one colleague remained behind on the telephone and two others decided to use the lift rather than the stairs.

When the office staff arrived at the meeting point no one appeared to have a list of the accounts staff personnel in the building and there was general discussion as to who was in today. After 20 minutes in the cold, with no instructions being issued, three of the accounts staff decided to return to their desks.

Write a memo to the personnel manager, Karen Jones, detailing any problems that you noted with this evacuation procedure and any recommendations that you may have. Use the blank memo below.

```
MEMO

To:

From:

Date:

Subject:
```

Task 8

With your background knowledge of health and safety procedures the accounts manager has asked you to give a brief presentation to the accounts staff on the use of the fire extinguishers in the building. You have noted that there are three types of fire extinguisher, water, carbon dioxide and powder.

Prepare notes for a brief presentation on the use of each of these types of fire extinguisher.

Task 9

One weekend you were considering your week's work and realised that you had spent some time during the previous week searching for files, your calculator and stationery that you needed which were all within your work area but were currently hard to find due to a general state of disorganisation within your work area. You have vowed to clear up your work area on Monday morning and you are making notes to yourself about how you could improve your work area. Your work area consists of a desk, computer and screen, printer, filing cabinet, wall shelves and a set of drawers.

Draft notes about how you could organise your work area to increase your efficiency and give a more positive image of your own working effectiveness.

Task 10

Once you have tidied and organised your work area you discover that whilst the computer screen is in the correct place for comfort now this does mean that in the afternoons there is some glare from the sunshine through the window. You notice that there is a blind on the window but you have never seen anyone close it.

You also realise that one of the reasons why you tend to feel sleepy in the afternoons is that the office is so warm. You have checked the thermostat on the air conditioning unit and this is set at 20 degrees celsius.

A further problem that you have with concentration is that a colleague who sits next to you by the window tends to open it in the afternoons and you find the traffic noise from outside a distraction.

Finally having moved your computer screen this is now flickering which is causing you problems with your eyes and you can feel the start of a headache.

Draft notes as to how you should deal with each of the factors which affect the efficiency and effectiveness of your work.

Task 11

A new binding machine has arrived in the office this morning and the old one has been removed. The accounts manager has just asked you to bind 10 reports for an urgent meeting which he has this afternoon. He has said to you that the new binding machine is just like the old one so you should get on with it straight away. However, when you examine the new machine you discover that it does not look familiar in any way.

How should you deal with this situation and why?

UNIT 23
ACHIEVING PERSONAL
EFFECTIVENESS

The performance criteria tested in this practice simulation are:

Element 23.1

A identify and prioritise tasks according to organisational procedures and regulatory requirements

B recognise changes in priorities and adapt resources, allocations and work plans accordingly

C use appropriate planning aids to plan and monitor work progress

D identify, negotiate and co-ordinate relevant assistance to meet specific demands and deadlines

E report anticipated difficulties in meeting deadlines to the appropriate person

F check that work methods and activities conform to legal and regulatory requirements and organisational procedures

Element 23.2

A   communicate with other people clearly and effectively, using your organisation's procedures

B   discuss and agree realistic objectives, resources, working methods and schedules and in a way that promotes good working relationships

C   meet commitments to colleagues within agreed timescales

D   offer assistance and support where colleagues cannot meet deadlines, within your own work constraints and other commitments

E   find workable solutions for any conflicts and dissatisfaction which reduce personal and team effectiveness

F   follow organisational procedures if there are difficulties in working relationships that are beyond your authority or ability to resolve, and promptly refer them to the appropriate person

G   treat others courteously and work in a way that shows respect for other people

H   ensure data protection requirements are followed strictly and also maintain confidentiality of information relating to colleagues

You are allowed 3 hours to complete your work.

Correcting fluid may be used but should be used in moderation. Errors should be crossed out neatly and clearly. You should write in black ink not in pencil.

DATA

Your name is Justin Spring and you have recently been employed as an accounts assistant by Reeves Ltd, a company which produces and sells a variety of educational children's' toys.

Task 1

Given below is the job description that was given to you on your employment and was discussed with the personnel manager.

JOB DESCRIPTION

Job title:	Accounts assistant
Job summary:	General financial and management accounting duties
Job content:	Enter daily sales invoices into computer
	Enter daily cash/cheque receipts into computer
	Enter daily cash/cheque payments into computer
	Prepare monthly bank reconciliation
	Deal with daily petty cash claims
	Enter petty cash details in computer weekly
	Assist in preparation of weekly payroll
	Other ad hoc financial and management accounting matters
Reporting structure:	Accountant – Patrick Fellows
Hours:	9.00am to 5.30pm Monday to Friday
	1 hour for lunch
Training:	Necessary training to be provided
Prepared by:	Personnel manager
Signed by:	Justin Spring

You are required to list your daily, weekly and monthly routine tasks.

Task 2

On Friday 27 February 2006 you arrive at work knowing that you have not only your routine sales invoice entries to make in the computer (normally takes about 2 hours) and cash/cheque receipts and payments to enter into the computer (normally takes about 2 hours), petty cash claims to deal with (normally only about 30 minutes per day) but also the monthly bank reconciliation which normally takes about 2 hours and must be completed by 5.00pm. The petty cash entries to the computer should also be made today (normally about 1 hour) but these can be postponed until Monday. The cash/cheque receipts and payments for the day must be entered into the computer before the bank reconciliation can be completed but the sales invoice entries can be put off until Monday.

When you arrive at your desk you find the following additional work:

- the accountant has asked you for a list of sales invoices sent out to a particular customer for a meeting at 1.00pm today – you estimate that this will take you about 1 hour to compile.

- the personnel manager has left a message warning you that at the end of the sales conference this afternoon at about 3.00pm there will be most of the sales representatives arriving with you for their petty cash claims to be processed. You anticipate that this will take a further 30 minutes of your time on top of the normal petty cash claims for the day.

Determine the order in which you would perform the tasks required of you for the day. Briefly explain why you have given the tasks the prioritisation that you have.

Task 3

At about 11.30 am you get a telephone call from the sales director who needs an analysis of salesman's expenses to date for the last six months for a meeting at 4.00pm this afternoon. This task should take about 1 hour to complete.

Reschedule your day to reflect this change in priorities.

Task 4

On Monday 1 March Patrick Fellows, the accountant, calls you into his office. He would like you to prepare a special report regarding payroll costs. You will require files from the archives that must be ordered two days in advance. Patrick believes that given your current workload the research for the report should take two days and the analysis and writing of the report a further three days. The report must be typed which will take half a day, checked and proofed a further day of your time, ten copies printed which will take 3 hours of printer time and finally bound which should require a further half day. Printing and binding can be done together provided that there are two people doing the job, one printing a copy and then the other binding it. This joint task would take half a day. The report is required by Patrick for a meeting on Monday 15 March at 9.00pm.

Produce a planning schedule showing how you would complete this task on time.

Task 5

On Friday 5 March you are told by the personnel manager that you must attend a training course on Thursday 11 March from 9.00 am to 5.00 pm.

What assistance would you seek in order to complete the report from the previous task on time?

Task 6

If you are given the assistance that you require in the task above show how the report can be completed on time.

Task 7

On Monday 22 March 2006 you are asked to take part in a team project that will take about one month as well as your normal daily, weekly and monthly tasks. The team is to provide detailed costings for a new line of children's' toys. The team is made up of three accounts assistants a, a senior accounts assistant and the team leader who is the cost accountant. The costings must be ready for the monthly Board meeting on Wednesday 21 April 2006.

Your task within the team is to analyse the labour costs of similar products which it is estimated will take about three weeks of your time. Your estimates will then be given to the senior accounts assistant who will collate these with figures from the other accounts assistants. The figures are required by the senior accounts assistant by Tuesday 13 April 2006.

On Tuesday 6 April at the weekly project team meeting one of the other accounts assistants timidly admits that she had forgotten that the following weekend was the Easter weekend and that due to not being at work on either the Friday or the Monday she would not be able to produce all of the figures regarding materials costs for the new products. She believes that she can analyse the figures by the next day but due to her other work commitments will not have time to input them to the computer on Thursday, the last working day of the week. You know that you are likely to have some spare time on Thursday as you are ahead with your routine tasks and have completed the project tasks.

What would you do in this situation and why?

Task 8

Once the marketing director has received the costings from the project team he has sent you the following memo:

MEMO

To: Justin Spring, Accounts assistant

From: Marketing director

Date: 20 April 2006

Subject: Overheads

Thank you for your part in preparing the costings for the new product line. I have one concern which is the subject of overheads.

I notice that there are four categories of overheads in the costings:

- variable production overheads

- fixed production overheads

- selling and distribution overheads

- administration overheads

Please could you explain to me what each of these categories of overheads is made up of.

You are to write a memo in reply to the marketing director (who is not an accountant) explaining each category of overhead. Use the blank memo below.

MEMO
To:
From:
Date:
Subject:

Task 9

Later in the week you find that you have three additional tasks to perform as well as your routine duties.

i)   Deal with a customer who has taken a cash discount which is not allowable as the invoice was not paid until after the discount period had ended.

ii)   Deal with an IOU that has been put into the petty cash box for £10 from one of the administrative staff.

iii)   Provide the production manager with total overtime hours for the previous week from the payroll.

For each task determine what would be the most appropriate method of communication ie, memo, letter, telephone call, fax, e-mail etc.

Task 10

Since you started working for Reeves Ltd you have had some personal conflicts with one of the other accounts assistants, George Moss. Since day one he has constantly picked on you as the most recent recruit forcing you to make his coffee and do his photocopying for him. However, recently things have got worse and you now find that when George cannot finish his own tasks on time (which happens fairly frequently) he asks you to help him complete them. To date you have been happy to help as you tend to find that you manage to finish your own tasks within the working day fairly easily. However, you are now beginning to realise that George is fundamentally lazy and he appears to be handing over tasks to you so that he can spend more time chatting to colleagues and on the telephone. You do not want to seem un-cooperative by refusing to help George but you do feel that you are being used by a less than conscientious colleague.

How would you deal with this situation?

Task 11

One day at work you receive the following two requests:

i)   a customer calls asking for the bank details of one of Reeves Ltd's employees stating that the customer wishes to pay a cheque into the employee's bank account. You can find this information from the payroll.

ii)   one of the senior accounts assistants has asked you to photocopy the notes for a training course that another rival company uses. You notice that the course notes have the copyright symbol on them.

Explain how you would deal with each of these requests and why.

REVISION COMPANION UNITS 22 & 23

Health & safety and personal effectiveness answers

1 The Health and Safety Commission is a government body with overall responsibility for health and safety. The job of the commission is to protect everyone in Great Britain against risks to health or safety arising out of work activities, to sponsor research, to promote training, to provide information and an advisory service and to submit proposals for new or revised regulations and approved codes of practice.

The role of the Health and Safety Executive is to help the Health and Safety Commission ensure that risks to people's health and safety from work activities are properly controlled. The Executive is staffed by people from a range of different backgrounds including administrators, lawyers, inspectors, scientists, engineers, technologists and medical professionals.

2 As many as you can remember from the following list:

HEALTH

Ventilation	the workplace must be adequately ventilated with fresh, clean air – either natural air or a ventilation system
Temperature	in a workplace where employees are largely sitting, such as an office the temperatures should be at least 16 degrees Celsius (13 degrees if the work involves physical effort)
Lighting	sufficient to enable people to work and move about safely
Cleanliness	the workplace and furniture, furnishings and fittings should be kept clean as well as floors, walls and ceilings
Waste	waste should be stored in suitable receptacles and removed as necessary
Personal space	each employee in a room should have a minimum of 11 cubic metres of free space to allow them to move about with ease
Workstations	must be suitable for the people using them and for the work – employees should be able to leave them swiftly in an emergency
Seating	should give adequate support for the lower back and footrests should be provided for workers who cannot place their feet flat on the floor

SAFETY

Maintenance	equipment should be maintained in efficient working order
Floor surfaces	should not have holes or be uneven or slippery

Entry/exit routes	all entry and exit routes and routes of passage must be safe
Staircases	a handrail should be provided on at least one side of every staircase
High places	if there is a danger of employees falling from a height then safety rails or other guards must be installed
Falling objects	materials and objects need to be stored and stacked in such a way that they are not likely to fall and cause injury
Glass	where necessary should be made of safety material or protected against breakage
Windows	openable windows should be capable of being opened, closed and adjusted safely and when open should not be dangerous
Doors/gates	doors and gates should be suitably constructed and fitted with safety devices if necessary
Escalators	escalators and moving walkways should function safely, be equipped with necessary safety devices and one or more emergency stop controls
WELFARE	
Toilets	toilets and washing facilities should be kept clean and adequately lit and should have hot and cold or warm water, soap and clean towels or other means of drying
Water	an adequate supply of wholesome drinking water should be provided
Clothes	space should be provided for workers' own clothes and as far as is reasonably practical a facility for drying clothes
Rest areas	rest areas should be suitable and sufficient and should have enough seats with backrests and tables for the number of workers likely to use them at any one time
Eating	there must be facilities for employees to eat in the workplace although food need not necessarily be provided
First aid	first aid must be available normally in the form of a trained first aider and a first aid box

3   Control of Substances Hazardous to Health

4   A hazard is a condition that exists that could potentially cause harm whereas a risk is the likelihood of this hazard causing harm. Therefore, a hazard might be an unmarked step up between two offices and the risk is the likelihood that an employee might trip on the step.

5   **Step 1**   Look for the hazards

     Step 2   Decide who might be harmed and how

     Step 3   Evaluate the risks and decide whether existing precautions are adequate or more should be done

     Step 4   Record the findings

     Step 5   Review the assessment and revise it if necessary

6   Employees' responsibilities under the Health and Safety at Work etc Act are:

     ■   to take reasonable care of their own health and safety

     ■   to take reasonable care of the health and safety of others who might be affected by their actions

     ■   to co-operate with the employer in order to meet health and safety requirements

7   i)   This is probably a hazard that you can deal with yourself either by tucking the carpet back in or trimming the frayed piece of carpet.

     ii)   This is a security hazard that you would not be capable of dealing with. Alert your colleague to the potential danger and ensure that the computer is shut down. Then advise the maintenance department of the problem and suggest that your colleague uses an alternative computer terminal until the problem has been dealt with.

     iii) This is a security hazard as payroll details are private and confidential. You should inform your supervisor or the head of payroll immediately.

     iv)   This is another security risk and the maintenance department should be informed immediately.

     v)   14 degrees is below the legal level for offices of 16 degrees. However, as you have not been instructed in how to alter the temperature you should not try to do this yourself but instead inform the office supervisor.

     vi)   There are a number of actions required here. Firstly the coffee on the floor must be wiped up in case anybody slips on it. The coffee machine should be switched off and you should attach a notice saying temporarily out of order. Finally the office supervisor or maintenance department should be informed so that it can be mended.

1 An employer with more than 10 employees is legally bound to keep an accident book.

2
- go to Jennifer, take the files from her and find her a chair to sit on
- shut the desk drawer
- find a qualified first aider
- stay calm and remember as many details of the incident as possible

Date	Name of injured person	Details of accident (time, place, description and witnesses)	First aid treatment	Further action required
14/1/06	Jennifer Cage	10.30am Accounts department Jennifer walked into an open desk drawer whilst carrying a pile of files Witness Sasha Grimes	Leg cleaned and dressed by first aider	To be checked by first aider in one weeks time

3 The types of incidents that should be reported and recorded are:

- death or major injury – this includes any major fractures, amputations, dislocations, loss of sight, burns, electrocution and chemical poisoning. This relates to an employee, self-employed person or member of public on the premises

- over three day injuries – injuries that requires the employee to be off work for three days or over

- work related diseases – example might include Repetitive Strain Injury (RSI), skin diseases, lung diseases and infections such as legionnaires disease

- dangerous occurrences – incidents which could have resulted in injury eg. explosions, collapses, radiation, vehicle collisions

4

Health and Safety at Work etc Act 1974
The Reporting of Injuries, Diseases and Dangerous Occurrences Regulations 1995

HSE
Health & Safety
Executive

Report of an injury or dangerous occurrence

Filling in this form
This form must be filled in by an employer or other responsible person.

Part A

About you
1 What is your full name?

Penny Vincent

2 What is your job title?

Human resources manager

3 What is your telephone number?

01132 486 111

About your organisation
4 What is the name of your organisation?

JJ Donald Engineering

5 What is its address and postcode?

Park House
Industrial Estate
Crawley
GW3 4XN

6 What type of work does your organisation do?

Manufacture engineering products

Part B

About the incident
1 On what date did the incident happen?

21 / May /2006

2 At what time did the incident happen?
(Please use the 24-hour clock eg 0600)

09.30

3 Did the incident happen at the above address?

Yes ✓ Go to question 4

No ☐ Where did the incident happen?

☐ elsewhere in your organisation - give the name, address and postcode

☐ at someone else's premises - give the name, address and postcode

☐ in a public place - give the details of where it happened

If you do not know the postcode, what is the name of the local authority?

4 In which department, or where on the premises, did the incident happen?

Warehouse

Part C

About the injured person
If you are reporting a dangerous occurrence, go to Part F.
If more than one person was injured in the same incident, please attach the details asked for in Part C and Part D for each injured person.

1 What is their full name?

Patrick Spence

2 What is their home address and postcode?

42 High Street
Horsham
GW15 5NT

3 What is their home phone number?

01323 661 661

4 How old are they?

24

5 Are they

✓ male?

☐ female?

6 What is their job title?

☐☐☐

7 Was the injured person (tick only one box)

✓ one of your employees?

☐ on a training scheme? Give details:

☐ on work experience?

☐ employed by someone else? Give details of the employer:

☐ self-employed and at work?

☐ a member of the public?

Part D

About the injury
1 What was the injury? (eg fracture, laceration)

Fracture ☐☐

2 What part of the body was injured?

Leg ☐☐

3 Was the injury (tick the one box that applies)

- [ ] a fatality?
- [x] a major injury or condition? (see accompanying notes)
- [ ] an injury to an employee or self-employed person which prevented them doing their normal work for more than 3 days?
- [ ] an injury to a member of the public which meant they had to be taken from the scene of the accident to a hospital for treatment?

4 Did the injured person (tick all the boxes that apply)

- [ ] became unconscious?
- [ ] need resuscitation?
- [x] remain in hospital for more than 24 hours?
- [ ] none of the above?

Part E

About the kind of accident
Please tick the one box that best describes what happened, then go to part G.

- [ ] Contact with moving machinery or material being machined
- [ ] Hit by a moving, flying or falling object
- [x] Hit by a moving vehicle
- [ ] Hit by something fixed or stationary

- [ ] Injured while handling, lifting or carrying
- [ ] Slipped, tripped or fell on the same level
- [ ] Fell from a height
  How high was the fall?

  [_____] metres

- [ ] Trapped by something collapsing
- [ ] Drowned or asphyxiated
- [ ] Exposed to, or in contact with, a harmful substance
- [ ] Exposed to fire
- [ ] Exposed to an explosion
- [ ] Contact with electricity or an electrical discharge
- [ ] Injured by an animal
- [ ] Physically assaulted by a person
- [ ] Another kind of accident (describe it in part G)

Part F

Dangerous occurrences
Enter the number of the dangerous occurrence you are reporting. (The numbers are given in the Regulations and in the notes which accompany this form.)

[_____]

Part G

Describing what happened
Give as much detail as you can. For instance

- the name of any substance involved
- the name and type of any machinery involved
- the events that led to the incident
- the part played by any people.

If it was a personal injury, give details of what the person was doing. Describe any action that has since been taken to prevent a similar incident. Use a separate piece of paper if you need to.

Patrick Spence was working in the warehouse by a forklift truck whilst preparing products for despatch.

The forklift was reversing and the driver did not see Mr Spence step out behind him.

The driver has since been cautioned and all forklift truck drivers have been warned to be extra vigilant particularly when reversing.

All warehouse staff have also been warned to look out for moving vehicles within the warehouse area.

Part H

Your signature

Penny Vincent

Date

22 / 05 / 06

Where to send the form
Please send it to the Enforcing Authority for the place where it happened. If you do not know the Enforcing Authority, send it to the nearest HSE office.

For official use
Client number	Location number	Event number

[ ] INV   REP [ ] Y [ ] N

5   Draft presentation – evacuation procedures

When an evacuation takes place either as a drill or in response to a real emergency there are a number of basic procedures that each employee should follow. These procedures should alway be followed whether or not the evacuation is a real emergency or it is believed to be just a drill.

- leave the building by the designated route as quickly as possible

- stay calm at all times and remember that in the case of a fire the lifts should not be used

- go immediately to the designated assembly point and ensure that any visitors or others on the premises who do not know where to go are directed

- pay particular attention to any people being evacuated with special needs, for example wheelchairs or those with other disabilities

- respond when your name is called by myself as the Safety Officer as I will have a list of all employees who were in the building

- do not return to the building until instructed to do so by a senior official or myself

6   Under the Fire Precautions Act 1971 and the Fire Precautions (Workplace) Regulations 1997 (amended 1999) employers must:

- provide an appropriate number of suitable fire extinguishers

- install fire detectors and fire alarms where appropriate

- train employees how to deal with fighting a fire – ie. explain which type of fire extinguisher to use

- provide adequate and well signed emergency routes and exits

- communicate evacuation procedures to employees

- ensure that all fire fighting equipment is regularly maintained

7   Water extinguisher   Use for wood, paper, textiles
                                      Do not use for flammable liquids or electrical fires

Carbon dioxide extinguisher   Use for flammable liquids or electrical fires
                                      Do not use for wood, paper, textiles

Powder extinguisher   Use for all types of fire
                                      Do not use on computers as these will be ruined

8   Practical measures that should be taken to avoid a fire in the office include the following:

- keep the workplace clear of combustible materials or waste

- keep rubbish away from smoking areas or machinery that is likely to get hot

- never obstruct a fire escape route

- never prop open Fire Doors – these are fire resistant and are designed to stay shut unless escaping through them

- make sure that all Fire Exit signs can be seen

- only smoke in designated areas

- ensure that any flammable materials or substances are properly stored

1   Effectiveness is about getting the job done. You will be effective at work if you can carry out the tasks that are assigned to you. In terms of the organisation as a whole this will be viewed to be effective if it achieves its objectives such as profit targets, sales targets and a motivated workforce.

Efficiency is getting the job done with the minimum amount of resources. This means ensuring that the tasks that are undertaken are done in the quickest manner and with the minimum possible use of resources.

2   Examples of conditions that may not be contributing to the effectiveness and efficiency of your work and that of your colleagues:

- temperature in the office – too hot or too cold
- lighting – natural or artificial
- sunlight and reflection
- noise
- not enough space
- queues for services such as using the photocopier or fax
- flickering computer screens
- flickering light bulbs

3   The main characteristics of an organised work area are:

- it is clean and tidy
- the employee knows where everything he needs can be found quickly
- everything can be reached easily
- the computer is correctly set up
- the chair is the correct height for the desk and computer
- the filing system is such that not only the employee but other relevant employees can find what they need

4   Most organisations will have official or unofficial policies regarding the appearance of employees work areas. The main reason for this will be to give a good impression of the office and those who work in it.

In an office where there is little contact with suppliers, customers or the general public the rules may be fairly relaxed. However, in an office where suppliers, customers or other outsiders are regularly present then it is likely that there may be more strict policies regarding the appearance of the work area.

It is important that such policies are followed as they have been set for the purpose of giving the correct impression of the department, office or company as a whole. In other cases the policies may also have been set in order that other colleagues are not offended by any personal material that colleagues may have on show in their work area.

5   i)   In such a situation there is nothing that you would be authorised to do about this problem yourself but it would be advisable to discuss the problem with your supervisor or line manager. It may be possible to move your work area to a position that is further away from the photocopier and therefore quieter.

    ii)   Again this is not an action that you would normally be authorised to undertake. Instead you should persuade your colleague to discuss the problem with her supervisor or line manager and hopefully it can be arranged for her desk to be moved provided that this does not affect the effectiveness and efficiency of others in the office.

    iii)   Probably the first action here would be to discuss the matter with the colleague concerned or perhaps with other colleagues to discover whether they have the same problem with the loud personal telephone calls. If the problem cannot be resolved by personal contact then you may feel that you need to discuss the matter with your supervisor or line manager.

    iv)   Before turning up the thermostat it would be courteous to ask your colleagues whether they find it cold in the office as well. It may be that you feel the cold more than normal and that your other colleagues are perfectly happy with the temperature therefore to turn the air conditioning down without consulting them would not be contributing to their effectiveness and efficiency.

    v)   This is a matter that you should raise with your supervisor or line manager. It will not be your role to empty the waste paper bin but overflowing rubbish, particularly near a machine which becomes hot such as a photocopier is a definite safety hazard.

6   **Draft regulations for use of photocopier**

- to be switched on at the start of the day by the first person in the office

- to be switched off at the end of each day by the last person to leave the office

- no unauthorised copying

- no copying of copyright material without reference to supervisor (copyright material has © symbol)

- when 'paper out' symbol shows replace paper in cassette

- when 'toner out' symbol shows contact accounts supervisor

- when 'paper jam' symbol shows contact accounts supervisor

- if 'maintenance light' symbol shows refer to financial controller

1 Routine tasks are the daily, weekly and monthly tasks that make up an employee's basic job description. Unexpected tasks are other tasks that in the course of a working day or week an employee is asked to perform over and above his/her routine tasks.

2 Unexpected tasks may arise for a number of reasons. This includes one-off jobs for a more senior staff member, cover for an employee who is off sick or being instructed by a manager to help a colleague with a task in order to meet a deadline.

3 An urgent task is one that needs to be done for a deadline in the very near future. An important task is a task that is your responsibility to complete but it may not necessarily be urgent.

4 **Urgent and important tasks**

These are tasks that must be done in the very near future and which are important to yourself and to other people in the organisation. For example, if you are asked to produce a report for a meeting tomorrow morning.

Urgent but not important tasks

These are tasks which if not done will not be a major problem but they are necessary and are required to be done in the near future. For example, as a junior accounts assistant one of your responsibilities is to ensure that there is always coffee in the kitchen. You notice this morning that there is only one spoonful left therefore it must be replaced so although urgent it is not important in terms of the organisation as a whole.

Not urgent but important

These are tasks which are important but they do not necessarily have to be started immediately as there is a little time before they are due. For example if by the end of the week you need to produce a petty cash summary for the accountant for last month if today is Monday although the task is important it is not urgent although it will become so on Friday if not yet done.

Not urgent and not important

These are tasks that are not required to be done for any particular timescale. They must be done but can be done at any time when perhaps you are less busy. For example, routine tasks such as packing up out of date files to be stored in the archives.

5   Clearly the meeting with the personnel manager is important and must take place between 2.00pm and 2.30pm. As this is the last Thursday of the month then three hours of your time will have to be spent producing the monthly statements. There are also two unexpected tasks:

- production of the breakdown of sales for the accountant
- producing the account balances for your colleague

As well as this you will also need to find the time to carry out your normal routine tasks.

Plan of action

The production of the monthly statements is both urgent and important and should take priority.

The sales breakdown for the accountant and the production of the account balances for your colleague are both important, but provided that your timing estimates are accurate, could both be fitted in tomorrow morning. Therefore, the remainder of Thursday can be spent carrying out your routine tasks although the filing of the sales invoices and credit notes could be carried over until tomorrow.

Thursday

Prepare monthly statements

Carry out other routine tasks other than filing

Friday morning

9.30am   Produce account balances required

10.00am   Prepare sales breakdown for accountant

11.00am   Continue with routine tasks and catch up with yesterday's filing

6   The simplest form of planning aid is a to do list or tick list. You simply write down each task that is required of you for the day, preferably in prioritised order. Then as each task is completed tick it off from the list. At the end of the day if there is anything left unticked on the to do list then it must be carried over to tomorrow's to do list and fitted into tomorrow's tasks and priorities.

Keeping a diary is a useful way of ensuring that events or meetings are not missed. Diaries can be paper-based or electronic and can be used in combination with to do lists. The purpose of the diary is to make a note of any scheduled event or meeting as soon as you know about it and then refer to the diary on a regular basis to ensure that you do not miss the event or meeting.

Planning schedules are used for more complex tasks or projects. They tend to be used when the project involves a number of separate tasks and some of those tasks must be completed before others can be started. The planning schedule should make it quite clear when each task is to be started.

7   **Planning schedule**

Wednesday 7 Feb   Requisition files
Thursday 8 Feb   Research
Friday 9 Feb   Analysis
                 Inform typist that report will be in 13 Feb
Monday 12 Feb   Analysis
Tuesday 13 Feb   Typing
Wednesday 14 Feb Checking and proofing

8   An action plan is a very detailed planning tool which can be used for complex and usually longer term projects. It will contain a lot of detail and will be monitored on a regular basis to ensure that things are going to plan or if they are not how the situation can be rectified. An action plan will normally contain the following:

- details of each task which is part of the project
- start date of each task
- completion date for each task
- person responsible for each task
- in some cases the expected and actual costs

9   If a deadline for a task has been set then it will have been set for a reason usually due to the fact that the person for whom the task is being performed will need the information by a certain time either for a meeting or for use in another task or project.

If you believe that you cannot meet a specific deadline that has been set for a task then you should immediately inform the person for whom you are performing the task. The importance of this is that the person for whom the task is being performed can then perhaps change their own deadlines for which the task was required or can arrange help or additional resources which mean that you can meet the original deadline.

10   There are four main stages to obtaining assistance for the purpose of meeting a deadline.

Firstly you must recognise that you need help or additional resources and that without them you will not meet the deadline. Secondly you must identify what additional resources are required for you to meet the deadline – this may be additional man hours or additional computer time etc. The additional resources required must then be negotiated with the appropriate manager which will include any reasons why you have fallen behind schedule in the first place. Finally you must co-ordinate any additional resources that are negotiated to ensure that they do enable you to meet your deadline.

11   The eight guiding principles from the Data Protection Act 1998 are as follows:

- personal data should be obtained and processed fairly and lawfully
- personal data should be held only for specified purposes
- personal data should be adequate, relevant and not excessive for those purposes
- personal data should be accurate and kept up to date
- personal data should not be kept for longer than is necessary
- personal data should be available to the individual whose data is being held
- personal data should be kept securely
- personal data should not be exported to countries outside the European Union unless it will be adequately protected in that country

12 i) Under copyright law you are not allowed to photocopy the training manual as it has the copyright symbol. Therefore, you should explain this to the accounts assistant and not carry out the photocopying.

ii) You would have to refuse this request as it is personal data which cannot be divulged to anyone.

iii) Again this request would be declined as this is personal data and as such should not be divulged.

answers to chapter 5: MAINTAINING GOOD WORKING RELATIONSHIPS

1   There are a number of advantages of working as part of a team rather than on an individual basis:

- **additional resources** – within a team there are likely to be individuals with different types of skills and techniques which can be used by the whole team

- **inspiration** – it is often the case that if a number of people are involved in a task or project then they can inspire each other and this may encourage individuals to be more creative and hard working

- **motivation** – the overall goal of the team and the help and support of individuals within the team can often provide additional motivation to team members in their work

2   As part of a team it is highly likely that the tasks that you perform will have an effect on other team members. Information that you provide will be used by other members of the team and they cannot complete their tasks until you have provided that information or completed your tasks. Therefore, schedules and timetables must be set by the team leader to ensure that there is full integration of the work of all members of the team. It is always important to meet deadlines as they will have been set for a purpose and within a team it is important that each individual meets their commitments according to the schedules set in order for the team to achieve its objectives.

3   Communication is about putting across your message in the most appropriate form and ensuring that that message is fully understood.

4   i)   telephone

    ii)   note or e-mail

    iii) face to face

    iv)   letter

    v)   memo, e-mail or possibly a more formal report

5

MEMO

To: Non-accountant

From: Accounts assistant

Date: 15 January 2006

Subject: Trade and cash discounts

When goods are sold to a customer they will normally be sold at the list price. However, some long-standing or bulk purchasing customers are allowed a trade discount in appreciation of their loyalty and custom. A trade discount is a percentage deduction from the list price of the goods which is shown on the invoice.

A cash or settlement discount is not an amount that is deducted from the value of the goods on the invoice. Instead the customer is offered the opportunity to pay the invoice within a certain period of time, say 10 days rather than the normal credit terms of 30 days. It is the customer's choice whether or not they accept the cash discount. If the customer decides to pay the invoice within the stipulated period, 10 days, then they will deduct the cash discount percentage from the invoice total and only pay the remaining amount.

I hope that this has been helpful.

---

6   If you are trying to influence someone, for example if you disagree with their solution to a problem and are putting forward your own solution, then you will need to be assertive without being aggressive and put forward your views clearly. Also be seen to be listening to the other party's arguments as nothing is more difficult to deal with than someone who will not accept that other people have ideas as well!

7   Grievances within the workplace might include the following:

- a serious case of harassment

- examples of unfair treatment by managers such as an employee not being promoted due to race, gender or disability

- an employee being given an unfair workload

- an employee being blocked for promotion

- unfair pay such as a male employee being paid more for the same work than a female employee

8   In this instance it would appear that the member of the sales ledger staff is divulging confidential information about one of the company's customers to an outsider. This is a serious breach of confidentiality and you should report the matter to your line manager as soon as possible.

1 S Specific
   M Measurable
   A Agreed
   R Realistic
   T Time-bounded
   E Evaluated
   R Reviewed

2 Despite the fact that you might be setting your personal development objectives yourself in many cases the achievement of these objectives will require the commitment of resources from your employer. This may be simply the loss of your time while you study or go on a training course but will also encompass the direct costs of your development. Therefore, it is important that, where necessary, any personal development objectives are agreed with the appropriate person which will often be your line manager or human resources manager.

3 i)   AAT website address is www.aat.org.uk

   ii) AAT magazine website address is www.accountingtechnician.co.uk

SKILLS BASED ASSESSMENT 1

UNIT 22
SUGGESTED ANSWERS

ANSWERS

Task 1

- Health and safety policy statement to sign
- Health and safety poster
- Name of health and safety officer
- Names of first aiders
- First aid box

Task 2

Employees have responsibilities under the Health and Safety at Work etc Act:

- to take reasonable care of their own health and safety

- to take reasonable care of the health and safety of others who might be affected by their actions

- to co-operate with the employer in order to meet health and safety requirements

Task 3

i)   If a drawer is left open it is easy for someone to trip over it and hurt themselves. Therefore, it would be appropriate to quietly point this out to your colleague asking her to keep it shut.

ii)   This is a security issue as confidential documents should not be left around where they can be read by anyone. Your course of action should be to inform the accounts manager of the situation immediately.

iii) This is a matter that should be raised with the accounts manager. It is company policy to shred various documents and part of the health and safety duties of the employer is to keep all machinery and equipment in good working order.

iv)   The trailing wire is a safety hazard but it would appear to be a hazard that you can put right yourself. Attempt to deal with this by carefully putting the wire under the carpet; however if this is not possible then you should inform the accounts manager who will deal with the maintenance department.

v)   Fire doors should not be propped open and therefore you should ensure that it is shut as you walk through it.

Task 4

MEMO

To: Karen Jones

From: Leon Hutton

Date: 20 January 2006

Subject: Risk Assessment

The Health and Safety Executive have issued practical guidance on risk assessment in the work place and have set out a five step plan for carrying out an assessment.

Step 1   Look for the hazards

Walk around the workplace and look afresh at what could reasonably be expected to cause harm. It is also recommended that you should ask the employees if they have noticed anything which is not immediately obvious but might be a hazard.

Step 2   Decide who might be harmed and how

Those that might be harmed are of course employees in general but bear in mind in particular young workers, trainees, pregnant women and staff with disabilities. There is also a responsibility to cleaners, visitors, contractors, maintenance workers etc who may not be in the workplace all of the time. Finally consideration should also be given to members of the public if there is a chance that they could be hurt by the organisation's activities.

Step 3   Evaluate the risks and decide whether existing precautions are adequate or more should be done

For each significant hazard the recommendation is to decide whether the risk is high, medium or low. The aim is to make all risks small by adding to the precautions already taken. For each hazard listed the precautions should meet legal requirements, recognised industry standards, good practice standards and should reduce the risk as far as is reasonably practical.

Step 4   Record the findings

In an organisation with more than five employees the employer must record any significant findings of the risk assessment. The significant hazards and the conclusions reached should be written down and the employer must tell his employees of his findings.

Step 5   Review the assessment and revise it if necessary

If a new significant hazard appears due to new machines, substances or processes then this must be added to the assessment. The assessment should be reviewed from time to time to make sure that the precautions are still working effectively.

I hope that this has been useful to you.

Task 5

You must of course report the missing light bulb to either the maintenance department directly or to the accounts manager. However, there is a further issue here in that other people might be affected by this if they use this staircase. Therefore, it would be necessary for you to warn others perhaps by putting up a temporary notice at the top of the staircase saying 'TAKE EXTRA CARE – NO LIGHT ON STAIRCASE'

Task 6

Date	Name of injured person	Details of accident (time, place, description and witnesses)	First aid treatment	Further action required
2006 20 Jan	Fran Davis	2.00 pm – Fran was working with the guillotine in the office and sliced skin off the end of two fingers. Witness Leon Hutton.	Wound cleaned and dressed by Charles Wells – first aider. Fran sent home.	Wound to be redressed by Charles Wells in three days

Task 7

MEMO

To: Karen Jones

From: Leon Hutton

Date: 21 January 2006

Subject: Evacuation procedure

As you know there was an emergency evacuation drill in the building this morning. I noticed a number of features which do need addressing for future evacuation procedures.

Initially there was no immediacy of action within the accounts department as everyone was discussing whether this was a drill or the real thing. Eventually the staff started to leave the office but one member of staff remained behind on the telephone. The accounts staff should be informed clearly that they should evacuate the building immediately whenever the alarm is heard.

It became clear during the evacuation that members of the accounts staff were uncertain of the escape route or the meeting place. This should be made clear to all staff and should be posted on the noticeboard.

Two accounts staff used the lift to evacuate the building. In the case of a fire the lift should never be used and again this should be made clear to staff.

There was no list of people in the office that day so that in a real emergency it would not have been clear whether all staff had been safely evacuated. It should be the responsibility of one member of staff to keep a list of personnel in the office each day and to take that list during any evacuation.

Finally some members of staff returned to their desks without being given an official all clear. Staff should be informed that they should never go back into the building until they have been told to do so by the Safety Officer or a senior member of staff.

I hope that this has been useful.

Task 8

Water extinguisher   Should be used for wood, paper and textiles fires
                                Do not use for flammable liquids or electrical fires

Carbon dioxide extinguisher Should be used for flammable liquids or electrical fires
                                Do not use for wood, paper or textiles

Powder extinguisher   Can be used for most types of fire
                                Do not use on computers as these will be ruined

Task 9

- Check your desk and chair are at the right height for each other to ensure comfortable working position.

- Computer screen, keyboard and mouse should be positioned so that body is not twisted to use it

- Screen should be in a position where there is no glare from the screen caused by lighting o sunlight

- All equipment used regularly, such as calculator and telephone, should be readily to hand

- Minimise piles of papers on desk

- Frequently used files in filing cabinet close to desk

- Frequently used forms and stationery should be in drawers to hand

- Ensure no inappropriate personal memorabilia on desk

- Tidy desk each evening to ensure organised start in the morning

Task 10

Glare from the screen could be eliminated by closing the blind. However, this will also affect other staf so they must be asked first. It may be that when the blind is closed some staff do not have enough natura light to work. If the other staff are happy then close the blind provided that it is not necessary to climb on anything to do so.

The air temperature in the office does appear quite high but before any action is taken you shoulc consult your colleagues. They may also feel that it is too warm but you must check with them first. I should be a simple job then to turn down the thermostat to say 16 or 17 degrees.

Discuss the situation with your colleague and explain your problem asking if the window could be kep shut. It may be that when the thermostat is turned down your colleague will have no need to open the window for air.

The flickering computer screen is certainly a hazard but it is not one that you can deal with yourself. You must inform the maintenance department or the accounts manager.

Task 11

Even though the job is urgent you should ensure that you read the manufacturer's instructions for the binding machine before using it. An employee has a legal duty to use all equipment provided by ar employer properly and in accordance with the instructions. As the task will now take a little more time then this should be explained to the accounts manager.

SKILLS BASED ASSESSMENT 2

UNIT 23
SUGGESTED ANSWERS

ANSWERS

Task 1

Daily tasks Enter sales invoices into the computer
Enter cash/cheque receipts into the computer
Enter cash/cheque payments into computer
Deal with petty cash claims

Weekly tasks Enter petty cash details into the computer
Assist in preparation of payroll

Monthly tasks Prepare bank reconciliation

Task 2

9.00am to 11.00 am Enter cash/cheque receipts and payments into computer
- this is high priority as it must be done before the bank reconciliation can be prepared

11.00am to 12.00 Prepare sales invoice listing for the accountant
- again this is high priority as it is needed for a meeting at 1.00pm

Note that the order of these two tasks could have been reversed to ensure that the accountant definitely got the figures on time.

12.00 to 1.00pm Lunch break

1.00pm to 3.00pm Prepare bank reconciliation
- this must be completed by 5.00pm

3.00pm to 3.30pm Deal with sales representatives petty cash claims
- an unexpected task which must be fitted in at this point

3.30pm to 4.00pm Deal with other petty cash claims for the day

You now have one and a half hours left until the end of the day and have completed all of the tasks that must be done today. During the remainder of the day you can start on the sales invoice inputs or complete the petty cash computer entries and then move on to the sales invoice inputs with the remainder being completed on Monday.

Task 3

9.00am to 11.00 am Enter cash/cheque receipts and payments into computer

11.00am to 12.00 Prepare sales invoice listing for the accountant

12.00 to 1.00pm Lunch break

1.00pm to 2.00pm Prepare analysis of sales representatives' expenses for sales director

2.00pm to 3.00pm Prepare first half of bank reconciliation

3.00pm to 3.30pm	Deal with sales representatives' petty cash claims
3.30pm to 4.30pm	Complete bank reconciliation
4.30pm to 5.00pm	Deal with other petty cash claims for the day
5.00pm to 5.30pm	Start either sales invoice computer entry or petty cash computer entry

Task 4

Mon 1 March	Order files
Wed 3 March	Research
Thurs 4 March	Research
Fri 5 March	Analysis
Mon 8 March	Analysis
Tues 9 March	Analysis
Wed 10 March	Typed
Thurs 11 March	Checked and proofed
Fri 12 March	Print and bind

Task 5

As you will be out of the office all day on Thursday 11 March this will leave you with half a day of report time missing. Typing the report should only take half a day on Wednesday 10 March therefore you could check and proof the report on Wednesday afternoon and Friday morning. This will however only leave you Friday afternoon to print the report and to bind it which cannot be done by you alone in the time available.

Therefore, you would need to seek help in printing and binding the report which would require half a day of another accounts assistant's time.

Task 6

Mon 1 March	Order files
Wed 3 March	Research
Thurs 4 March	Research
Fri 5 March	Analysis
Mon 8 March	Analysis
Tues 9 March	Analysis
Wed 10 March – am	Typed
– pm	Checked
Thurs 11 March	Training course
Fri 12 March – am	Checked
– pm	Printing and binding – 2 people

Task 7

As you are likely to have some spare time on Thursday then you should offer to help your colleague to input the figures to the computer that day. The entire project depends upon the figures being ready for Tuesday 13 April and you should offer assistance to ensure that the project team meets this deadline.

Task 8

MEMO

To: Marcus Field, Marketing director

From: Justin Spring, Accounts assistant

Date: 20 April 2006

Subject: Overheads

In general terms overheads are the expenses incurred by the business as opposed to the direct inputs to the products such as materials and labour time. These expenses tend to be classified according to the function and behaviour in order to improve the analysis of the cost figures.

Variable production overheads are expenses that are incurred within the factory and which relate closely to the product being manufactured. For example, the power costs of the machinery used for the product or the cost of the lubricant used on those machines.

Fixed production overheads are expenses incurred by the factory in general which cannot be specifically related to the particular product such as the total rent of the factory. Such fixed production overheads tend to be split up amongst all of the products and therefore each product bears a share of the expense.

Selling and distribution overheads are the expenses incurred in actually selling the product and delivering it to customers. This might include advertising and marketing costs and delivery van costs.

Administration overheads are all of the other expenses incurred by the business such as telephone and electricity bills. Again these cannot be related to a particular product and are therefore split up amongst all of the products.

I hope this has been helpful.

Task 9

i)   Customer and cash discount – letter

ii)   IOU in petty cash box – telephone call

iii) Overtime hours for production manager – memo or e-mail

Task 10

Initially you might talk to the other accounts assistants to find out if they had similar problems with George when they first joined the company and how they dealt with the problem. The next step would be to talk to George himself and explain that you are happy to help out in an emergency but not to do his work for him on a day to day basis.

If the situation does not improve after talking to George personally then you will have to consider reporting the matter to the accountant, Patrick Fellows.

Task 11

i)   Under the Data Protection Act this is personal data and should only be used for the purpose of making payments from the payroll. It is also highly confidential information and should not be disclosed to anyone. Therefore the customer's request must be denied.

ii)   As these notes have the copyright symbol on them then they must not be photocopied without written permission from the copyright owner, the rival company. This must be explained to the senior accounts assistant and you should not copy them.

COMBINED COMPANION

UNIT 21

WORKING WITH COMPUTERS

chapter 7:
USING COMPUTER SYSTEMS AND SOFTWARE

knowledge and understanding – general information technology

- the importance of carrying out simple visual safety checks on hardware and correct powering up and shutting down procedures

- how to save, transfer and print documents

- how to take back up copies

- causes of difficulties, necessary files which have been damaged or deleted, printer problems, hardware problems

knowledge and understanding – the organisation

- location of hardware, software and backup copies

- location of information sources

- the organisation's procedures for changing passwords, and making backups

- house style for presentation of documents

Performance criteria – element 21.1

- perform initial visual safety checks and power up the computer system

- use passwords to gain access to the computer system where limitations on access to data is required

- access, save and print data files and exit from relevant software

- use appropriate file names and save work

- back up work carried out on a computer system to suitable storage media at regular intervals

- close down the computer without damaging the computer system

- seek immediate assistance when difficulties occur

BUSINESS COMPUTER SYSTEMS

You may well be an experienced user of computers already, perhaps because of your previous education and perhaps because you have one yourself at home. In that case some of the contents of this chapter will be very familiar, but do not assume you know everything you need to know already.

- The most important thing to realise, when using a computer at work, is that the information it contains is crucial to the proper running of the business, so a much higher standard of care is needed than you might be used to on your own computer.

- Another important point to bear in mind for an accountant is that you may often be using computers that you are not used to, especially if your work involves visiting clients at their premises and using their computers and their data.

Hardware

As the name suggests, hardware is anything you can physically touch – a keyboard, a mouse, a monitor, a printer and so on.

Your computer at work may be a 'stand alone' machine like the one you have at home – in other words not directly connected to any other computers – but it is much more likely that it will be part of a network. The only difference, in terms of the actual machine, is that a computer on a network must have a network card and it may not have an internal modem.

Let's begin, therefore, by looking at the hardware components of a business computer system. Here's a diagram of a typical small business's network.

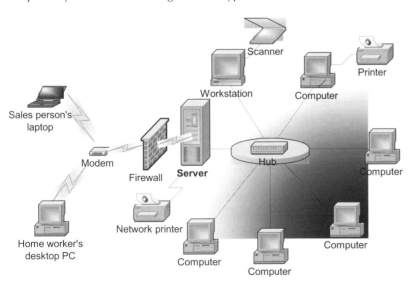

student notes✍

You may not be aware that your organisation's system has all these components and you may not even know where the server and the hub are – they may well be in another part of the building or in a different building.

- **Computers and workstations**: a monitor, a keyboard, a mouse and a box or tower containing disk drives (internal hard drive, floppy disk drive and CD drive) and all the electronics ('chips') that process data and make the computer work. A workstation is the same but it has a faster processor and more computer 'memory': they are used by graphic designers, web developers and the like.

  In old systems the computer user may just have a 'terminal' linked to a much more powerful computer elsewhere, in which case all you will see when you turn it on is a black screen with white or green text, not the gloriously coloured backgrounds and icons of computers that you are used to. Terminals are now relatively rare, but you may still have to go into 'terminal-mode' on a PC to operate some accounting systems.

- **Printers**: for printing out letters, accounting reports and so on. There may be a variety of types of printer for different purposes.

  - Laser printers, which work in much the same way as photocopiers, give the highest quality so you would use one of those for an important letter.

  - Accounting documents are often multipart forms such as invoices and these need to be printed out using some kind of impact printer such as a line printer – a printer that bangs a head or needle against an ink ribbon or (perhaps more usually, these days) directly onto special paper that is impregnated with a chemical that makes marks appear when the paper is hit.

- **Scanners**: these can be used to convert photographs into a form that can be read by computer. They can also read in printed materials and convert them into documents that can be read by text-editing programs (accuracy will depend how clean and clear the original copy is, and how complex the layout is).

- **Server and Hub**: a server is a powerful computer that controls the links between the desktop computers. For example it manages e-mail exchanges and provides services for (i.e. 'serves') the other computers. Services include storing data, enabling other computers to share it, handling queues for printers, and so on. The server will also be equipped with, or be connected to, backup devices such as tape drives. Connections are made through a hub, which in simple terms is a box into which all the connecting cables are plugged. All you usually need to do to connect to the hub and server is plug a wire into a socket in the wall and type in a password.

- **Firewall**: this is an important security component if the network in your organisation is also connected to the Internet. Firewalls may either be physical boxes, or the server may have a program on it (software) that performs the same function.

- **Modem**: this handles connections to an external telecoms network (usually the Internet, but larger organisations may have their own). Stand-alone computers will have an internal modem, but in a network connections are usually made via a separate modem connected to the server and protected by a firewall.

Activity 1

Draw a diagram of the components of the network in your own office, as far as you can. (If you work for a very large organisation you may have to restrict this to your own department or your own immediate colleagues.) It need not be a work of art - just use different-sized boxes for the different components - but make sure it is clearly enough labelled for someone other than you to understand it.

Software

Software means all the programs on your computer. Broadly speaking these can be split into the operating system (e.g. Windows) and applications (everything else).

The operating system (OS) does all the basic things that you take for granted, such as recognising input from the keyboard and the mouse, sending output to the screen, handling the location of files on the computer's hard disk, and controlling 'peripherals' such as printers.

Windows XP

Mac OS X

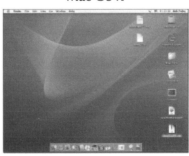

Unix (Sun Solaris)

student notes 🖎

Windows is by far the most common OS, but depending on the type of organisation you work for you may also come across various types of Unix (e.g. Sun Solaris, Linux), and/or the Apple Mac operating system (the latest version of which is also based on Unix). Unix tends to be used behind the scenes in some large organisations. The Mac OS is popular in creative organisations such as publishers, designers and advertising companies.

The majority of the screen illustrations in this book are taken from a computer running the latest version of Windows (Windows XP), although there are also some from a computer running Mac OS X.

Applications include all of the following.

- Browsers, of which most popular is Microsoft Internet Explorer.

- Email software, such as Microsoft Outlook.

- Word processing software: Microsoft Word is the most popular.

- Spreadsheets: Microsoft Excel is the most popular.

- Presentation software such as Microsoft PowerPoint

- Databases: examples include Microsoft Access for small-scale purposes and Microsoft SQL Server or Oracle for the larger-scale.

- Accounting packages, such as QuickBooks, Sage, Access Financials (nothing to do with the Access database) and many, many others.

Sage Line 50   **Microsoft Excel**

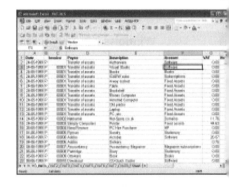

Basic applications are often bundled together into an 'office' package (such as Microsoft Office), which as a bare minimum will include a word processing package and a spreadsheet package, and perhaps also presentation software, email and a database package.

We'll take a closer look at some office applications later in this chapter. The whole of Chapter 9 is devoted to accounting packages.

Activity 2

Find out if there is a standard configuration for a computer in your organisation. For example does everyone have the same version of the same operating system? Does everyone have the same applications in the same versions?

POWERING UP AND SHUTTING DOWN

Switching on a computer is as easy as switching on any other piece of electrical equipment: just press the ON button! Actually, depending on the model, you may have to turn on more than one switch to get everything going, for example if the main computer and the monitor have separate plugs. That's a bit like your hi-fi, perhaps: with some models you have to turn on the amplifier separately from the CD player.

Bear in mind that just because the computer screen is blank, that does not necessarily mean the computer is turned off: if it is set to conserve power then the monitor will turn itself off after a certain time of inactivity. So just before you turn on a computer it is always wise to check that it is not already on. You can do this simply by moving the mouse or pressing the space bar: if the computer is already on you will hear the hard disk spinning up and the screen will soon come back to life.

Activity 3

Do you think it matters which order you switch on the monitor and the main computer? (Think of your hi-fi, say, or your TV and DVD player, if you are not sure.)

Safety

It's best to be SAFE with all electrical equipment, and that especially applies in offices because offices have a lot more 'traffic' than your living room - colleagues dropping in to discuss something, office cleaners who may need to get into corners and under the desk, builders and decorators maybe, or at worst intruders who have no business being there at all.

Being safe means making sure that you don't get injured YOURSELF and also taking care that there is no damage to the EQUIPMENT or to the DATA stored on it. You should also bear in mind the SAFETY OF OTHER PEOPLE.

Your own office may be very well-organised and your organisation probably already has proper safety procedures, but accountants often find themselves working in the offices of client organisations and using their computers. Some of your clients may not be as safety conscious as you are. Take special care in that situation.

Safety checks: main connections

VISUAL checks and common sense are all that are required of a user on a day-to-day basis. You are not expected to be a qualified electrician and you certainly should not start pulling the equipment apart or interfering with plugs and sockets.

 Probably the commonest problem with mains connections is overloading the circuit by plugging too many items into adaptors. Older buildings and buildings not originally designed to be offices are likely to be the worst offenders because there will not be enough sockets for all the electrical equipment a modern office needs.

There may be nothing you can do about this in the short term, if there are not enough sockets available for all the equipment being used, but you should certainly REPORT it.

Make sure plugs are fully plugged in, flush against the socket. Plugs can easily get pulled partially out of their sockets, for example if you move a piece of equipment or move the desk it is sitting on.

Plugs may be badly wired with the wires exposed where the cable enters the plug. Cables can also get worn or cut accidentally or they may overheat, and any of these problems might expose the wires underneath. The plug itself or the socket may be cracked, so look out for this. If it all seems to be held together with sticky tape then don't use it - that is not adequate protection!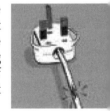

Everything you have learned already in this book about health and safety also applies of course. Watch out for trailing wires that might trip people up, precariously balanced cups of coffee, and so on.

Safety checks: connections between components

Computer cables and plugs are not normally dangerous in the same sense as mains cables. The main problem that is likely to occur with the cables and plugs for peripheral items such as printers and scanners, and even the keyboard and mouse, is that they are not plugged in fully, or not at all.

Most people these days have no idea how to operate a computer without a mouse, so you may well find yourself stuck if you turn on a computer without the mouse plugged in.

Once again, all that is normally required is a quick glance at the back of the computer to check that everything is plugged in properly.

Activity 4

Do you think it matters whether you plug the printer cable into the back of the computer before or after you switch on the computer? What about the network cable: must that be plugged in before you switch on?

Improper shut down

It is important to get into good habits when shutting down the computer. You should never just turn off the mains power. You risk corrupting data on the hard drive or, at worst, damaging the hard drive itself.

Although the results would rarely be catastrophic with modern computers and operating systems, it will at the very least waste your time. That's because the computer will know how badly you treated it, and it will strongly encourage you to do a full disk scan, to check that everything is still OK, the next time you turn it on.

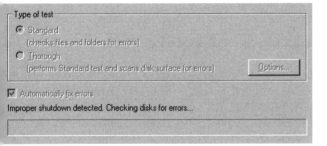

An improper shutdown may occur through no fault of your own, if there is a sudden power cut, say, or if someone else accidentally unplugs your computer.

You may also find that your program suddenly stops working for no apparent reason.

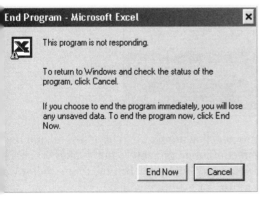

Problems like this are often caused as a result of computer memory problems: you simply have more programs and files open than the computer can deal with. There is rarely much you can do other than close down the program and restart, but if you are lucky the program will rescue as much of your data as possible: we'll come back to this later.

Shutting down applications

Before you shut down your computer it is best to shut down any applications that are running individually. Click on File and then choose Exit or simply click on the Close button ⊠ at the top right hand corner.

If you still have any files open in that application you will then be prompted to save them if you haven't done so already (you'll also be asked to give them a more meaningful name than the one suggested by the program, if you have not previously saved them: we'll cover file naming and saving a little later).

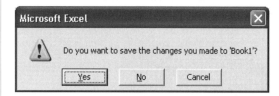

Take your time with this: it is ALWAYS worth saving a file unless you are absolutely sure you'll never need it again - you can always delete it later. Unfortunately you will forget this, from time to time - we have all done it - and there is nothing worse than realising that you have just said 'No' to saving an entire afternoon's work! You'll be more careful next time.

Shutting down the computer properly

Perhaps rather confusingly, for first time users, the correct way to STOP a Windows computer is to click on the START button.

Logging off is an option for computers that are set up to have several different users. It does not shut down the computer completely, but it takes you back to a log on screen. If someone else logs on they will be able to use their own files, but they will not be able to use, or even see yours.

If you choose to turn off, you can either put the computer into 'stand by' mode, or turn it off completely, or you can restart it. Stand by mode is useful for saving power and yet it means that your computer starts up again more quickly when you need it.

Restarting is often helpful if you have been doing a lot of work with a lot of different applications and, although you want to carry on, you first want to clear the computer's memory totally, to speed it up a bit. You may not be an Apple Mac user - most accountants aren't - but you may have to use one at a client's premises. If you need to turn it off there are similar options. To get to them you click on the Apple symbol (top left-hand corner).

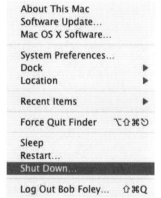

If you choose to shut down completely the operating system will check to see if there are any files still open that need to be saved and it will give you warnings about these. As mentioned, it is much better to shut down applications individually yourself, because then you don't feel as if you are being rushed to make these decisions.

PASSWORDS

Passwords and associated security measures, such as usernames, PIN numbers and 'memorable information', have become a familiar part of life, as more and more of us take advantage of facilities such as telephone banking and/or use the Internet to manage our affairs.

A good password is one that consists of both letters (some capitals, some not) and numbers and is at least eight characters long. We'll discuss password setting and password changing in more detail in Chapter 8.

At work you are likely to encounter passwords at several different levels.

student notes ✍

Logging on to the computer

You may need a password to log onto your computer in the first place especially if the computer you use is used by others too. For instance there may be a computer that can be used by anyone in the accounts department but only by one person to do sensitive payroll work.

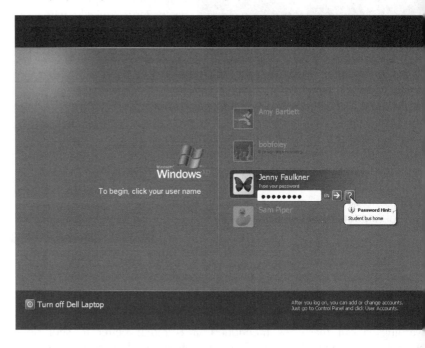

In this example, Jenny Faulkner may have an 'administrator' account enabling her to see everything on the computer while Amy Bartlett may have a more limited account that only lets her see her own files.

Note that the password itself should never actually appear on the screen: you will usually see a row of dots or asterisks. This is to stop anyone else who may be looking at your screen seeing what your password is. In fact, if you use text-based applications - and some accounting applications in large organisations still fall into this category - you may find you have to log in as in the following illustration.

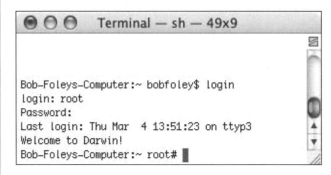

Note that although the user has clearly typed in a password successfully (because they have got a welcome message) nothing is shown on screen at all in the password line in a typical (Unix-based) system like this. This is an extra security measure: someone who caught sight of this screen would not even know how many characters the password contained.

Logging on to the network

In some systems your computer may start up in stand-alone mode and you will be required to enter a further password to log on to the network.

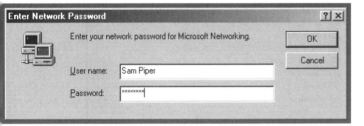

Opening an application

Sometimes you will need a password to open an application. You are very likely to encounter these if you use an accounting package. Your password may not give you full access to everything that can be done with an application.

- For instance you may be able to enter accounting transactions, but not be allowed to view payroll information, because that is considered to be extra-sensitive and is handled by your manager.

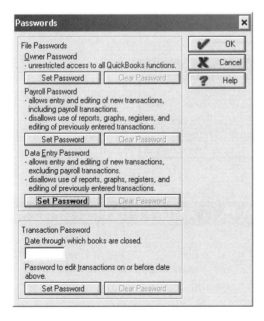

- ■ Or you may be allowed access to the purchase ledger functions, but not to the sales ledger, because the sales ledger is handled by another department.

Opening a file

To open a file you usually just have to double click on it, but you may sometimes have to enter a password to view or modify a specific document.

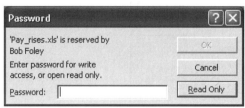

ACCESSING, SAVING AND PRINTING FILES

In a manual system you need to give a good deal of thought to the efficient physical storage of data. For instance you would normally organise the documents you need to keep and find again into different folders, and you may have different categories for different customers, different products, different geographical regions, and so on. Within the folders documents may be physically arranged in alphabetical order, or date order, or subject order, or probably some combination of all of these.

Many of the principles for organising files and data that apply in manual systems will also be used in computer systems, but because computer files are not physical documents there is a great deal more flexibility.

Computer file managers

Computers organise documents firstly by the 'drive' on which they are stored (for example the hard disk drive or the floppy disk drive) and the drive is divided into folders and sub-folders. This is equivalent to a room (the drive), containing filing cabinets (the folders), which contain lever arch files (sub-folders) in manual systems.

With a computer the number of folders and sub-folders is only limited by the size of the storage medium.

We limit our illustrations in this section to Microsoft Windows, but Apple operating systems and Unix graphical user interfaces such as Gnome and KDE work in almost exactly the same way.

Windows Explorer and Windows My Computer are more or less the same program; Windows Explorer is our preference.

For instance the folders and sub-folders on the hard disk of a computer owned by Southfield Electrical might look like this in Windows Explorer.

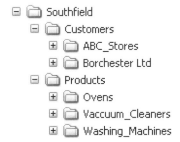

File management programs such as Windows Explorer allow you to sort folders and the files within folders according to four criteria: the name of the file; its size in bytes; the type of file; and the date and time last modified.

The list in the following illustration is ordered in alphabetical order of file name.

student notes✍

Activity 5

Study the illustration below. What other comments can you make about how the items are ordered.

Name ▲	Size	Type	Date Modified
backup.doc	24 KB	Microsoft Word Doc...	24/01/2005 17:26
Benson1.doc	1 KB	Microsoft Word Doc...	11/02/2005 17:43
Benson2.doc	10 KB	Microsoft Word Doc...	03/03/2005 15:04
Benson10.doc	5 KB	Microsoft Word Doc...	11/03/2005 17:43
Benson11.doc	38 KB	Microsoft Word Doc...	13/05/2005 17:43
Benson_Pres.ppt	37 KB	Microsoft PowerPoi...	04/04/2005 09:14
BensonPres.htm	35 KB	HTML Document	11/04/2005 12:27
BensonSales.xls	1 KB	Microsoft Excel Wor...	06/06/2005 17:43
Dean.doc	13 KB	Microsoft Word Doc...	09/01/2005 14:43
Dean-Baker.doc	5 KB	Microsoft Word Doc...	25/08/2005 16:01
Deans.doc	5 KB	Microsoft Word Doc...	28/03/2005 11:25
discount.xls	39 KB	Microsoft Excel Wor...	15/04/2005 17:27
Doc1.doc	2 KB	Microsoft Word Doc...	18/01/2005 10:22
Doc3.doc.doc	19 KB	Microsoft Word Doc...	28/02/2005 13:27
flowchart.jpg	1 KB	JPEG Image	06/06/2005 14:05
logo.gif	24 KB	GIF Image	09/05/2005 09:36
Maternity.doc	38 KB	Microsoft Word Doc...	12/01/2005 15:48
PRO_8245_05_1.doc	2 KB	Microsoft Word Doc...	11/02/2005 16:12
This file name is too long to b...	5 KB	Text Document	03/03/2005 12:14
UPPER.doc	8 KB	Microsoft Word Doc...	04/07/2005 15:01

With a computer you can sort and resort in ascending or descending order simply by clicking on the column title.

For instance here is the previous list reorganised by file type-indicated by the extension, .gif, .htm etc.-simply by clicking on the Type column heading.

Name	Size	Type ▲	Date Modified
logo.gif	24 KB	GIF Image	09/05/2005 09:36
BensonPres.htm	35 KB	HTML Document	11/04/2005 12:27
flowchart.jpg	1 KB	JPEG Image	06/06/2005 14:05
BensonSales.xls	1 KB	Microsoft Excel Wor...	06/06/2005 17:43
discount.xls	39 KB	Microsoft Excel Wor...	15/04/2005 17:27
Benson_Pres.ppt	37 KB	Microsoft PowerPoi...	04/04/2005 09:14
backup.doc	24 KB	Microsoft Word Doc...	24/01/2005 17:26
Benson1.doc	1 KB	Microsoft Word Doc...	11/02/2005 17:43
Benson2.doc	10 KB	Microsoft Word Doc...	03/03/2005 15:04
Benson10.doc	5 KB	Microsoft Word Doc...	11/03/2005 17:43
Benson11.doc	38 KB	Microsoft Word Doc...	13/05/2005 17:43
Dean.doc	13 KB	Microsoft Word Doc...	09/01/2005 14:43
Dean-Baker.doc	5 KB	Microsoft Word Doc...	25/08/2005 16:01
Deans.doc	5 KB	Microsoft Word Doc...	28/03/2005 11:25
Doc1.doc	2 KB	Microsoft Word Doc...	18/01/2005 10:22
Doc3.doc.doc	19 KB	Microsoft Word Doc...	28/02/2005 13:27
Maternity.doc	38 KB	Microsoft Word Doc...	12/01/2005 15:48
PRO_8245_05_1.doc	2 KB	Microsoft Word Doc...	11/02/2005 16:12
UPPER.doc	8 KB	Microsoft Word Doc...	04/07/2005 15:01
This file name is too long to b...	5 KB	Text Document	03/03/2005 12:14

- File size is usually rounded up to the nearest KB or MB. Sorting by file size can sometimes be a useful way of locating a file if you have forgotten its name but remember that it was a twenty page report, not a one page letter.

- File type is indicated by the file's extension: .doc for a Word document, .xls for an Excel spreadsheet, .htm or .html for a web page, and so on. The extension is usually added by the application that you used to create the file. You will quickly get familiar with the ones you use most often.

  Notice that Windows sorts in alphabetical order of its own name for the type of document, not in alphabetical order of file extension. So xls files appear above doc files because 'Microsoft Excel' comes before 'Microsoft Word' when alphabetically sorted.

  Again, sorting in ascending or descending order of file type is a useful way of locating a document if you know, for instance, that it is a graphic (e.g. a gif or a jpg file), but can't remember its name.

  If you rename a file and alter its file type you will probably get a warning telling you that the application that created the file may not be able to recognise it.

- Date modified speaks for itself. If you know that a matter was dealt with in June 2006, say, just click on the Modified column and sort the files in ascending or descending date order.

student notes✍

Activity 6

Janis wrote a letter to Mr Venables, who had called to complain about Product X, and saved it as 'moaner.doc'. She did not make a paper copy of the letter apart from the one she posted to Mr Venables. You are now dealing with a further call from Mr Venables, who wants to discuss Janis's reply. Janis is on holiday. How could you find a copy of the letter on Janis's computer? What advice would you give to Janis for the future?.

Computer searching

No matter how careful and well organised you are, every now and then you will forget where you saved a file or what its name was. Fortunately computers have built-in tools to help you.

If you were working on it very recently you may find that the application you used has a 'recent file list' under the File menu listing the most recently created files.

You can use the application's own search facility if it has one. For instance in Word if you click on File ... Open and then choose Tools ... Find you get a dialogue box like this.

student notes✍

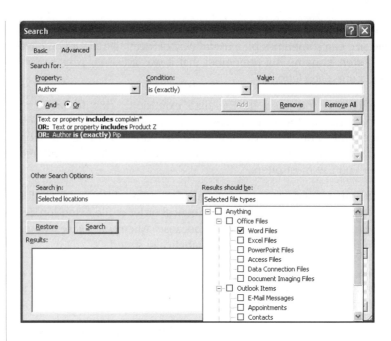

If you prefer you can also use the system's search facility. In Windows you access this by clicking on Start ... Search. Here is what you will see (in Windows XP) if you choose the advanced option.

You can restrict your search to specific time periods or file types or file sizes.

You can search either for a specific file name or for files containing specific text or both.

You can restrict your search to specific folders. You may know, for instance, that your file is somewhere in a folder called Work_in_Progress: it is much better and quicker to search only the few megabytes of files in this folder than to search the whole 80GB of your computer's hard drive!

You can ensure that sub folders are searched as well as the main folder (recommended).

You can make your search case sensitive (not recommended).

Wildcard characters can be used when you don't know what the real character is or you don't want to type the entire name.

There are two wildcard characters that you can use with a Windows search: the asterisk (*) and the question mark (?).

- Asterisk (*)

  You can use the asterisk as a substitute for zero or more characters. If you're looking for a file that you know starts with 'demo' but you can't remember whether it was just 'demo' or whether it had a longer name, type the following:

  demo*

  A Windows search will locate all files of any file type that begin with 'demo' including demo.ppt, Demonstration.txt, demos.doc, and demo005.doc. To narrow the search to a specific type of file, type:

  demo*.doc

  In this case, the search will find all files that begin with 'demo' but have the file extension .doc, such as demos.doc and demo005.doc, but not demo.ppt or Demonstration.txt.

- Question mark (?)

  You can use the question mark as a substitute for a single character in a name. For example, if you typed demo?.doc, the Find dialog box would locate the file demos.doc but not demo005.doc.

  You can also use wildcards in the "word or phrase' box, so if you had written a series of letters in Word to 'ABC Ltd', sometimes spelt 'ABC Limited', and saved them in different places you could locate them all by searching for files named *.doc containing text ABC L*.

  Wildcards are useful but take a little care and try to be as specific as you can. For instance if you search for all files containing text *er* that would probably include every file on your computer!

Naming and saving files

You should try to get in to the habit of doing a save every few minutes, to minimise the risk of losing data due to a computer or program failure or accidentally pressing the wrong key. Saving a file is simply a matter of clicking on the File menu, choosing the Save option and then deciding where to save the file, following organisational policy if necessary.

If you have never saved the file before you'll also have to decide what name to give it. On a computer file names are sorted in very strict alphabetical order (capitals are treated as lower-case letters), so some of the rules that you might expect don't apply. For instance a file named StJohn.doc will appear in the list with other files with names beginning with the letters 'ST' not with other files beginning with 'SA'.

On the other hand a useful trick, if you want a file to appear at the top of an alphabetically sorted list on a computer, is to put an exclamation mark at the front. For instance a file named '!zzz.doc' will appear at the top of a list of file that also include file names such as 'aaa1111_Plumbers.doc' because the exclamation mark comes first in the computer 'alphabet'.

If you are creating a series of files and you choose to give them the same name with sequential numbers you need to be aware that, when sorted in name order, 'file_10 doc' will appear immediately after 'file_1.doc', not, as you might expect, after file_9.doc'. (This does not happen in Windows XP.)

You can avoid this by adding a nought before single digit file numbers 'file_01.doc' (or if you are creating hundreds of files like this you will need to add two noughts: 'file_001.doc'). This is a good habit to get into in any document numbering system.

Activity 7

How are documents organised in an e-mail system such as Microsoft Outlook or Outlook Express?

The following characters are not allowed in file names or are restricted (the system will simply refuse to save the file if you use one of these in the name.)	
/	Forward slash
\	Back slash
|	Vertical stroke
?	Question mark
<	Less than or left angle bracket
>	More than or right angle bracket

The following characters should be used with care	
Space	Spaces are allowed but are generally best avoided. If you want to separate two words in a file name separate them with the underscore character (e.g. 'my_file')
.	Usually only one full stop is used, to separate the document name from its extension, which usually indicates the format of the document.
"	Double inverted commas are not allowed within the name. If you put them at the beginning and end of the file name but before the extension they will be ignored. If you save a Word document as, say, "my_file.txt" you will indeed end up with the file my_file.txt: in other words the Word extension .doc will not be used.
~	The tilde is allowed, but note that the system also uses this at the beginning of a file name to indicate a temporary file.

Certain characters are not allowed in file names. This varies a little depending on the system you are using, but the following rules will serve you well.

Maximum file name length depends partly which system you are using and partly where you are saving the file. You may find that you can save a file with a name of up to about 250 characters if you save it directly to the 'C' drive, but if you save it in a sub-folder you also have to take account of the number of characters in the name of the sub-folder.

File names longer than about 20 characters are not recommended in any case.

- They are difficult to read and take in at a glance.

- They are not acceptable to some types of compression or backup technology or to saving in certain formats, such as CD-ROM.

Older systems (DOS and Windows 3.1) were far more restrictive about file names: only eight characters were allowed, plus three for the file extension. You may still come across some programs that make you stick to the DOS rules and though it sounds restrictive it does make you take a lot of care with your file naming.

In general, you should follow the system of file-naming prescribed by your organisation if there is one. If not, try to give the file a name that would enable someone else to find it quickly.

Activity 8

Are there any rules for computer file naming in your organisation? What efforts are made to ensure that people stick to the rules?

If necessary you may have to conduct a brief audit of computer file-naming practices within your own department and make a note of any problems you identify.

If there are no rules, you may consider drawing some up for your own department to follow in future - but only after discussion with your colleagues and your manager. It is probably best not to rename all the old files if everyone already knows where to find them under the system currently in use.

Databases and accounting packages

Saving in a program such as a database or an accounting package is different to saving in a document creation program like a word processor. In such a package you will find that every time you make an entry or change anything your alteration is saved automatically, at that moment. There is therefore no need to go through further save procedures when you shut down, although you may want to make a backup copy (see below).

student notes✍

Transferring files

It's easy to save a file in the wrong folder if you are in a hurry, or you may decide to re-organise your files at a later date. Transferring a file is a simple matter of selecting it in your file manager and dragging it to the new location

- You can also use copy and paste options, although then you may run the risk of not knowing which is the most up-to-date version of the file.

- If you have the file open you can also use the File ... Save As option to save it with a different name in a different location.

Printing files

File ... Print is the option to choose: that's easy enough, but there are one or two other points to consider.

- Which printer to use? It may be a printer connected to your computer or a network printer. You may want to print to an impact printer if you are printing a multi-part document, or a laser printer if you are printing out a letter.

- Is the printer on? Is it loaded up with paper?

- If you are printing a lot of pages will this interfere with anyone else's work? It is polite to ask, if possible.

BACKUPS

One of the great advantages of electronic data is that it is possible to make identical copies of it – no matter how much there is – in a very short time. This is called backup: it ensures that if the worst comes to the worst, the effects of losing data are minimised.

Files can be physically lost, accidentally deleted or even stolen, and it is also possible for a file to become corrupted when it is written. A file might also be physically damaged and become unreadable.

It is important therefore to have procedures that enable data to be recreated if the original is lost or corrupted. To recreate a file you need to go back to the earlier version, re-enter any new data that has been added since that time and so create a new version of the up-to-date file.

Storage of backups

You can make a backup on your own hard disk, on the hard disk of a server, or on a separate storage device such as a floppy disk, a CD-R or a tape. Obviously, a backup on your own hard disk is of no value if the hard disk itself is damaged or the files are overwritten, so separate copies are preferable.

Back-up copies of accounting data should be stored off site, perhaps at a bank. This means that if there is a fire or a burglary at the business premises the back up copies will not be damaged or lost. In practice many organisations keep one set of back-ups on-site (for speed of access) and a second set at a separate location, just in case.

Creating a backup

Backups can be done in several ways.

- Some programs automatically retain the previous version of a file (perhaps with the extension .bak) so that you can return to it if you make a mess of the current version.

- Others, such as Microsoft Word and Microsoft Excel, can be set to make backups of all open files every few minutes, minimising the amount of work lost if the program crashes or there is a power cut.

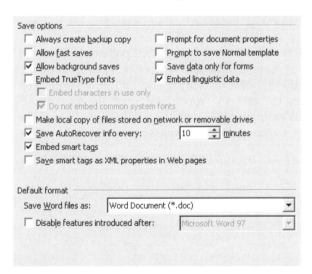

In the above illustration Word has been set to 'Save Autorecover info' every 10 minutes. This means that if the computer suddenly crashes or there is a power cut, then only a small amount of work will be lost. When you next open the program it will automatically detect that there was a problem with closing down and present you with a set of options such as the following.

student notes

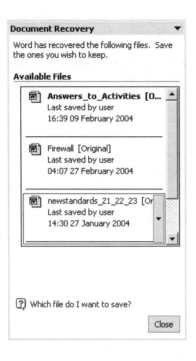

Compressed backups

If you have a lot of files to backup it is usually better to use a special backu
tool that also stores information such as each file's original location. Thes
will usually compress the data in the individual files so that the backup fil
takes up less space than a simple copy of all the files would take.

File compression works by finding repeated patterns in data and replacin
them with index numbers, which take up much less space. For example,
every occurrence of the words 'the', 'it' and 'and' in this book were replace
by the numbers 1, 2 and 3 it would be a much shorter book. Zip files ar
the best known example of file compression because they are widely use
on the Internet, to speed up file downloads.

Windows has its own backup utility, as illustrated on the next page.

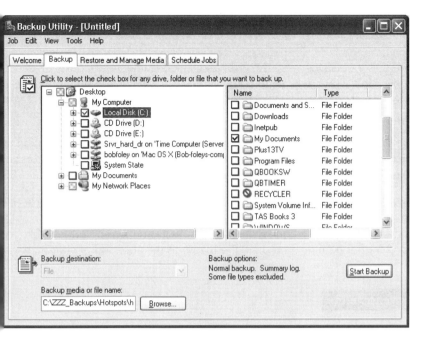

Some applications will also have their own backup facilities. Accounting packages almost certainly will. Here's an example from QuickBooks and you will see other examples in Chapter 9. Creating a backup is simply a matter of clicking on File … Backup and choosing a file name and location.

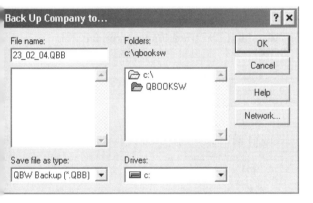

These type of backup files are also saved in a compressed format.

It is obviously safer to make backups on separate disks or other media, rather than on the machine's internal hard disk.

Activity 9

Check your organisation's general policy on data backup, if there is one, and note down the main points, or include an actual copy in your portfolio.

USING APPLICATIONS

There is not space here to give a detailed guide to the use of all the applications you are likely to come across. We will confine our comments to a few points that may be useful when you are preparing evidence for your portfolio.

We'll assume that you know that you can usually open an application by clicking on its icon on screen or by using the Start ... Programs option and selecting it from a list.

Any decent application will have help files and those should be your first port of call if you have difficulties. To get full use out of an application it may be necessary to go on a course dedicated to that program: if you feel that you need further training then draw the matter to the attention of your manager.

Spreadsheets

Spreadsheets are the best tool to use for preparing tabular data (text or numbers), for doing typical accounting calculations (adding up lists), and for simple analysis of tabular data, such as sorting lists in different orders. There may come a point when your data analysis needs are so complex that a database such as Access is a better option, but that is well beyond the scope of your current studies.

You should ensure that you know how to enter data into a spreadsheet, manipulate it in various ways and construct simple formulae.

Activity 10

Create a spreadsheet that demonstrates that you have the following basic skills. If necessary you should use the Help system in your spreadsheet to find out how to do them. Be sure to save your spreadsheet and include it in your portfolio.

For data you can take almost anything you have to hand: a supermarket bill, a phone book, or anything you like, so long as it is a list of text and numbers. You only need about five lines.

- Enter numbers and format them, for instance make them display as 1,234 (comma format) or 5.67 (to two decimal places) or as a percentage (25% instead of 0.25).

- Enter a column of dates such as 24/03/2004.

- Enter text.

- Insert extra columns and rows.

- Insert a new sheet.

- Select cells, copy and paste their contents and drag them to other parts of the spreadsheet.

- Sum a column of numbers.

- Use formulae to add, subtract, multiply and divide the contents of one cell by another cell.

- Automatically fill in data based on adjacent cells (look for "fill" in the Help file if necessary).

- Sort columns of data in different ways.

student notes✍

Word processing and house style

Many organisations have what is known as a 'house style' for letters, reports, presentations and similar output. This is a set of rules that specifies details such as page margins, hierarchies of headings, paragraph numbering system, spacing between paragraphs, fonts to use, size and placement of company logo, acceptable colours, and so on.

As you no doubt know, a word processing application makes it incredibly easy to add stylistic features to documents: you just select a piece of text and click a button.

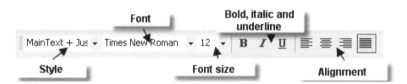

The only drawback is that it is so easy that it is tempting to go over the top and use these features to excess. Most day to day business documents will need no more than two or three styles. As a general rule, no matter how complicated the content of your document is, if it uses more than ten different styles in total, including styles for the overall title, the headings and sub-headings, you are probably going too far.

A typical house style for a letter and for a fairly complex report is shown on the next page.

- Headings. There is a 'hierarchy' of headings: there is an overall title and the report as a whole is divided into sections. Within each section main points have a heading in bold capitals, sub-points have a heading in bold lower-case and sub-sub-points have a heading in italics. (Three levels of headings within a main section is usually

student notes ✍

considered the maximum number that readers can cope with.) It i
not necessary to underline headings.

- References. Sections are lettered, A, B and so on. Main points ar
  numbered 1, 2 and so on, and within each division paragraphs ar
  numbered 1.1, 1.2, 2.1, 2.2. Sub-paragraphs inherit their reference
  from the paragraph above. For instance the first sub-paragrap
  under paragraph 1.2 is numbered 1.2.1.

- Fonts. Word processors offer you a wealth of fonts these days, but
  is best to avoid the temptation. It is often a good idea to pu
  headings in a different font to the main text, but stop there: tw
  fonts is quite enough!

Our example is not the only way of organising a report, of course: you migh
choose to reference sub-paragraphs 1.2(a), 1.2(b) and so on, or you ma
simply use bullet points. You might use roman numerals, although we advis
against this. If your report turns out to be longer than you expected and yo
get up to paragraph XLVIII you are likely to confuse many of your reader
unless they happen to be Romans!

Typical letter layout

```
                                          Letterhead (company
                                          logo, address, phone
                                          number, email address)
Mr David Gilmour
Purchasing Manager
ABC Ltd
Address 1
Address 2
Address 3
Post code

Date
Reference

Dear Mr Gilmour
Subject

Text of letter

Yours sincerely



Your name
```

Report layout for a fairly complex report

# TITLE		Arial 28 pt Bold Capitals
## SECTION A		Arial 18 pt Bold Capitals
1 MAIN HEADING		Arial 14 pt Capitals Bold
1.1 Paragraph		Times New Roman 10 pt
Sub-heading		Arial 12 pt Bold
1.2 Paragraph		
1.2.1 Sub-paragraph		Times New Roman 10 pt Indented
1.2.2 Sub-paragraph		
Sub-sub-heading		Arial 10 pt Italic
1.3 Paragraph		
Sub-heading		
1.4 Paragraph		
2 MAIN HEADING		
2.1 Paragraph		
etc.		
## SECTION B		
etc.		

Activity 11

What are the key elements of the house style(s) used in your organisation? If there aren't any house styles already you may wish to develop some. Find good examples of existing documents of various types (letters, reports etc.) and define a style for each element, including fonts used, font sizes, space between paragraphs and so on.

Once you've worked out all the styles you may like to go further and create some word processing templates for future use.

DEALING WITH DIFFICULTIES

We have already mentioned many of the difficulties you are likely to encounter in day-to-day computer work and suggested what you should do.

- Hardware problems: for instance if things are not plugged in properly.

- Software problems: for instance if an application stops working or the computer as a whole crashes.

- Lost or corrupted files: for which backups are essential.

Problems beyond these are best sorted out by an expert, not by pressing every key, not by hitting the computer, not by just switching off at the mains.

student notes🖎

Seeking assistance

The best way to demonstrate competence is to know who to ask, to be patient if that person is busy with other matters, and to find something else useful to do in the mean time (how about that manual filing you've been putting off for days?)

One last point: the person you ask for help is likely to ask you what you were doing just before the problem occurred, so make a note of that. If there is an error message of some kind on the screen, leave it there if possible, or at least make a note of what it says before you click OK or Cancel.

CHAPTER OVERVIEW

- computers at work are usually connected to other computers and to a server in a network. Hardware is anything you can physically touch – keyboard, mouse, screen and so on

- software can be split into operating system software (such as Windows XP) which controls all the basic operations, and applications software such as word processing programs, spreadsheets and accounting packages

- visual safety checks include checking plugs and cables and the general arrangement of the computer, using common sense

- files, programs and even the equipment can be damaged if you do not shut down correctly. Shut down applications first and then use the proper procedure for shutting down: do not just switch off the power

> **KEY WORDS**
>
> **Hardware** computer equipment
>
> **Stand alone computer** a computer not connected to any other computer
>
> **Software** computer programs
>
> **Password** a set of letters and numbers used to gain access to a computer or to a program
>
> **Backup** a duplicate copy of a file or files (possibly in compressed format)
>
> **House style** guidelines for the presentation of documents, letters, reports and so on in a specific organisation

- passwords may be required at various levels: to log on as a user, to log on to a network, to start up an application or to access an individual file

- files can be accessed using the computer file manager, which arranges them in a hierarchy of folders and offers you different views. Computers have sophisticated searching facilities if you forget the name and location of a file

- file names should be chosen in accordance with organisational policy, and wherever possible they should give some indication of the file's contents

- backups are an important measure to minimise the loss of data. They may be a simple duplicate copy or they may be compressed files. Backups should usually be stored in a separate location to the original files

- in any business role you will need basic skills with spreadsheets and word-processing packages, and you will need to be aware of the house style for preparing documents in your organisation

HOW MUCH HAVE YOU LEARNED?

1   How is a stand alone computer different from one that is part of a network?

2   What does an operating system do?

3   What are the two main applications included in an office package?

4   If you performed visual safety checks on your computer yesterday morning do you need to do so again today? Explain your answer.

5   What should you do before turning off the mains power to your computer?

6   A colleague has left a file for you to work on in a shared folder on the network. However, when you try to access this file you get the following message. What is the most likely reason?

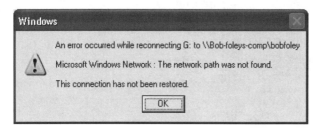

7   Is "123" a good password? Explain your answer.

8   Give two reasons why a password might place limitations on your access to a computer program.

9   What are the different ways in which a computer file manager can sort files?

10   Why is the asterisk useful when searching for files?

11   You are attempting to print a ten-page document when you get the following message on your screen. What should you do?

12   Some of your data gets damaged, but fortunately you have backup from three days ago. How would you actually use this backup?

chapter 8:
MAINTAINING THE SECURITY OF DATA

───── chapter coverage 📖 ─────

We've talked about security in general earlier in this book, but this chapter is specifically concerned with the security of data. Not only is your organisation's data highly valuable for business reasons, but also there are certain cases where you may actually be breaking the law if you lose it, or misuse it, or let it fall into the wrong hands.

✍ risks to data

✍ password policy

✍ data protection

✍ copyright

✍ retention of documents

✍ healthy, safe, secure and well-organised computing

knowledge and understanding – general information technology

- the purpose of passwords

- different types of risk, viruses, confidentiality

- relevant security and legal regulations, data protection legislation, copyright, VDU legislation, health and safety regulations, retention of documents

knowledge and understanding – the organisation

- location of hardware, software and back up copies

- organisational security policies

Performance criteria – element 21.1

- ensure passwords are kept secret and changed at appropriate times

- ensure computer hardware and program disks are kept securely located

- identify potential risks to data from different sources and take steps to resolve or minimise them

- maintain security and confidentiality of data at all times

- understand and implement relevant legal regulations

RISKS TO DATA

Information held on computers needs to be protected from accidental or malicious damage and from interference and prying eyes. Interference may be just casual – someone playing around with your machine when you're not there – but it can still result in damage, disruption or loss of files.

It is especially important to keep accounting data secure, because it is needed to run the business properly, it is commercially sensitive and in some cases (eg payroll data, customer's personal data) it may be highly confidential).

Physical risks

The computer hardware itself may be stolen or damaged and so may backup disks. Dangers such as fire and liquid, badly arranged desks and offices, unauthorised intruders – and what you can do to avoid such dangers – were covered in the earlier chapters on health, safety and security. However there are some additional points to make when we are considering computers and data.

- You may find that your computer is security tagged in some way. This doesn't prevent it from being stolen, but it may deter a thief because it increases the risk of the computer – and the thief – subsequently being traced.

- Some organisations go as far as to bolt or chain computer equipment to the working surface. However, this still may not prevent determined burglars with some computer knowledge from opening up the computer boxes and removing the most valuable components, such as the central processing chip, the memory chips, the hard disk and so on.

- Floppy disks are vulnerable to physical damage by bits of dust or grit, heat or liquid. Floppy disks are magnetic media, and strong magnetic fields can destroy or distort the data stored on them. This doesn't often happen. but cases have been know known of disks being damaged by being stood on top of powerful loudspeakers (speakers contain large magnets).

- Optical disks (CDs and DVDs) are more difficult to damage than floppy disks, but don't make the mistake of thinking they are indestructible. They are sensitive to heat, and greasy finger marks and scratching.

student notes✍

Activity 1

People are often careless with their computers. Suggest a few simple rules that you could apply at work to protect computer hardware from damage.

Precautions against viruses

A virus is a piece of software that infects programs and data and replicates itself to other computers. Viruses need an opportunity to spread. The programmers of viruses therefore place viruses in the kind of software which is most likely to be copied and circulated. Above all this includes e-mail messages, but some free files or software (programs such as amusing screensavers that you may be tempted to download from the Internet, for instance) may also be infected.

A virus can be activated very easily – often simply by opening an infected e-mail message – and it may have a number of very unpleasant effects.

- It may send itself on – without your knowledge – to everyone in your e-mail address book.

- It may slow down the operation of your computer so much that it becomes virtually unusable.

- It may delete particular files.

- It may wipe or reformat the entire hard disk.

- It may install and start up a program that could do any number of things – display a message, dial a premium phone number (at your expense), alter your files in some way, disable a particular program, send your data to someone who may misuse it, and so on.

If a virus enters a large networked system the damage can be enormous. Files, data and system software can all be attacked. Most organisations therefore respond in several ways.

- By operating firewalls (covered later)

- By banning staff from introducing any disks that haven't been virus-checked by the IT department, or by preventing use of disk drives for floppies and CDs altogether

- Above all, by using virus protection software, which is always on and which watches out for and destroys suspicious items, or at least stops them before they do any damage

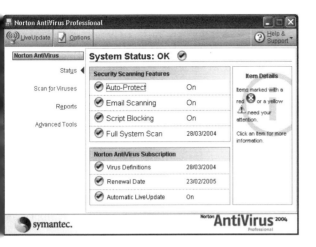

You can help yourself simply by being careful. Never install any software at all unless you are absolutely sure it is safe to do so. Never open an e-mail with an attachment unless you trust the person who sent it and you are absolutely sure that the attachment is safe.

Most organisations that provide e-mail services (Internet Services Providers, ISPs) now encourage you to log on to your mail on the Internet, so that you can see what email is awaiting you before you download it to your computer and check anything that does not look quite right. With any luck you will be entirely prevented from downloading suspect attachments.

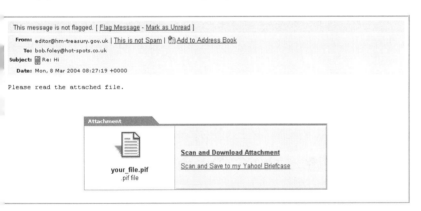

Of course the people who create viruses are always working on new and more deadly ones, so there is a constant race between attackers and defenders. All computer users should check for updates to their anti-virus software very frequently – at least once a week – and run a system scan equally often.

You should also be aware of hoaxes. These are not viruses at all, but simply spoof warnings that such and such a document or program contains a virus. Hoaxes are sent in the form of unsolicited e-mail ('spam') to unsuspecting persons and they encourage people to forward the message to anybody else they can think of that might be affected.

Hoaxes do not do any harm in themselves. Their creators simply think it is amusing or desirable to create panic and waste the time of individuals and organisations.

Hoaxes are likely to be spotted by spam controls, either on your own computer or at your ISP, but just in case one gets through to you make sure you are not the one foolish enough to send it on to all of your colleagues and friends.

Hacking and firewalls

Hacking is an attempt to gain unauthorised access to a computer system over the telephone network. Hackers may try to access personal information on your computer. They may install code on your computer that destroys files or causes malfunctions. They can also use your computer to cause problems on other computers on your network.

The best protection you can get against this is to install what is known as a 'firewall'.

- A software firewall (for example Zone Alarm, Norton Internet Security) runs on your computer in the background. The most recent operating systems, such as Windows XP have a built-in firewall.

- A hardware firewall is generally a small box which sits between your computer and your modem. A business network is more likely to have a hardware firewall since these can protect more than one computer at once.

- It is, of course, possible to use both types.

Firewalls have always been important but they have become much more so as more and more people have broadband connections to the Internet that are 'always on' (to a hacker, 'always on' means 'always vulnerable').

The main problem with firewalls is that it can take time to get them configured exactly as you want them. Until you have done this they may attempt to prevent you from doing things that you are quite sure you want to do, like collecting your email or sharing files with other computers on the network.

Activity 2

What option would you choose if the following alert suddenly appeared on your computer screen?

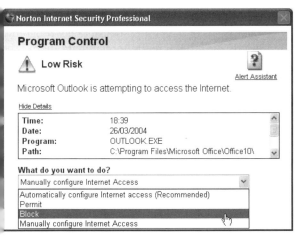

Data recovery

When data items are 'lost' – for instance if you delete a file accidentally – don't panic immediately. Your files can sometimes be recovered even when they seem to have disappeared completely.

This is possible because of the way a computer's filing system works.

When you save a file, the operating system first looks for space on the disk. A large file may be broken up into several smaller chunks to fit various gaps on the disk. The system then identifies the electronic 'addresses' of each storage location, and tags them so that the file can be listed in the file directory.

When you delete a file, the system does NOT delete the actual data, only the address. The data remains, but is now invisible to the file manager system. Later on some data may be stored on top of the original data, but until this happens, the original material can often be recovered.

Your first action should be to check the contents of the Recycle Bin (or 'Trash' on an Apple Mac – the icon illustrated above).

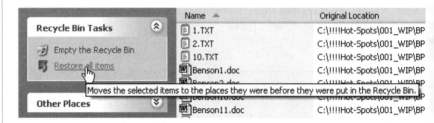

If you are lucky, recovering the data may be a simple matter of clicking on the Restore option.

It is surprisingly difficult to destroy the data on a disk by normal (non-violent) means. Experts can often recover items of data using special utility programs, even after very determined efforts have been made to eliminate them. The process can be slow and expensive, and the data may be corrupt to some extent, but when the need is great enough (for instance in a criminal case such as fraud), it may be possible.

The persistence of computer data can therefore present a security problem of its own. Only physical destruction or repeated over-writing or reformatting of the whole disk can remove all traces of data files. Organisations that are very security sensitive may prefer to destroy rather than resell obsolete computers, for this very reason.

Backups

We've emphasised the importance of backups already in the previous chapter, but it won't hurt to repeat the point. Frequent backups, stored safely away from the original data, are the best precaution of all.

PASSWORD POLICY

The purpose of a password is to prevent users from getting access to things that they are not authorised to access or that they do not need to access.

> ## Activity 3
>
> Think about the data and information held on your own computer. Are there any files that you would prefer your colleagues not to have access to?
>
> A useful approach is to attach a password to a screen saver. The original screen can only be restored by keying in the password. But besides passwords what other options can you think of to keep people away from your data?

As mentioned in the last chapter, an ideal password is at least eight characters long and consists of a random combination of letters (both capitals and small letters) and numbers. For example pkTd8z3A.

Assuming you use a password like this it is important to ensure that the Caps Lock key is not on when you are typing your password, otherwise you will get the small and large letters the wrong way round and your password will be rejected.

Problems with passwords

Passwords are useful as a protection against non-expert snoopers and against accidental alterations, though they may not prevent a file from being deleted. The basic password systems that some popular programs use: for instance you can freely download software from the Internet that enables you to 'crack' the passwords used by older versions of Microsoft Office programs with ease.

Passwords are regarded as an inconvenience by some and they can be a problem.

- Many people use a password that is fairly obvious, such as their nickname, or the name of a partner or child, or something that can easily be found out about them, such as their date of birth

- Others choose a less obvious password (e.g. pkTd8z3A) and then forget it altogether

- Many people write down their password where others can easily find it. Putting it on a Post-it note and sticking it to the computer itself is very common!

- People may simply tell others what their password is

student notes ✍

Password policy

Organisations can set down a password policy, instructing people not to reveal their passwords to others but this is difficult to enforce. It is difficult to avoid these problems altogether, but some measures can be taken.

- The organisation can set up the system so that passwords must be a certain length, may not be a real word, and must contain a mixture of letters and numbers.

- The organisation can impose passwords on people and not allow individuals to change them.

- The organisation can insist that passwords are changed at regular intervals – say every three months. The system itself may do this anyway. For example a Windows XP system is set up to require that passwords are changed every 180 days.

Changing passwords

If it is suspected that any password has been discovered by, or revealed to an unauthorised person it should be changed immediately.

Note that you will be asked to enter your current password before you can change it. This is to prevent others changing your password without your knowledge.

Forgetting your password

If you find it very difficult to remember a password you may be allowed to set a password hint. Inevitably this is less secure, because if the hint reminds you it may well help someone else to work out your password. 'Son's name age' is not a good password hint if your password is 'David11' and you happen to have an eleven year old son called David! Either make sure that neither your passwords nor your hints are this obvious or don't use hints at all.

If you forget a system or program password your only option may be to ask someone with a higher level of access to the system or program to reset it for you. In other words a new password will be chosen for you so that you can access the item, and then you will be able to change it yourself to something you can remember.

THE DATA PROTECTION ACT 1998

We all like a bit of privacy and data protection legislation recognises this by placing some constraints on organisations that collect, store and use information about people. The latest version in the UK is the Data Protection Act 1998.

Activity 4

Why do you think people might object to organisations keeping information about them?

The Act is concerned with 'personal data', which is information about living, identifiable individuals. This can be as little as a name and address: it need not be particularly sensitive information. If it IS sensitive (explained later) then extra care is needed.

The Act gives individuals (data subjects) certain rights and it requires those who record and use personal information (data controllers) to be open about their use of that information and to follow 'sound and proper practices'

This means that organisation must follow the eight Data Protection Principles. These are listed and explained in the table on the next page.

If an organisation holds personal information about living individuals on computer or has such information processed on computer by others (for example, its accountants or auditors) the organisation probably needs to 'notify' under the Data Protection Act 1998.

'Notify' means that the organisation has to complete a form about the data it holds and how it is used and send it, with an annual registration fee, to the office of the Information Commissioner.

Organisations have obligations if they receive a written request from an individual asking to see what data it holds about them, or to obtain a copy of it, or to be given an explanation of what it is used for, or who it is given to. The organisation must deal with the request promptly, and in any case within 40 days. The organisation is entitled, if it wishes, to ask for a fee of not more than £10 in which case the 40 days does not begin until this is received.

The eight data protection principles. *Data must be...*

1. Fairly and lawfully processed

2. Processed for limited purposes

These two principles mean that when an organisation collects information from individuals it should be honest and open about why it wants the information and it should have a legitimate reason for processing the data.

3. Adequate, relevant and not excessive

Organisations should hold neither too much nor too little data about the individuals in their list. For instance, many companies collect date of birth or age range information from their customers, but in many cases all they actually need to know is that they are over eighteen.

4. Accurate

Personal data should be accurate and up-to-date as far as possible. However if an individual provides inaccurate information (for example lies about their age) the organisation would not normally be held to account for this.

5. Not kept longer than necessary

There are only exceptional circumstances where personal data should be kept indefinitely. Data should be removed when it is no longer required for audit purposes or when a customer ceases to do business with you.

6. Processed in accordance with individual's rights

Individuals have various rights including the following.

- The right to be informed of all the information held about them by an organisation

- The right to prevent the processing of their data for the purposes of direct marketing

- The right to compensation if they can show that they have been caused damage by any contravention of the Act

- The right to have any inaccurate data about them removed or corrected.

7. Secure

Organisations should make sure that they provide adequate security for the data, taking into account the nature of the data, and the possible harm to the individual that could arise if the data is disclosed or lost.

- Measures to ensure that access to computer records by staff is authorised (for instance a system of passwords).

- Measures to control access to records by people other than staff. For instance care should be taken over the siting of computers to prevent casual callers to the organisation's premises being able to read personal data on screen. Also there should be procedures to verify the identity of callers (especially telephone callers) seeking information about an individual.

- Measures to prevent of the accidental loss or theft of personal data, for example backups and fire precautions.

8. Not transferred to countries that do not have adequate data protection laws

If an organisation wishes to transfer personal data to a country outside the European Economic Area (EEA) it will either need to ensure there is adequate protection (e.g. a Data Protection Act) for the data in the receiving country, or obtain the consent of the individual.

The Data Protection Act 1998 also covers some records held in paper form. These do not need to be notified to the Commissioner, but they should also be handled in accordance with the data protection principles. A set of index cards for a personnel system is a typical example of paper records that fall under the Data Protection Act 1998.

Sensitive data

The Act defines eight categories of sensitive personal data. If an organisation wishes to hold personal data falling into these categories it is likely that it will need the explicit consent of the individual concerned. It will also need to ensure that its security is adequate for the protection of sensitive data.

Here are the eight categories.

- The racial or ethnic origin of data subjects

- Their political opinions

- Their religious beliefs or other beliefs of a similar nature

- Whether they are a member of a trade union

- Their physical or mental health or condition

- Their sexual life

- The commission or alleged commission by them of any offence

- Any details of court proceedings or sentences against them

Activity 5

Consider whether your own work involves processing data about individuals, and if so find out about your own organisation's data protection policies and guidelines.

COPYRIGHT

Copyright law is highly specialised, so we are only going to consider matters that it might be useful to know for day-to-day office work or which are of general interest.

Copyright is a way of ensuring that the creators of a work have an exclusive right to use it, and also have the right to stop others from using the work without their permission.

Copyright can be owned by an individual, a group, or an organisation.

There is no need for an author to register copyright with anybody. Usually publishers will mark the work with the international copyright symbol ©, but this is not actually necessary: copyright applies as soon as the material is 'recorded' (in writing, on a cassette tape, on a computer screen etc.) as opposed to just being in the creator's brain.

The Copyright, Designs and Patents Act 1988

The main legislation (in the UK) is The Copyright, Designs and Patents Act 1988 (CDPA 1988), which covers the following types of 'work'.

- Published materials of all kinds, including text in newspapers, books, magazines, marketing brochures and websites

- Musical works

- Images, paintings, drawings, photographs, and so on

- Sound recordings, films, broadcasts

- Computer programs (for instance any software you use at work)

Most other countries have similar legislation, so don't think you can avoid copyright issues if you copy material from, say, a Canadian website.

Copyright generally applies for a period of 70 years from the end of the calendar year in which the author dies (The Duration of Copyright and Rights in Performances Regulations 1995).

Does it affect you?

Copyright covers the 'form or expression' of an idea, not the idea itself: it covers the way the words or notes or visual images are arranged, not what they convey.

In other words, if you pick up some new ideas about doing your job from this book you can't be prevented from discussing those ideas with your colleagues in a meeting. However, if you copy paragraphs from this book and try to publish them in YOUR OWN book, without the permission of the publishers or author of this book, you are infringing copyright and could be sued for damages.

For the purpose of gathering information at work or for your portfolio you should be aware that under CPDA 1988 copying includes STORING the copyright work in any medium by electronic means. Fortunately, many websites include their own notification that gives you permission to download pages and store them on your computer for, perhaps, 30 days, and perhaps to print out a single copy.

Activity 6

Visit the BBC's website and read the Terms and Conditions in full. Get into the habit of doing this for any other website that you obtain information from regularly – just in case you are breaking the law!

Popular fallacies

There are certain provisions in CPDA 1988 relating to the use of short passages, the use of material for educational purposes and its use for private research. But, contrary to popular belief, there are NO exceptions that you can safely rely on when you are 'borrowing' material.

- Do NOT assume you can copy material if you just use a sentence or two.

- Do NOT assume you can copy material if you are only using it for educational purposes.

If there is a dispute the courts will consider the author's rights and the issue of fairness, and this will be different in every case. It is certainly not up to the person copying the material to say what is fair and what is not.

Photocopying

It is normally permissible to photocopy a few pages of someone else's work for research (either commercial or non-commercial) or private study, but again this is subject to the notion of 'fair dealing'

It is not considered fair, for example, to make a single copy of a whole book (even if it is only a short one), or to make lots of copies of extracts from a book to circulate to every member of your department, say, or to a class of students.

The use of photocopying for educational purposes is limited to 1% of a work in every three months, unless a licensing agreement has been entered into with the publisher and author.

Letters and other works written by you

If you write a private letter, you own the copyright. The recipient is not entitled to publish it without your permission (unless you write to somebody that normally publishes readers' letters, like a newspaper). This also applies to your e-mails or postings on an Internet notice board.

If, in the course of your job, you write something (a letter, a report, a training programme and so on) you have created it for your employer, and your employer almost certainly owns the copyright.

The same normally applies to any other 'work' you create as part of your job (for instance a word processor macro), unless you have an agreement to the contrary.

DOCUMENT RETENTION

There are legal obligations to keep certain documents for certain lengths of time. The Limitations Act 1980 (or the 'Statute of Limitations') deals with documents in general and many business records are covered by specific legislation such as company law, tax law, contract law, charity law, consumer law, employment law, pensions law, health and safety law, and so on.

The table below shows recommended retention periods for various types of documents, but if in doubt you should always seek advice from your manager.

Activity 7

Do you think that e-mails sent by or received by businesses need to be kept? Explain your answer.

DOCUMENT	RETAIN FOR ...
Accounting and banking records	
Ledgers, invoices etc	6 years
Cheques and bills of exchange	6 years
Paying-in counterfoils	6 years
Bank statements	6 years
Instructions to banks (e.g. standing orders)	6 years
Employee Records	
Staff personnel records	6 years after employment ends
Personnel records of Senior Executives	Permanently
Job applications (rejected candidates)	Up to 1 year
Time cards and piecework records	6 years
Payroll records	6 years
Expense claims	6 years
Medical records	Permanently
Accident book	Permanently
Insurance	
Correspondence about claims	3 years after claim is settled
Insurance schedules	7 years
Public Liability, Product Liability and Employers Liability policies	Permanently
Contractual and Trust Agr eements	
Simple contracts, e.g. with customers or suppliers	6 years after contract expires
Contracts under seal (e.g. related to land and buildings)	12 years after contract expires
Trust deeds (e.g. a mortgage)	Permanently
Statutory returns, records and registers, board meetings	
All statutory registers	Permanently
Notices, circulars and board minutes	Permanently

HEALTHY, SAFE, SECURE AND WELL-ORGANISED COMPUTING

Possibly the biggest threat to the security of the data that you are responsible for at work is ... YOU! If you are not taking enough care – because you are tired, or unwell, or your mind is elsewhere, or you are just having a bad day – there is a very good chance that you will make mistakes, accidentally delete or overwrite a file, spill coffee and so on.

We mentioned the Display Screen Equipment regulations earlier, but it will be fitting to conclude this chapter with a more detailed look. The regulations are not just about flickering computer screens (VDUs). A lot of good advice about efficient, healthy, safe and secure computer work is condensed into the table in the next page.

HOW DO YOU WORK?

Getting comfortable

- Adjust your chair and VDU to find the most comfortable position fo your work. As a broad guide, your forearms should be approximately horizontal and your eyes the same height as the top of the VDU.

- Make sure you have enough work space to take whatever documents or other equipment you need.

- Try different arrangements of keyboard, screen, mouse and documents to find the best arrangement for you. A document holder may help you avoid awkward neck and eye movements.

- Arrange your desk and VDU to avoid glare, or bright reflections on the screen. This will be easiest if neither you nor the screen is directly facing windows or bright lights. Adjust curtains or blinds to prevent unwanted light.

- Make sure there is space under your desk to move your legs freely. Move any obstacles such as boxes or equipment.

- Avoid excess pressure from the edge of your seat on the backs of your legs and knees. A footrest may be helpful, particularly for smaller users.

Keying in and using a mouse

- Adjust your keyboard to get a good keying position. A space in front of the keyboard is sometimes helpful for resting the hands and wrist when not keying.

- Try to keep your wrists straight when keying. Keep a soft touch on the keys and don't overstretch your fingers. Good keyboard technique is important.

- Position the mouse within easy reach, so it can be used with the wrist straight. Sit upright and close to the desk, so you don't have to work with your mouse arm stretched. Move the keyboard out of the way if it is not being used.

- Support your forearm on the desk, and don't grip the mouse too tightly.

- Rest your fingers lightly on the buttons and do not press them hard.

Reading the screen

- Adjust the brightness and contrast controls on the screen to suit lighting conditions in the room.

- Make sure the screen surface is clean.

- In setting up software, choose options giving text that is large enough to read easily on your screen, when you are sitting in a normal, comfortable working position. Select colours that are easy on the eye (avoid red text on a blue background, or vice versa).

- Individual characters on the screen should be sharply focused and should not flicker or move. If they do, the VDU may need servicing or adjustment.Posture and breaks

- Don't sit in the same position for long periods. Make sure you change your posture as often as practicable. Some movement is desirable, but avoid repeated stretching to reach things you need (if this happens a lot, rearrange your workstation).

- Most jobs provide opportunities to take a break from the screen, e.g. to do filing or photocopying. Make use of them.

- If there are no such natural breaks in your job, your employer should plan for you to have rest breaks.

- Frequent short breaks are better than fewer long ones.

student notes

CHAPTER OVERVIEW

■ both equipment and data need protecting from risks such as physical damage, theft, unauthorised interference and viruses

■ computer viruses can be a serious problem. The best solution is to keep anti-virus software running constantly on your computer and make sure that it is updated at least weekly. Firewalls are essential if the organisation's systems are connected to the Internet

■ data that is accidentally deleted from a disk can often be recovered, providing the user acts quickly

■ unauthorised access to computers and data can be prevented with security hardware, passwords and simple precautions like switching the machine off when not in use

■ passwords are a good means of protection but they are not without problems: they can easily be forgotten and can easily be revealed to non-authorised persons. Passwords should be changed regularly, and changed immediately if they are discovered by a non-authorised person

KEY WORDS

Virus a piece of software that infects programs and data and replicates itself to other computers

Hacking an attempt to gain unauthorised access to a computer system over the telephone network

Firewall a piece of software or a hardware device that can deny access to hackers

Personal data information about living, identifiable individuals

Sensitive data data about an individual that an organisation may not hold without explicit consent

Copyright a way of ensuring that the creators of a work have an exclusive right to use it, and also have the right to stop others from using the work without their permission

■ the Data Protection Act 1998 is concerned with information about living, identifiable individuals. The Act gives individuals certain rights and it requires organisations that record and use personal information to follow the eight Data Protection Principles

■ copyright law places constraints on whether you can store and reuse most types information in its original form. The creators of a work have an exclusive right to use it, and also have the right to stop others from using the work without their permission

■ the Display Screen Equipment regulations cover a number of aspects of healthy, safe and efficient working, such as taking regular breaks and organising your work area

HOW MUCH HAVE YOU LEARNED?

1   What are the main carriers of computer viruses?

2   How could you reduce the risk of viruses entering your organisation's computers?

3   What action do you think you need to take if you see a message such as this on your screen?

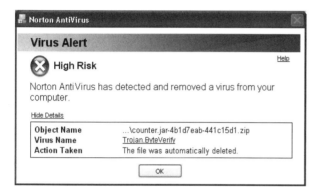

4   If you saw the following message on your screen what option would you click? Explain your answer.

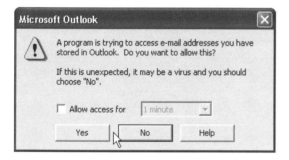

5   When you tell a computer to delete a file, what actually happens, and why may it be possible to recover the file?

6   What are the eight data protection principles?

7   You believe that a credit card company may hold incorrect information about you in its computer files. What are your main rights under the Data Protection Act 1998?

8   Copyright legislation prevents you from re-using other people's ideas. True or False? Explain your answer.

9   If you don't have a copy of the latest version of Microsoft Office on your home computer, is it allowable to take home the program disks from your organisation and install them at home? Explain your answer.

10 How long must most accounting data be retained for? Why?

11 What aspects of your working area are covered by the VDU regulations besides the screen itself?

chapter 9:
COMPUTERISED ACCOUNTING SYSTEMS

chapter coverage

You will be required to prove your competence in the IT aspects of accounting by providing evidence from your workplace or by completing a simulation. The AAT has indicated that simulations should include a series of exercises involving the operation of an accounting package - entering customer and supplier details, posting a few basic transactions such as journals, invoices and credit notes, and obtaining reports and print-outs.

This chapter explains how you might do the computerised accounts parts of a typical simulation in a typical accounting package. It is by no means a comprehensive guide to computerised accounting, and we only look at Sage, which is just one of many packages that you might use. We use Sage because it is the most popular package amongst small/medium- sized businesses in the UK, and because most colleges also use it for training purposes.

There are a large number of illustrations in this chapter, so don't be put off if it seems a bit long: it should still be quick and easy to read, so just enjoy the pictures!

The topics covered are:

✍ accounting packages

✍ simulations

✍ company data and the main ledger

✍ customer and supplier data

✍ journals

✍ entering invoices

✍ payments and receipts

✍ bank reconciliations

✍ print-outs

✍ error corrections

Unit 21

knowledge and understanding – general information technology

- how to save, transfer and print documents
- how to take backup copies

knowledge and understanding – the organisation

- location of hardware, software and back up copies
- location of information sources
- the organisation's procedures for ... making back ups

Performance criteria - element 21.1

- access, save and print data files and exit from relevant software
- use appropriate file names and save work
- back up work carried out on a computer system to suitable storage media at regular intervals

As far as actually **using** a computer to do something, the requirements are indicated in Units 1 to 4.

Units 1 to 4

Each of these units includes the following items.

knowledge and understanding – accounting methods

- methods of coding data/organisational coding systems
- operation of computerised accounting systems including output

The potentially enormous scope of the second item is indicated in the range statements for Units 1 to 4 as follows:

Range statements

Computerised coding systems (Elements 1.1, 2.1)
Relevant computerised records for prime entry (Elements 1.1, 2.1)
Computerised ledgers (Elements 1.1, 2.1, 3.1)
Computerised statements (Element 1.1)
Computerised cash processing (Elements 1.2, 2.2, 3.1)
Computerised bank reconciliation (Elements 3.1)
Computerised journal (Element 3.2)
Computerised control accounts (Element 3.2)Computerised trial balance (Element 3.3)

ACCOUNTING PACKAGES

Accounting packages range from simple analysed cash book style packages like Microsoft Money or Quicken to heavy-duty Enterprise Resource Management systems used in very large organisations. Huge organisations often have a system that has been built for them specially, made up of components from a variety of software suppliers, or written for them on a one-off basis.

Obviously we cannot even begin to cover the vast range of available packages, but we can illustrate the features of a typical package, and the most popular one in the UK amongst small to medium sized businesses is called Sage.

Sage produce a variety of accounting packages: Sage "Line 50" is the best known and the illustrations in this chapter are taken from a recent version of that package (version 10). Sage "Instant" is a cheaper product, with fewer features, but otherwise it looks exactly like Sage Line 50 and works in exactly the same way. In the remainder of this chapter we will just use the word "Sage" to refer to either Sage Line 50 or Sage Instant.

Hands-on

Most colleges use Sage for training purposes, even though they may not have the very latest version (currently version 12). If possible we strongly recommend that you sit at a computer equipped with a version of Sage as you read through this chapter.

Most of the activities assume that you are doing this and can practise the tasks we describe as you go along. We will also assume that you are using the data provided by BPP, which your lecturer can obtain from the BPP website (visit http://www.bpp.com/aat/companions and follow the links).

Finding your way about: terminology

We'll assume that you know what we mean when we say "menu" and "button", but there may be some other terms that you are not sure of, so here is a quick guide, just in case.

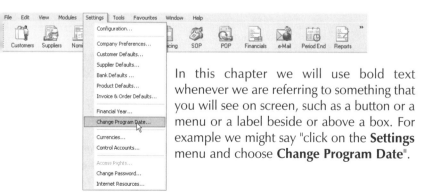

In this chapter we will use bold text whenever we are referring to something that you will see on screen, such as a button or a menu or a label beside or above a box. For example we might say "click on the **Settings** menu and choose **Change Program Date**".

student notes ✍

You won't actually be using the menus much: the buttons on the toolbars will be your main starting point. Here is the main toolbar that you see when you open up Sage, with the Customers button highlighted.

Individual parts of the program have their own toolbars.

Most of what you do involves you making entries in "fields" - for example the A/C field and the **Date** field in the next illustration.

Sometimes you need to select a "tab" to view the part of the program we refer to. For instance in this example the Activity tab is selected.

Finally, make sure that you know where the **TAB** key is on your keyboard (usually above the Caps Lock key) and also that you are aware of the function keys (**F1**, **F2** and so on, usually along the top). The **Esc** key is also very useful for closing windows quickly.

Defaults

Computerised packages make extensive use of "defaults", which are the entries it thinks you want to make. When you start entering data you will often find that Sage has done some of the work already, using the default options that would normally be chosen. This saves a great deal of time, but you should always glance at the default entries in case they are not the ones you want. This will become clearer as you start using the package.

SIMULATIONS

You may be asked to do an AAT simulation, or the one in this book, or your college may create simulations for you.

A simulation will involve a number of tasks that test your competence in the various matters described in chapters 7 and 8 (passwords, physical safety and so on), possibly some spreadsheet and word processing tasks (such as a memo on data protection issues), and a series of accounting package tasks, which are the subject of this chapter.

Before you start...

Before you start your lecturer should tell you what opening data you can expect to see when you open the package. You may be given a new "blank" company, or some data may already have been set up for you, or you may be required to restore the correct data yourself from a backup file (see below).

Also before you start you should find out from your lecturer what the arrangements are for making your own backups and for printing out your work.

Advice for lecturers on administrative matters such as these is available from the BPP website, together with Sage backup files to help get you started. Lecturers should visit http://www.bpp.com/aat/companions and follow the links.

Here's how to tackle the accounting package part of a simulation in outline.

- Open the accounting package and login if necessary.

- Ensure that you have the correct opening data.

- Set up or change any overall company details required, as instructed.

- Check that the main ledger has all the accounts you need and create new ones if not.

- Check that the sales ledger and purchase ledger have all the accounts you need and create new ones if not.

- Post the transactions and complete the other tasks, following the instructions in the simulation.

Backing up and restoring

We've already discussed the importance of backups in computing in general and of course this also applies to the data in your accounting system.

Unlike a program such as a word processor or a spreadsheet, when you make an entry in an accounts package that data is saved immediately. That means that you could post an invoice, say, then close down the program without backing up. Your invoice would not be lost: it will still be there when you next open the program.

In Sage a backup is created by clicking on the **File** menu and choosing **Backup**: not exactly difficult! You'll be asked if you want the program to check your data first, and it is worth doing this occasionally, though usually you'll probably choose not to.

Then you will need to choose a name for your backup file and a location.

The program suggests the name SAGEBACK.001 by default, but you can choose any name you like: ask your tutor if there is any particular style of file name that you should use (for instance SIMULATION.ABC, where ABC are your initials).

In the example above the backup will be saved in a folder on a server. Again, you should ask your tutor about the location you should use.

You only need to backup the **Data Files**, so deselect any other options in lower part of the screen, if necessary.

Restoring data is just as easy: click on **File** and then **Restore** and locate your backup file.

Bear in mind, though, that when you restore from a backup this will overwrite any data that is currently held in the program's data files, so take care with this. If you post a transaction and then restore an old backup your transaction will be lost.

You may well be asked to restore a backup before you start a simulation, because this is an excellent way of making sure that everyone starts from the same point, with the same opening balances, the same nominal ledger structure and codes, and so on.

Activity 1

Restore the BPP backup file SFE_04.000. Your lecturer will tell you where to find this, or visit http://www.bpp.com/aat/companions and follow the links.

A typical simulation

The following example is based closely on the sample simulation recently issued by the AAT.

Situation

SFE Merchandising is a new business that has been set up by Charlize Veron, one of Southfield Electrical's former marketing staff. Charlize is an expert on store layout and management of stocks and she intends to sell her skills and knowledge, on a consultancy basis, to medium and large retailers to help them to optimise their sales.

Charlize has started her new venture as a sole trader and has taken on some of the risk herself. However, SFE Merchandising is part -financed by Southfield Electrical, and may well be acquired by them if this new venture is a success.

Initial enquiries have been so promising that Charlize has already voluntarily registered for VAT and intends to run the standard VAT accounting scheme, not VAT cash accounting.

The business commenced trading in January 2004.

Tasks to be completed

It is now 31 January 2004 and you are to complete the following tasks ...

There may be around 20 tasks involving setting up data, entering journals, posting sales and purchase transactions, obtaining print outs and so on. You will be provided with a series of documents such as invoices, cheques, etc. We'll show you how to deal with all of this in the remainder of this chapter.

COMPANY DATA AND THE MAIN LEDGER

When you first open the accounting package you may have a blank company, with just a basic nominal ledger. Your first task in that case is to set up the new company's details and main ledger accounts.

You will find it very helpful if it is possible for you to have Sage open on your computer as you read through the remainder of this chapter, so open it now if you can.

student notes✍

Financial year

The first thing that you must do is ensure that you are in the correct financial year. In Sage the financial year and its starting month are always shown at the foot of the screen, together with other information.

You are told in the scenario that the financial year starts in January 2004 and this is what it should say at the foot of your screen. If not, you must change it by choosing the **Settings** menu then **Financial Year** … and entering the correct information.

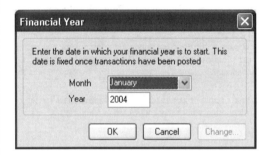

You will only be able to change the financial year if no items have yet been posted. This information is shown at the foot of the screen too, next to the financial year. It should say 0, for this scenario, because we are starting a new business. If it does not say 0 on your screen you should consult your lecturer.

(The program date will initially show the computer system date (i.e. "today's date, according to the computer's clock), but you can change this if you like as we will see later.)

Company data

The name and address details of the business should then be entered. This information will appear on any documents you produce with the package such as reports and invoices, so make sure it is accurate and is spelled correctly.

The scenario only tells us the name of the business, so for the rest of the information you will have to look through the scenario data and find company document such as a sales invoice.

Let's assume you find an invoice such as the following (extract only).

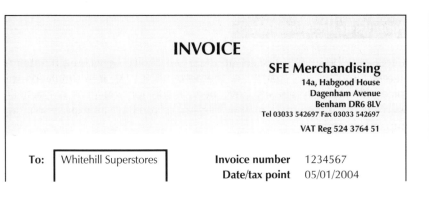

The invoice heading gives us all the extra information we need. To enter this in Sage choose the **Settings** menu and then **Company Preferences** (it doesn't matter that this is not actually a "company").

Then you simply enter all the information you've found. Use the **TAB** key on your keyboard to move between different lines. Alternatively you can click in each line, but this will really slow you down, so get into the habit of using **TAB** immediately. (Almost all accounting packages work in this way.)

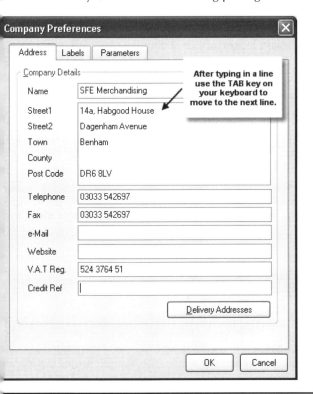

Activity 2

You must do Activity 1 before you attempt this. Ensure that the financial year is January 2004 and enter the company details shown above.

student notes ✎

Accounts in the main ledger

When a new business is first set up there is a choice between a number of different templates or "charts" for the accounts (COA). In a simulation this choice will probably already have been made for you (it is not actually possible to open the program otherwise, unless you have an expensive multi-company version).

Nominal Charts

```
General Business - Standard Chart of Accounts.
Accountancy & Financial Practitioners.
Charities or Other Non-Profit Making Organisatio
Medical Practitioners.
Legal Practitioners.
Agricultural Producers or Traders.
Garage and Vehicle Services.
Hotels, Restaurants & Guest Houses.
Building Trade
Transport, Travel & Haulage Services.
I wish to create my own layout of accounts.
```

The chart used will depend on the type of business. For instance if "General Business" is chosen the main ledger will only contain one account for sales, initially, whereas if "Hotels, Restaurants and Guest Houses" is used for the initial chart of accounts there will be several separate sales accounts for "Restaurant Meals", "Alcoholic Beverage Sales" and so on.

You are not confined to using the accounts that you are given by the program when you first set up the company. Certain accounts must always remain because the program will not be able to operate otherwise, so you will not be able to delete the main bank account, the debtors and creditors control accounts, VAT accounts, and certain other essential accounts. But you can delete any non-essential accounts (so long as you have not yet posted any transactions to them), and you can rename them and add as many new ones as you wish.

New accounts and simulations

When you are doing a simulation you may not have all the main ledger accounts you need at first, so it is worth having a good read through the whole thing and checking that the accounts you will need have been set up. You can create new ones as you go along, if you like, but that runs the risk of distracting you from the transaction you are trying to post, so we recommend that you do it in advance.

If the simulation includes a purchase invoice for stationery, for instance, check that there is already an "Office stationery" overheads account before you start to post the invoice. The tasks may actually ask you to do this. For instance you may be instructed to work through the invoices provided and write the relevant main ledger codes on them.

To do this in Sage, simply click on the **Nominal** button. Depending on which version you are using you may initially see an "analysed" list like the following.

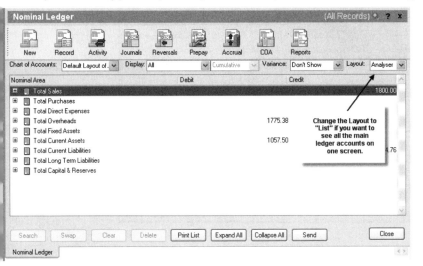

If this is what you see in your version, use the drop down menu at the top right to change the **Layout** to "List": this will allow you to see all the nominal accounts available. (The ones shown in the next illustration, incidentally, are the nominal ledger accounts that cannot be deleted in Sage.)

Look through the list and you will see that there is not yet a suitable account for stationery, so you will need to create one.

Click on the **New** button and the program will take you through the Nominal Record Wizard. It is possible to set up new accounts without using the wizard, but we strongly discourage this, because that can very easily lead to problems in the way the program handles your new main ledger accounts when it is producing reports and financial statements.

The first step is to decide on the **Name** of your new account and choose what **Type** of account it is.

student notes

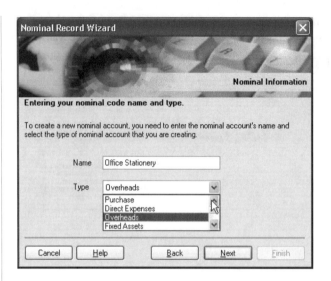

Activity 3

Adam was in a huge hurry to post a transaction because he'd just had a text message from a girl he met last night and he wanted to answer it. He wasn't quite sure what nominal account to use, anyway, so he created a new account named "L8R". Why might this cause problems later on?

The types of account you can choose from the screen above coincide with the main categories of accounts that are shown on the Profit and Loss account (Sales, Purchase, Direct Expenses, Overheads) and the Balance Sheet (Fixed Assets, Current Assets, Current Liabilities, Long Term Liabilities, Capital and Reserves).

On the next screen you can further refine the **Category** of account (the options available will depend on the type of account you are setting up) and choose an account code (**Ref**). In fact the program will suggest a code depending on the choices you have made so far, and we strongly recommend that you accept this.

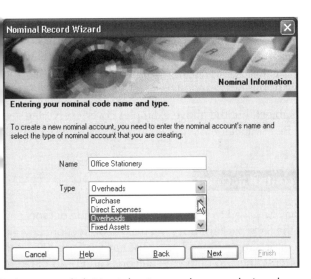

When you click **Next**, having made your choices here, you will be asked if you want to enter an opening balance: you should always choose the **No** option, otherwise you will end up with a balance in the Suspense account, too.)

Activity 4

Using the BPP data which you restored in Activity 1, create a main ledger account for Office Stationery. Refer to the explanations above for details of how to do this.

VAT rates

Accounting packages deal with VAT by means of codes for the various different types of transaction that may occur. Sage calls these "Tax Codes" and you will find that the following VAT rates are set up for you automatically.

Tax code	Used for
T0	Zero-rated transactions, such as books, magazines, and train fares. (Think of the code as "T Zero" - then you will never confuse it with the code for exempt transactions.)
T1	Standard rate (currently at 17.5%). Some standard-rated items that catch people out are taxi fares (but only if the taxi driver is VAT-registered), restaurant meals, and stationery. You can only reclaim VAT if you have a valid VAT invoice: if not use code T9.
T2	Exempt transactions such as bank charges and insurance, postage stamps, professional subscriptions
T9	Transactions not involving VAT, for example wages, charitable donations, internal transfers between accounts (for instance from the bank to the petty cash account). Also used if the supplier is not VAT-registered or if you do not have a valid VAT invoice.

There are also codes for transactions with organisations in the EC (outside the UK), because these need to be shown separately on a VAT return, but we don't need to go into that at this level. You may also be aware that there is a reduced rate of 5% for certain things such as domestic electricity, but this does not normally apply to business expenditure.

VAT is a very complex subject, but the above examples cover everything you are likely to encounter in a simulation.

Non-trade debtors control account

It is possible that you may be asked to deal separately with trade debtors and non-trade debtors, but the Sage package does not make a distinction: anyone to whom you grant credit is simply treated as a customer in Sage. (You can assign different types of customers to different categories and/or to different 'departments', but that is beyond the scope of your present studies.)

If you wish you could create your own non-trade debtors account. You would then have to post invoices to it using journals rather than using the neater invoicing options, and receipts would be posted as ordinary receipts (like bank interest, for example) rather than receipts from customers.

In a simulation it is probably simpler and safer to treat the non-trade debtor as an ordinary debtor and make a note that you did so because Sage does not have a non-trade debtor control account.

CUSTOMER AND SUPPLIER DATA

Before you can post any transactions you will also need to set up accounts in the sales ledger and the purchase ledger.

Once again we recommend that you set up all the accounts you need before you start posting any transactions.

In a simulation (and in real life) you will find the details you need on the documents you have to hand: the business's own sales invoices and its suppliers' purchase invoices.

Codes

The first decision you will need to make is what kind of codes to use. In Sage the default behaviour of the program is to use the first eight characters (excluding spaces and punctuation) of the full name of the customer or supplier, so if you enter 'G. T. Summertown' as the name the package will suggest that you use the code GTSUMMER.

This is a very clear and easy to use coding system because the code actually contains information about the account to which it refers. If you just gave this customer the code '1' that may be fine when you only have a few customers, but if you have thousands it's most unlikely that you would know who, say, customer 5682 was, just from the code.

The program will not allow you to set up two customers or two suppliers with the same code, so if you had a customer called 'G. T. Summerfield' as well as one called 'G.T Summertown' you would get a warning message suggesting that you use the code GTSUMME1. For this reason many businesses actually introduce numbers into their coding systems. For example you could use the first five letters of the name and then the numbers 001, 002 and so on for subsequent customers or suppliers with the same first five letters in their name (GTSUM001, GTSUM002, and so on).

Of course, in real life you may simply have to use the coding system prescribed by your organisation, but in a simulation the choice is yours. We recommend an alphanumeric system, since this shows that you understand the issues.

Activity 5

Do you think it is possible for a customer and a supplier to have exactly the same code? Explain your answer.

Entering the account details

We'll illustrate setting up a supplier account: the process is identical for customers.

If you click the Supplier button on the main toolbar this gives you a new set of buttons.

New   Record   Price List   Activity   Aged   Invoice   Credit   Dispute   Phone   Labels   Letters

To set up a new account you can either use a Wizard (click on New and enter as many details as you have available) or set the account up directly, by clicking on Record.

student notes

The details will be found on the supplier invoice and you should enter as much information as you have: If the invoice shows an email address, for instance, be sure to type it in, even though you may not have email addresses for other suppliers. Take care with typing, as always. When you are happy that everything is correct click on Save and Close.

You'll then see your new supplier listed in the main Supplier window.

To look at this account again, just select it in this window and click the Record button. The first time you do this, you will probably get the following message.

To rectify this click on the Credit Control tab for this record.

Put a tick in the appropriate checkbox at the foot of the screen, and then save the record.

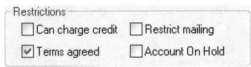

Activity 6

Set up a supplier account based on the following details from the heading of an invoice. Decide on an appropriate coding system yourself.

McAlistair Supplies Ltd
52 Foram Road
Winnesh
DR3 5TP
Tel. 06112 546772 Fax: 06112 546775
E-mail: sales@mcalisupps.co.uk
VAT No. 692 1473 29

Customer and supplier defaults

By default when you set up a new customer account the transactions you enter will be posted to the Debtors Control Account (debit gross amount), the Sales Tax Control Account (credit VAT amount) and the Sales account (credit net amount).

Again, by default when you set up a new supplier account the transactions you enter will be posted to the Creditors Control Account (credit gross), the Purchase Tax Control Account (debit VAT) and the Purchases account (debit net).

For sales this is most probably exactly what you want to happen, unless you are specifically instructed that different types of sales should be posted to different main ledger accounts.

For purchases, however, it would probably be better to set a different default for the expense depending on the type of purchase: you'd want to post a stationery supplier's invoices to the stationery account, but an insurance company's invoices to the insurance account.

To change the defaults, just open the supplier record and click on the Defaults tab. In the box labelled **Def. N/C** you can set the main ledger account to which all transactions with this supplier will be posted, unless you specify otherwise when you actually post a transaction. To see a list of all available accounts click on the arrow   at the right of the box or just press the **F4** key on your keyboard. In the next illustration we are setting the default for McAlistair Supplies to Office stationery.

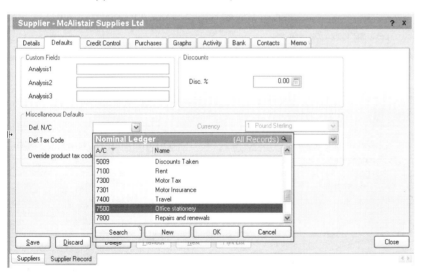

Obviously it helps if you have created an Office stationery account already. You can set one up from this screen if necessary, but we don't recommend it: it's much safer to set up all new nominal accounts using the appropriate Wizard, as mentioned earlier.

JOURNALS

If you are setting up a new business the first entries you are likely to make will be done via a journal, to set up any opening balances. As a bare minimum there will probably be some money in the business bank account, and this needs to be reflected in the accounts.

To post a journal in Sage click on the **Nominal** button and then on **Journals**.

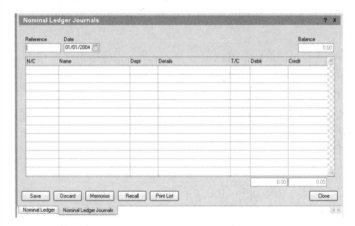

This screen looks reassuringly similar to a journal slip in a manual system, but all you need to do in a computerised system is fill in the slip and click on **Save**. All the entries to the 'books' will then be made in one go without any further effort from you.

Let's suppose your simulation asks you to post the following journal, to set up the opening cash balances.

	Dr	Cr
Bank	2,750.00	
Petty Cash	250.00	
Capital		3,000.00

This is how it might look on your screen (the comment and arrows are added by us, of course).

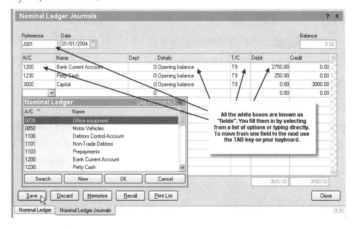

The table below explains what to do as you work through each entry field, in the order in which the TAB key will take you through them.

SCREEN ITEM	HOW IT WORKS
Reference	Type in the journal slip number you are given, if any. Journals should be numbered consecutively, so you may need to check to find out the number of the previous journal. If this is the first ever journal, choose your own coding system and make sure it has room for expansion. For example "J001" allows for up to 999 journals in total.
Date	By default this field (box) will show the program date, but you should change it if that is not correct (see below). Pressing the **F4** key, or clicking the ▦ button will make a little calendar appear.
N/C	Enter the main ledger code of the account affected, or press **F4** or click the ⌄ button to the right of this field to select from a list.
Name	This field will be filled in automatically by the program when you select the nominal code.
Dept	Leave this blank. Departments can be used in Sage for a variety of data analysis purposes, but we won't be using this feature.
Details	Type in the journal narrative. In the second and subsequent lines you can press the **F6** key when you reach this field, and the entry above will be copied without you needing to retype it. This can save lots of time.
T/C	The VAT code, if applicable. For journals this will almost always invariably be T9 (transaction not involving VAT)
Debit/Credit	Type in the amounts in the correct columns. If it is a round sum, such as £250 there is no need to type in the decimal point and the extra zeros.

It is completely impossible to post a journal if it does not balance.

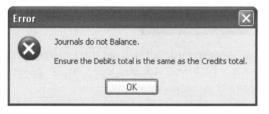

Error ☒

❌ Journals do not Balance.

Ensure the Debits total is the same as the Credits total.

[OK]

Activity 7

Enter the journal shown above.

The importance of dates

By default Sage sets the date of transactions to the current date according to your computer's clock, but this may well not be the date you want to use, especially if you are doing a simulation.

It is vitally important to enter the correct date when you are using a computerised system, even if you are only doing a practice exercise, because

student notes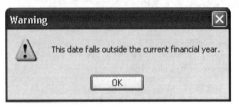

the computer uses the date you enter in a variety of ways – to generate reports such as aged debtors reports, to reconcile VAT, and so on.

If you get the date seriously wrong you will get a warning like the following.

However, if you enter the month as 02 when you meant 12 the program will allow you to do this without complaining at all, so long as the financial year is correct.

The best way to avoid this kind of error, especially when doing a simulation, is to use the facility to set the program date before you enter any transactions.

Select the **Settings** menu and then **Change Program Date**.

If you are doing a simulation we recommend that you set the program date to the last day of the month for which you are supposed to be posting transactions. That way you can never go seriously wrong.

Once you set the program date Sage will use it as the default date until you change it again or shut down the program. This has no adverse effect on any other programs you may be using and even within Sage the date will revert to the computer clock date the next time you use the program. (Remember that you will need to set the program date again if you shut down and then restart.)

Activity 8

Change the program date to 31 January 2004 and check that you have done so correctly by looking at the foot of the screen.

Then close down the program. You should backup your data when prompted to do so, using a file name that includes your own initials. Ask your lecturer where you should save the backup file. Don't skip the backup, because we are going to overwrite your current data in the next activity.

ENTERING INVOICES

You may be feeling that you have been working quite hard but not actually got anything much done yet! This is one of the few off-putting things about accounting packages: it may take quite a while to set everything up properly before you can really get started.

If you get a bit frustrated just remember that you only have to set all these details up once. In future the fact that all the data is available at the touch of a button will save you a vast amount of time, so it really is worth the initial effort.

Purchase invoices

Purchase invoices are created by your suppliers, whereas sales invoices are documents that you need to create yourself. That means that it is usually simpler to enter purchase invoices so we'll deal with those first.

In Sage click on the **Suppliers** button on the main toolbar and then on Invoice on the Suppliers toolbar.

As ever you use the **TAB** key to move between different parts of the screen.

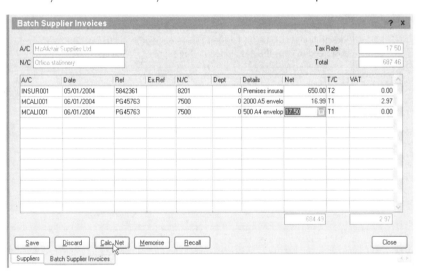

You can enter a number of different invoices from different suppliers on the same screen, and you can enter each line of an invoice separately. Obviously you would need to do this if the invoice is for a variety of items that need to be coded to different nominal accounts.

To repeat the same entry in consecutive lines just press the **F6** key on your keyboard when you reach the appropriate field. For example most of the third line in the above illustration can be entered like this, since the details are mostly the same.

The table below explains what to do as you tab through each entry field. Pay particular attention to the **Net**, **T/C** and **VAT** fields.

SCREEN ITEM	HOW IT WORKS
A/C column	Select the supplier account from the drop down list (press the F4 key to see this, or click on the ⬇ button). The A/C box at the top left of the screen will show the full name of the supplier you select, so you can che ck to make sure you have the right one.
Date	The program date will be entered by default, but you can change this if you wish. Press **F4** to see an on-screen calendar.
Ref	Type in the supplier's invoice number.
Ex Ref	Leave this blank.
N/C	This will show the default code for this supplier (the N/C box at the top left of the screen will show the name of this account). If you need to change it press **F4** or click the ⬇ button to see a list of main ledger accounts.
Dept	Leave this blank.
Details	Type in a brief but clear description of the item and be sure that your description would be understood by someone other than you. Usually you will just need to copy the description on the supplier's invoice.
Net	Enter the net amount of the invoice, excluding VAT. If the invoice has several lines you can enter each line separately but you should use the same Ref for each line. The ▦ button in this field will call up an on screen calculator. Alternatively, type in the gross amount and press the **F9** key on your keyboard (or click **Calc. Net**), as shown in third line in the above illustration.
T/C	The VAT code, as explained earlier. Type in or select the appropriate code for the item.
VAT	This item will be calculated automatically, depending on the tax code selected. Check that it agrees with the VAT shown on the actual invoice. You can overtype the automatic amount, if necessary. You may need to do this if the VAT is affected by settlement discount.

When you have entered all the invoice details you post them simply by clicking on **Save**. This will post ALL the required accounting entries to ALL the ledgers.

I don't believe it!

The first time you do this you will probably not quite believe that double entry to all the ledgers can be so incredibly easy. Check for yourself by looking at the individual accounts.

To check the main ledger click on **Nominal** (and change the **Layout** to **List** if necessary). Depending on which type of transaction you posted you should then select either the Sales Ledger Control Account or the Purchases Ledger Control Account and click on **Record**. Choose the **Activity** tab and you will see something like this.

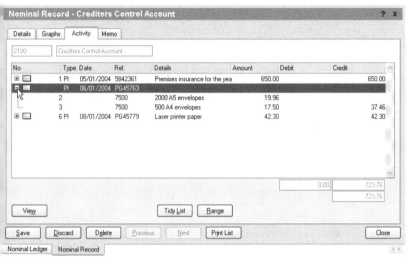

Notice that you can 'drill down' to see full details of any transaction by clicking on the plus sign button ⊞ to the left, just like in Windows Explorer when you want to know the contents of a folder.

If you drill down you can see the other side of the double entry. In the example above transactions 2 and 3 were credited to account 2100 and the net amount was debited to the expense account 7500 while VAT was dealt with by a debit to the Purchase Tax Control Account.

To check that the correct amounts have also been posted to the subsidiary ledger, simply open the record for the relevant customer or supplier and choose the **Activity** tab.

student notes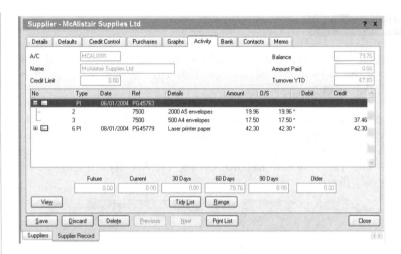

Finally, if you just want a quick look at the transactions you've posted, clic on **Financials**, which shows you a list of all of them, numbered in the orde in which you posted them. This can be very useful on occasions: for instanc if you can't remember the reference number of the last journal you poste you can quickly check using this screen.

Activity 9

So long as you have already done the previous activity, where you took a backup, restore the BPP file SFE_04.001. This includes all the postings you should have made so far and some additional items, to set you up to do the remaining activities.

Post an invoice from McAlistair Supplies dated 6 January 2004 for 2000 sheets of A4 paper (net price: £20.35) and a box of 100 blue biros (gross price: £9.99). The invoice number is PG45783.

Write down the total amount of VAT, as calculated by the program.

£_____

Sales invoices if no invoice is produced

Some businesses create sales invoices using a different system from their accounts package – a word processor, for instance.

If that is the case then sales invoices are entered in exactly the same way as purchase invoices, as you can see from the illustration: click on **Customers** then **Invoice** and enter the invoices in a batch.

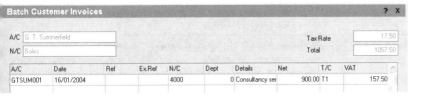

Sales invoices if the system creates the invoice

If you use your accounting package to produce printable invoices the procedure is a bit more involved. You begin by clicking on the **Invoicing** button on the main toolbar and then on the **New/Edit** button.

A screen like this will appear and you tab through the fields and make entries as described below.

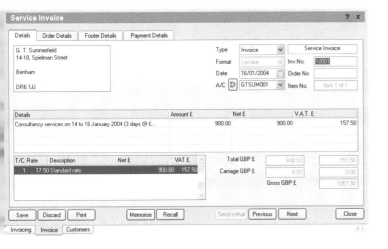

student notes🖎

SCREEN ITEM	HOW IT WORKS
Type	The basic choices are Invoice and Credit. (There may be other options, depending which version of Sage you are using.)
Format	You can choose between a Product invoice if you sell items of stock or a Service invoice if not. If you choose the product option you need to select what items of stock to sell from a product database that you have already set up. It is unlikely that your simulation will require this.
Date	This will be the program date, but you should change this if n ecessary.
A/C	The code for the customer you are invoicing. As usual you can just select from a list: press the **F4** key.
Inv Number	By default this will say **<AutoNumber>**, meaning that Sage will look up the number of your last sales invoice and add one. You can change this if you like but we recommend that you use the automatic option except for the very first invoice that you enter.
Details	Type in a description of what the invoice is for. Make sure this is clear: remember that this invoice will be sent to the customer.
Amount	For services, type in the total amount of the invoice. If you were producing a product invoice you would have the option to enter a unit cost and a quantity: Sage then does the multiplication for you.
Net and VAT	These fields are c alculated automatically.

Once you have entered the details you can click on **Save**, but unlike any other part of the program this does not mean that entries are immediately made in the ledgers. Click on **Close** to return to the main invoicing screen which will now show the invoice you have just created.

Notice that the **Printed** and **Posted** columns are blank at present.

The system works like this because for many businesses sales invoicing and updating the ledgers is the very last stage of the more complex process of Sales Order Processing. However, this feature is only available in the most expensive versions of Sage, so we will not cover it here: it may well not be available in the version you are using.

To print out the invoice select it and click on the **Print** button: it will still not be posted however, so if there is a mistake you can change it and print it again.

To post the invoice you must select it and click on the **Update** button.

This will produce a report which you can just preview on screen or print out (for instance your manager might want to see a list of all new invoices) and ALL the ledgers will now be updated, as you can now see from the **Yes** in the **Posted** column on the Invoicing screen.

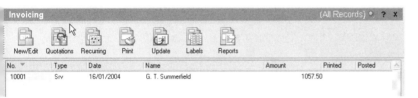

Credit notes

Supplier credit notes are posted in exactly the same way as supplier invoices except that you begin by clicking on **Supplier** and then the **Credit** button, instead of the Invoice button. The entries you make will appear in red, as a visual reminder that you are creating a credit note.

Customer credit notes can be posted in this way too, if no printed credit note is required. If you do want something you can print you can use the **Invoicing** button, choose **New/Edit** and then select **Credit** as the **Type** of transaction.

The procedure is then exactly the same as for a printed sales invoice. If you use this method don't forget that you still have to **Update** the ledgers, not just create and save the credit note.

PAYMENTS AND RECEIPTS

Your simulation is likely to provide you with details of a series of cheques to enter into the accounts – both cheques that you have sent to suppliers and cheques received from customers.

Take care that you know which is which. If it is a cheque that you have paid out to a supplier you may only be shown the cheque stub (that's all you would have in practice, after all), like this.

Date ....

Payee ....

....

....

....

£ ....

000001

If it is a cheque that you have received from a customer you may be shown the cheque itself.

Lloyds TSB   30-92-10

Benham Branch   Date _____

Pay_____

_____

_____

FOR WHITEHILL SUPERSTORES

You can tell that this is a receipt because the name below the signature (here Whitehill Superstores) will be the name of one of your customers.

Alternatively you may be shown a paying-in slip: notice that this may include payments from several different customers.

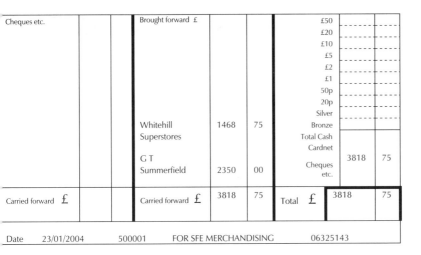

Cheques etc.			Brought forward £			£50		
						£20		
						£10		
						£5		
						£2		
						£1		
						50p		
						20p		
						Silver		
			Whitehill	1468	75	Bronze		
			Superstores			Total Cash		
						Cardnet		
			G T				3818	75
			Summerfield	2350	00	Cheques etc.		
Carried forward £			Carried forward £	3818	75	Total £	3818	75

Date   23/01/2004   500001   FOR SFE MERCHANDISING   06325143

Supplier payments

When you pay a supplier it is important to allocate your payment to invoices shown as outstanding in the purchase ledger. Sage makes this very easy.

To post a payment to a supplier click on **Bank** on the main toolbar and then on the **Supplier** button (NOT the **Payment** button).

The next screen looks like a cheque at the top, but the bottom half shows you details of any outstanding invoices on this supplier's account.

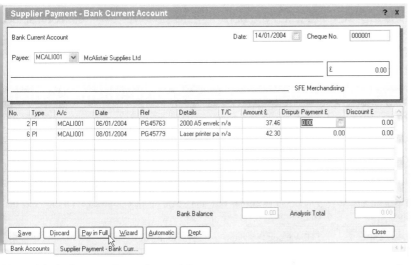

The table below explains the quickest way to post a payment to a supplier. Press TAB to move from one field to the next.

269

student notes✍

SCREEN ITEM	HOW IT WORKS
Payee	Select the code for the supplier you want to pay.
Date	This will show the program date, but you can change this if necessary.
Cheque No.	Type in the number of the cheque. Take care because accuracy here will help you with disputes and bank reconciliations.
£ box	Though it may seem odd, leave this as 0.00 and just press the TAB key
Payment £ (first line)	When you reach this box don't type anything! Just click on the **Pay in Full** button at the foot of the screen.
Discount £	TAB will skip this and move down to the next line.
Payment £ (second line)	When you reach this box don't type anything! Just click on the **Pay in Full** button at the foot of the screen.
Save	This will post the payment to ALL the ledgers.

Using this method the amount of the cheque, shown in the £ box in the top half of the screen, updates each time you click on Pay in Full. The program is also clever enough to write the amount in words.

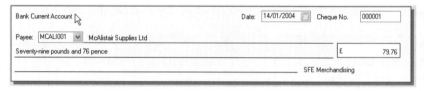

You don't need to pay all the outstanding invoices if you don't want to: just click on **Save** when you've paid the ones you want.

This is the quickest way of posting a payment in ordinary circumstances.

There may be times when you don't want to pay invoices in full. For instance you may decide to pay the supplier in the illustration above only £50 because of some problem with the items supplied. In that case, proceed as follows.

SCREEN ITEM	HOW IT WORKS
Payee	As before.
Date	As before.
Cheque No.	As before.
£ box	Type in £50.00
Payment £ (first line)	When you reach this box don't type anything! Just click on the **Pay in Full** button at the foot of the screen.
Discount £	TAB will skip this and move down to the next line.
Payment £ (second line)	When you reach this box don't type anything! Just click on the **Pay in Full** button at the foot of the screen. Sage will know better than to try to pay this invoice in full: it will work out how much of the £50 is left after paying the first invoice and allocate the remainder to the second one.

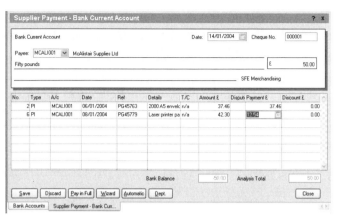

A further possibility is that there will be a credit note on the account as well as invoices. Not surprisingly, **Pay in Full** is the answer to this, too. When you reach the credit note line click on **Pay in Full** and the amount of the cheque will be reduced by the correct amount.

Activity 10

Post a payment made with cheque 158002 to Davidson Ltd. The total amount of the cheque is £230.59. You should allocate this to outstanding invoices as best you can.

Customer receipts

When you receive money from your customers it is again important to allocate your payment to invoices shown as outstanding in the subsidiary ledger.

To record a receipt from a customer click on the **Bank** button and then the **Customer** button (NOT the **Receipt** button).

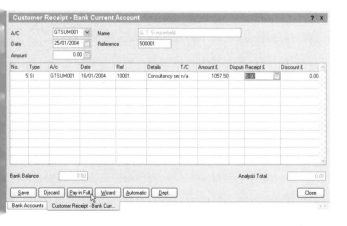

student notes✍

Although this screen looks slightly different to the payment one it works in exactly the same way, and we recommend that you use it in exactly the same way – in other words, rely on the **Pay in Full** button.

One important point to remember when posting receipts is that you should use the paying-in slip number (if you have it) for the **Reference**. This makes it much easier to do bank reconciliations, because typically several cheques will be paid in on a single paying-in slip and the bank statement will only show the total, not the individual amounts.

Activity 11

Post a receipt from Biddlecombes for £1250. This was paid in using paying-in slip 500001 dated 16 January 2004. You should allocate this to outstanding invoices as best you can.

Other payments and receipts

Some payments and receipts do not need to be allocated to customers or suppliers. Examples include payments like wages and receipts such as VAT refunds.

If your simulation includes transactions like this you should post them by clicking on **Bank** and then **Payment** (or **Bank** and then **Receipt**).

Payment

Receipt

Here's an example of how a loan from the bank might be posted to the accounts. You will have to decide which nominal code to use. Note that transactions like this will often not involve VAT, in which case the **T/C** code to use is T9.

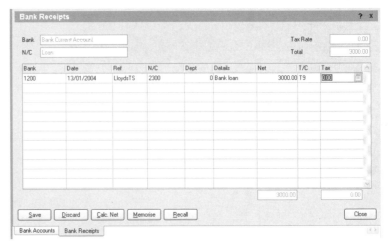

The screen for posting payments such as wages is exactly the same.

Petty cash

Petty cash transactions are posted in exactly the same way as bank transactions except that you use the nominal code for Petty Cash in the **Bank** column. Also, take care to use the correct code for VAT with petty cash expenditure. Refer to the list given earlier in the chapter if you are not sure.

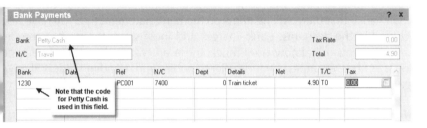

BANK RECONCILIATIONS

As you know, it is important to carry out a bank reconciliation on a regular basis to ensure that you have posted all the transactions you should have posted and that this has been done correctly, both by you and by the bank.

In Sage this can be done on-screen. Click on **Bank** and then **Reconcile**.

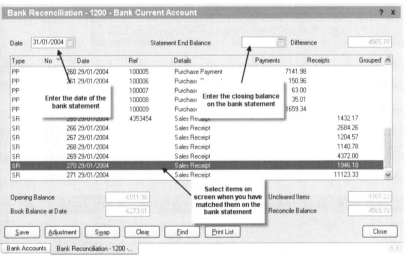

SCREEN ITEM	HOW IT WORKS
Date	Set this to the same date as the date of the statement received from the bank (probably the date of the last transaction shown on the statement).
Statement End Balance	Type in the closing balance on the bank statement, using a minus sign if the account is overdrawn.
Difference	This field is updated by the program as you select transactions on screen. The aim is to make this box show 0.00.

Selecting items on screen is just like physically ticking them off on the statement. When you have matched everything on the bank statement and the **Difference** is zero just click on **Save** and the selected transactions will be marked as reconciled. That is all there is to it, apart from a few additional points below.

Adjustments

Even if you have posted all your transactions fully and perfectly there is a good chance that there will be items on the bank statement that you have not included in the accounts. Bank charges and interest are the most common examples: you only know how much these are when the bank statement arrives. Other examples include direct debits and standing orders if you haven't already posted these in another way (e.g. by journals).

For such items click on the **Adjustment** button and enter the details, then click on **Save**.

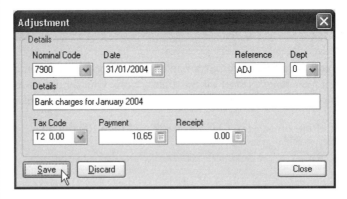

Make sure you use the correct tax code. Do not to use this option to post any amounts that include VAT. Post such items in the normal way and then start the bank reconciliation again.

You cannot use this method to post payments to/receipts from credit suppliers/customers because the subsidiary ledgers and the relevant VAT control account will not be updated. You will get a warning if you try to do this.

Grouped receipts

As we mentioned earlier, businesses often pay several cheques into the bank on the same paying in slip and bank statements only show the total of the paying-in slip, not the individual items.

It is therefore helpful to use the paying-in slip number as the **Reference** when posting receipts: you can then set up Sage to group the items together when doing a bank reconciliation. This option can be found in the **Settings** menu (you can turn it off and on as often as you wish).

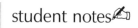

PRINT-OUTS

When you have finished entering transactions the next task in your simulation is likely to be to print out some reports.

Sage offers you a large number of different reports and you can create others of your own if you wish, containing any information you choose. Although the pre-prepared reports that are available in Sage don't all have names that you will immediately recognise from your knowledge of manual accounting systems, rest assured that everything you are likely to be asked to produce in a simulation can easily be found.

One or two print-outs, such as customer statements, have their own buttons, but in general to generate and then print a report you open the part of the program you want a report on and choose the **Reports** button.

(Don't click the **Reports** button on the main toolbar: that opens a separate program called the report designer, and that is beyond the scope of your current studies.)

Here's an example of the range of Customers reports that you could create. To get to this screen click on **Customers** then **Reports**.

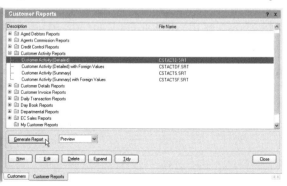

In recent versions of Sage the reports are organised into separate folders by subject, as in the illustration. In older versions this screen is laid out a bit differently and it simply lists all the reports in alphabetical order, so you may have to do a bit of scrolling around before you find the one you want.

When you have found your report, select it and check that the initial output will be a **Preview**. This allows you to take a look at what will be printed out on screen before actually sending it to the printer. It is especially important to preview your report if you are sharing a printer (as you are likely to be if you are doing a simulation) because otherwise you may clog up the printer queue with output that you do not want at all.

The next step is to click the **Generate Report** button. Usually you will get a set of further options such as the following.

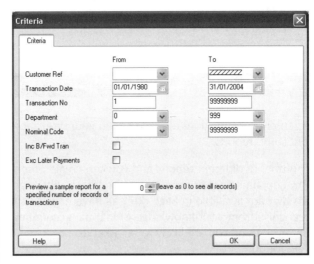

The default settings shown in the illustration will produce a report on ALL customer accounts up until the date specified, but if you wish you can specify that you only want a report on a specific account, or range of accounts, by making selections in the **Customer Ref** boxes. You can also restrict your report to cover a specific period by making entries in the **Transaction Date** boxes.

We suggest that in a simulation you simply check that the **To** date is the last day of the month for which you have entered transactions and leave everything else as shown above. If you have already set the program date to the last day, then that will be shown as the default entry already, so you just have to click on **OK**.

The preview will then appear on screen and once you have had a look through and are happy that it shows the information you want you can click a **Print** button to print it out.

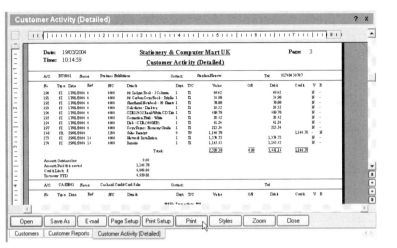

Invoices and statements

Some print-outs assume that you are using pre-printed stationery. For example a customer statement will look like this (extract only) in an on-screen preview.

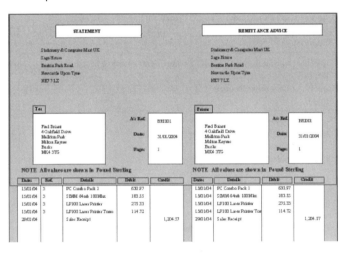

However, if you do not have pre-printed stationery in your printer you won't get any of the shaded parts or the neat boxes and lines: all you will see on your print-out will be the words and figures on plain white paper. This is obvious if you think about it, but we mention it because it still surprises and disappoints new users.

Print-outs in simulations

Here's a list of the print-outs you are most likely to be asked for in a simulation and how to obtain them in Sage.

PRINT-OUT REQUIRED	HOW TO GET IT	WHICH REPORT TO CHOOSE
Audit trail	Click on **Financials**, then on **Audit**	The **Summary** type of audit trail with **Landscape Output** is the most useful. Just click on **OK** when you are asked for **Criteria** and you will get a list of ALL transactions in the order in which they were posted.
Aged Debtors	Click on the **Customers** button then the **Reports** button and (if necessary) open the **Aged Debtors Reports** folder	Aged Debtors Analysis (Detailed)
Customer Statements	Click on the **Customers** button and then the **Statement** button	A4 Stat with Tear Off Remit Adv. Individual & All Items
Bank reconciliation statement	Click on the **Bank** button, then the **Reports** button and (if necessary) open the folder **Reconciled and Unreconciled Transaction Reports.**	Bank Statement — Reconciled and Un-reconciled
Sales and Sales Returns Day Books	Click on **Customers**, then **Reports** and (if necessary) open the folder **Day Book Reports**.	Day Books: Customer Invoices (Detailed) Day Books: Customer Credits (Detailed)
Purchases and Purchases Returns Day Books	Click on **Suppliers**, then **Reports** and (if necessary) open the folder **Day Book Reports**.	Day Books: Supplier Invoices (Detailed) Day Books: Supplier Credits (Detailed)
Journal Day Book	Click on **Nominal**, then **Reports** and (if necessary) open the **Day Book Reports** folder	Day Books: Nominal Ledger
Subsidiary (sales) ledger	Click on **Customers**, then **Reports** and (if necessary) open the **Customer Activity Reports** folder	Customer Activity (Detailed)
Subsidiary (purchases) ledger	Click on **Suppliers**, then **Reports** and (if necessary) open the **Supplier Activity Reports** folder	Supplier Activity (Detailed)
Main ledger	Click on **Nominal**, then **Reports** and (if necessary) open the **Nominal Activity** folder	Nominal Activity Reports
Trial Balance	Click on the **Financials** button, then on the **Trial** button	Choose Printer when asked about Print Output, unless you only want to preview the report on screen.

Activity 12

Make sure the program date is set to 31 January 2004 and then preview a Sales Day Book report and an Audit Trail, following the instructions above.

ERROR CORRECTION

If you make an error when you are making your entries it is not the end of the world.

Errors made when setting up customer and supplier accounts can be corrected simply by opening the relevant record and changing the data.

Errors made when typing in the details of a transaction (references, descriptions etc.) can be corrected by clicking on the File menu and then on **Maintenance ... Corrections**. A list of all the transactions you have posted so far will appear and you can select the one you want to change. Click on Edit and change the details as appropriate.

Some corrections that you can make in this way have a bigger effect on the underlying records than others. For example if you try to change the date or the amounts or account codes for a transaction the program may let you do so, but to guard against fraud it will also post a record of what has been changed, and you will be able to see this if you click on the **Financials** button: the correction will show up in red.

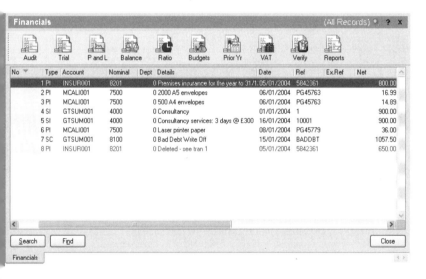

Write offs

If you need to write off a transaction altogether, for example if it is decided that a customer will never pay, there are a variety of wizards to help you get the double entry correct and make the appropriate changes to the subsidiary ledgers.

If you need to do this click on the **Tools** menu and choose **Write Off, Refund, Return**. A variety of options are available, as illustrated below.

student notes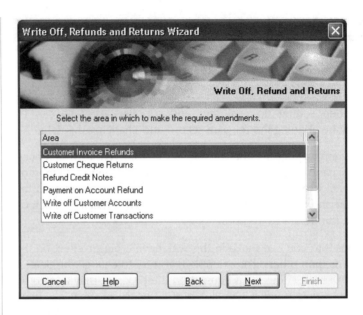

Write Off, Refunds and Returns Wizard   ☒

Write Off, Refund and Returns

Select the area in which to make the required amendments.

Area
Customer Invoice Refunds
Customer Cheque Returns
Refund Credit Notes
Payment on Account Refund
Write off Customer Accounts
Write off Customer Transactions

[Cancel]   [Help]   [Back]   [Next]   [Finish]

For you it is just a matter of working through wizard choosing the appropriate options. When you click on **Finish** however, the program will do all the necessary double entry automatically.

1162 SC	A1D001	4000	1 Refund - 1	24/01/2004	REFUND	60.72
1163 SI	A1D001	9999	1 Allocation - 1	24/01/2004	REFUND	71.08
1164 JD		9999	1 Refunds (S) - A1D001	24/01/2004	REFUND	71.08
1165 JC		1200	1 Refunds (S) - A1D001	24/01/2004	REFUND	71.08

Starting over

All of us have a bad day sometimes, and you may find that you make a complete hash of all the entries you make. Or someone else may have been using the package, and got everything wrong.

If this happens it may well be better to start again rather than trying to correct all the mistakes, possibly making things worse.

To do so, of course, you need to have made a backup of the data as it was before all the errors were made. You can then simply restore the correct data and start posting your new entries again.

Try not to make a habit of this though. There is no advantage in using a computerised package if you need three goes before you get it right. The key is to slow down a bit when you are entering data, and make sure you are getting it right.

CHAPTER OVERVIEW

- accounting packages range from the very simple to the very complex. Sage's products are the most popular packages in the UK

- simulations will typically involve setting up new customer and supplier accounts, posting journals, invoices, payments and receipts, and obtaining printouts

- it is essential to make sure that you are posting transactions to the correct financial year

- new main ledger accounts should be set up using the accounting package's 'wizard' to ensure that the new account is dealt with correctly in the chart of accounts

- VAT is dealt with by assigning the correct code to a transaction

- new customer and supplier accounts should be given consistent and meaningful codes

- you should use the keyboard as much as possible (rather than the mouse) when entering data. The TAB key, the ESC key and the function keys (e.g. F4 and F6) will greatly speed up your work

- payments and receipts should be allocated to outstanding invoices

- all the printouts that you are likely to require are available as pre-prepared reports

- there are various facilities for error correction, but it is best not to make errors in the first place!

KEY WORDS

Field a box on screen in which you enter data or select from a list (similar to a spreadsheet cell)

Defaults the entries that the accounting package knows will normally be made in a particular field

Backup a compressed file created to ensure that data is not lost

Restore the process of overwriting the data currently held in the program with different data

Chart of accounts a template that sets out the main ledger accounts and how they are organised into different categories

Tax code Sage's term for the code to be used for VAT calculation

Program Date the date that is used for any transactions that are posted unless a different date is entered (it need not be the same as 'today's' date)

Activity the transactions that have occurred on an account

Pay in Full a slightly misleadingly-named button that helps to allocate payments and receipts to outstanding invoices

HOW MUCH HAVE YOU LEARNED?

1   What is a 'field' in an accounting package?

2   What do you understand by the term 'default'?

3   Before you shut down an accounting package it is essential to save your work. True or false? Explain your answer.

4   What happens when you restore a backup file?

5   When is it not possible to change the financial year of an accounting package?

6   Why is it important that details such as company name and address are entered with no mistakes or typing errors?

7   What is a chart of accounts?

8   In an accounting package there will usually be codes for at least four different types of transactions. What are these types?

9   What must be done before a supplier credit invoice can be posted?

10 How would a supplier invoice be assigned to the correct main ledger account?

11 If you attempt to post a journal that does not balance the difference will be posted to the suspense account. True or false? Explain your answer.

12 Why is it so important to enter the correct date for a transaction?

13 If a purchase invoice has five separate lines should these be posted individually or is it sufficient just to post the invoice totals?

14 When you receive a payment from a customer this is posted using the Receipt button. True or False? Explain your answer.

15 If you have not yet been able to work through this chapter while sitting in front of a computer equipped with Sage, come back later and do all the activities.

ANSWERS TO CHAPTER ACTIVITIES

CHAPTER 7 Using computer systems and software

1   Your answer should be in the form of a diagram like the one in Chapter 7, though you need not be as artistic.

2   You may well find that your organisation has a mixture of Windows 95, Windows 98, Windows ME, and Windows XP computers. You may well find that some people are using the very latest version of Microsoft Office whereas others have an older version. Typically computers are updated on the basis of need: the people who need the latest features in Excel will have the new version, while those who never do any calculations may not have it at all. On the other hand, office politics have a part to play: managers may have a newer, better computer than their staff, even though they don't really need it.

3   The order of switching things on only matters in a practical sense. If you were switching on your hi-fi it would be best to get the amplifier going first because otherwise you might miss the beginning of the music. Likewise for practical reasons it is best to switch on the computer monitor first – so you can see the messages on screen that tell you what the computer is doing.

4   You should always make sure the mouse and keyboard are plugged in before switching on, but it normally does not matter if you plug in other items afterwards. (This depends upon your operating system to a certain extent.) You may sometimes get a message saying a certain item can't be found.

If you use a network printer you may have no idea whether it is plugged in or not, because it is in another room, but this can usually be sorted out after you've switched on.

5   You may have spotted a number of things.

- The file extension (.doc, .xls and so on) is not taken into account at all.

- Benson_Pres.ppt comes before BensonPres.htm, indicating that the computer thinks that the underscore character comes before P in the alphabet.

- The three files beginning with 'Dean' are treated as they would be in a manual system.

- No account is taken of whether the initial letter is a capital or a small letter.

- It is possible to include a full stop in a file name, before the one that indicates the file type (Doc3.doc.doc)

6   Your search options depend on the information provided when the document was created and saved. If you create a file in Microsoft Word, for example, there are options (under File …

Properties) to give it not just a file name, but also other summary details such as a subject, author name, category and keywords. The computer will then be able to search for all files that fit any of these criteria: all files with the subject 'customers', for example, or all files that fall into the category 'complaints' or include the keyword 'Product X'.

In Janis's case, however, it seems unlikely that she bothered with extra file properties. If you can work out where Janis normally saves her letters the best bet initially is to find out the date of the letter to Mr Venables (ask him) and sort Janis's files in date order. This may restrict the search to just a few documents, but you may still need to look through several files before you find the one you want.

In future Janis must be encouraged to think of others and use a clearer system. If the file had been given the name 'venables.doc' and saved in a folder called 'complaints' this would give another person a reasonable chance of locating the file fairly quickly. Janis could also be encouraged to use the 'subject', 'category' and 'keyword' options.

7   In an e-mail system all the documents are of the same type (e-mails) and they are typically organised into folders (Inbox, Sent items) under headings such as 'From' (or 'To'), Subject, and Received date (or Sent date).

You can improve on this basic system by adding your own sub-folders. For instance all internal memos could be put in a different folder to e-mails received from customers, and the customer sub-folder could be further sub-divided by name or customer type.

8   Your answer and your actions will depend on the file-naming system in use in your own organisation.

9   Again, this depends on what goes on in your own organisation. If you are not working at present there may be a system for backups of student data at your college: find out about this instead.

10   This is a hands-on activity. Additional help and sample files can be found on the BPP website (visit http://www.bpp.com/aat/companions and follow the links).

11   Again this depends on your workplace policy. If you are not in work at present you might like to look at the letters and so on you receive from an organisation you deal with, such as your bank, and see if you can work out their house style.

CHAPTER 8 Maintaining the security of data

1   The over-riding rule is: don't do anything that you wouldn't do to your TV at home. We could add some more rules.

- Don't place drinks or other liquids on or near the computer

- Don't place the computer where it can easily be knocked or kicked or where it is subject to strong vibrations or electro-magnetic fields

- Don't move the computer around more than strictly necessary

- If you have to move the machine – even to insert or remove a plug at the back – save and close all current files and switch the machine off first

2 In this example it would be quite alright to choose either of the options 'Permit' or 'Automatically configure Internet access' because the program that is trying to access the Internet is a tried and trusted email program from Microsoft. This is an example of what may happen when you first install a firewall: it will need some configuration before it knows what Internet connections you are prepared to allow without question.

3 Switching off the machine when it is not attended is the simplest method. This prevents casual snoopers from reading files on the screen. Unfortunately, this won't always be possible or desirable, especially if you move around a lot and the machine is needed continuously.

Some users 'disguise' their most sensitive files by giving them uninformative filenames or placing them in unexpected parts of the directory. This is hardly perfect: the chances are that after a while the user will not be able to find the files either! And in any case a search based on file content might well reveal the file and its location if the snooper had some inkling of the secrets about you that he or she was trying to discover.

4 Many people feel unhappy about their personal details being retained by commercial organisations. Here are some of the concerns that people have.

- Incorrect details may be entered, causing anything from minor irritation to significant financial problems

- A list or database may be sold to other organisations, who then try to sell various goods and services to the people on it

- 'Personalised' mailings have arrived addressed to someone who has recently died, causing great distress to the surviving partner

5 Personal data may be kept for any of several dozen different reasons; however, the data of main interest under the Act are kept for sales, marketing and promotional purposes. If you believe that you or your department are holding data that should be registered, or you are unsure what can be disclosed to whom, you should discuss the matter with your line manager.

6 This is an activity for you to do next time you connected to the Internet.

7 E-mail is considered to be the electronic equivalent of a letter. So if the correspondence is the type that would be kept if it were in paper form (for example an e-mail making an offer or communicating acceptance of an offer) then yes, the e-mail should be kept for a certain time (usually 6 years), under contract law and consumer law.

CHAPTER 9 Computerised accounting systems

1 This is a hands-on activity. Don't skip it because otherwise you might not get the right answers when you do Activities 2 to 8.

2 This is a hands-on activity. You will need to change the financial year from January 2000 to January 2004, and you can do so, because no transactions have yet been posted. Take great care to make sure you type in the company details correctly.

3 Adam could easily forget to give the account a proper name next time he uses the package and in future he may not have any idea what sort of expense should be recorded in that account. Nobody else who uses the system will have a clue either. The moral of the story is: don't use abbreviations that others might not understand, and take care with spelling too. A bit of care will save time in the long run.

4   This is a hands-on activity. The Name should be Office Stationery (watch your spelling!), the Type is Overheads, the Category is Printing and Stationery. Assuming you got all of those right Sage will suggest the Refn (account number) 7500, and you should accept this. There is no opening balance to enter.

5   It is possible for a customer and a supplier to have the same code, because it is quite possible that a business will both sell goods and buy goods from the same person.

6   This is a hands-on activity. If you use the new supplier wizard you will be asked for a lot of information, but you can just leave any details that you don't have blank or accept the defaults suggested. When you have finished open your record (make sure that terms are agreed, if necessary) and check the details on screen against those given. We used the account code MCALI001.

7   This is a hands-on activity. Make sure that your journal has an appropriate reference and that each line has a description (use the F6 key for the second two lines). You can check your journal by clicking the Financials button, or by looking at the Activity tab of the main ledger accounts affected, if you wish.

8   This is a hands-on activity. An example file name would be SFE_A08.XYZ, where A08 stands for Activity 8 and XYZ are your initials, but be sure to ask your lecturer about the file name you should use. If you save the backup to a floppy disk, keep it safely and put a label on it: it is evidence of your competence!

9   This is a hands-on activity. Don't skip it because otherwise you will not get the right answers when you do Activities 10 to 12. Make sure you have restored the correct data: there should now be 8 transactions and you can check by glancing at the foot of the screen or by clicking on Financials.

   Use the F6 key when entering the second line of the invoice, to save typing. The total VAT is £5.05 (£3.56 on the first item, which was given net, and £1.49 on the second, where we told you the gross amount). Don't forget that you can use the F9 button to calculate the net amount.

10   This is a hands-on activity. Be sure to use the Bank ... Supplier option, not Bank ... Payment. We deliberately did not tell you the date of the cheque to make you think about the importance of dates: you should have chosen a date after the date of the invoices you are paying, in other words after 15 January 2004. The cheque should be allocated to the second two outstanding invoices using the Pay in Full button: if you do this correctly it will add up to £230.59.

11   This is a hands-on activity. Be sure to use the Bank ... Customer option, not Bank ... Receipt. The customer has paid an amount that does not precisely match any specific invoices. In the absence of other information you should allocate it to outstanding invoices in date order. Type in the amount £1,250 in the Amount field and then tab down and click on Pay in Full for each invoice. The first one will be paid in full, but there will only be £192.50 left to pay the second one.

12   This is a hands-on activity. If you would also like to see a Trial Balance, to see the results of all your work in terms of debits and credits, click on Financials and then Trial.

CHAPTER 7 Using computer systems and software

1 A stand alone computer is one that is not directly connected to any other computers, so it cannot share files or exchange internal e-mail with colleagues' computers. As a rule the only difference in terms of the actual machine is that it need not have a network card and that it will probably have its own internal modem. A networked computer doesn't need a modem, because it connects to the outside world via the server's modem.

2 The operating system does all the basic things that you take for granted, such as recognising input from the keyboard and the mouse, sending output to the screen, handling the location of files on the computer's hard disk, and controlling 'peripherals' such as printers. Although we call them 'basic' these are actually very complex things, especially file handling, and they all rely on the operating systems' management of the computer's memory. You only really appreciate what the operating system normally does when it stops doing it: i.e. when the computer crashes!

3 Word-processing software and spreadsheet software. These are sometimes known as the original 'killer applications' – the applications that made personal computers so successful and essential in business from around 1990 onwards. Depending on your own age and experience you may be surprised at how recently this happened. It is difficult to imagine life without these software tools now.

4 Yes, you should perform your safety checks every time you start up the computer if you have been away from your desk, because you have no idea what may have been happening in your office since you left it. You can probably be a bit more relaxed at home, assuming you know that no-one has been at your computer since you last used it yourself.

5 Before switching off at the mains you should save all open documents, quit any programs that are open and then use the computer's shut down option, so that the computer can close down anything else that may be running behind the scenes. If someone else is connected to your computer (if you share a folder, say) it would be polite to tell them that you are about to shut down. (If someone is still connected you will normally get a warning message telling you so.)

6 This has most probably occurred because your colleague's computer is not turned on. If not, there may be a problem with the network as a whole (for instance the server may have been stopped and is restarting). You should talk to your colleague first, and if that does not solve the problem ask around to see if others are having problems with the network: they may know about the problem and may already have reported it. If not, then it is up to you to contact the network administrator.

7 '123' is a really terrible password. It is far too short, and that makes it easy for password cracking programs to find it very quickly (there are relatively few combinations of three characters). It is numeric only, so only 10 characters have to be tried. Worse the numbers are in numerical order, so it would be one of the first possible combinations tried. If this is your password you may as well say goodbye to your data.

8   One possible reason for limiting your access is to prevent you from viewing data that is considered to be confidential. The other reason might be that you simply don't need to have access to certain parts of the program, because your job does not require you to use them, and it is simpler and safer if you don't have the opportunity to interfere with them.

9   File managers can sort files in alphabetical order of file name, in order of file type, in order of file size, and in order of date last saved. In each case this can be done in ascending or descending order.

10   The asterisk can be used as a 'wildcard' to stand for any number of unknown characters. This makes it easier for you to search for files assuming you can make an educated guess at the file name, or a word or phrase of its contents, in the first place.

11   We suggest that you cancel your current attempt to print and just print out a single test page – preferably one with a lot of text on it. You can look at this to find out whether or not it matters about the margin settings, and if not go ahead with your original intention. However, if your test sheet shows that some data will not appear on the printed page you will have to adjust the margins. At least you will have wasted only one sheet of paper, not ten, and you will have saved yourself some time.

12   Before you restore an old backup it is a good idea to take a backup of whatever data you currently have, if possible, even if there are errors in it. Then at least you will be no worse off if there is also a problem with the old backup.

Next restore the three-day-old backup (this will overwrite your current data) and check that you now have the correct information as of three days ago. Put away the three-day old backup in a safe place, just in case you need it once again.

Then, re-enter whatever data was added or changed since the last back up.

Finally, take a fresh backup, as at today's date, and store it safely. (It is probably also best to delete the backup you took at the start of this process.)

CHAPTER 8 Maintaining the security of data

1   E-mail attachments are now the main carriers of viruses.

2   Your organisation should be running anti-virus and anti-spam software right across the network, full time. It should also install firewall hardware or software. Any e-mail file attachments should be scanned at the server before being passed on to the intended recipient and suspect attachments should be removed (this can be done automatically).

Individuals should not be allowed to install programs of any kind on their computers. If individuals have Internet access this should be controlled and monitored and ideally restricted to approved sites (although this is difficult to control). Ideally individuals should not be allowed to use floppy disks or CDs at all, but this may not be practical.

All staff should be made aware of the risks and the procedure to follow if someone suspects that they have a computer virus should be set down and known to everyone.

3   If you read the message you can see that you don't actually need to take any action because the threat has been deleted automatically by the anti-virus software.

However, before you click on OK and get on with your work it would be wise to make a note of what you were doing on your computer just before this alert appeared, and a note of what the message says (the quickest way is just to press Print Screen and then open a new Word document and press Control + V), then draw the matter to the attention of your system administrator.

4   You should definitely click No. Programs that access your stored e-mail addresses may well be viruses that are trying to spread.

In fact this particular example was generated because Norton Anti-Spam was handling an unsolicited e-mail and Microsoft Outlook detected this and raised the alarm. In other words Outlook did not know that Norton's intentions were benign. So this is also an example of the difficulties that may arise if different programs are not configured to work with one another.

However, there is absolutely no way of knowing that it was a configuration problem, just from the illustration we gave you, so the correct answer is that you should click No.

5   When you delete a file the system initially 'moves' it to the recycle bin (which may not involve moving it physically), and if you delete it from there the system only deletes its address – the set of binary numbers that tell the computer where the file is located on the hard disk. The file then becomes invisible to the file manager system, but it may still be on the hard disk. This means that it may still be possible to recover it using special utility programs.

6   Data must be:

1. Fairly and lawfully processed
2. Processed for limited purposes
3. Adequate, relevant and not excessive
4. Accurate
5. Not kept longer than necessary
6. Processed in accordance with individual's rights
7. Secure
8. Not transferred to countries that do not have adequate data protection laws

7   You have the following rights.

■ The right to be informed of all the information held about you by the organisation

■ The right to prevent them from processing their data about you for the purposes of direct marketing

■ The right to compensation if you can show that the you have been caused damage by any contravention of the Data Protection Act

■ The right to have any inaccurate data about you removed or corrected.

8   This is false. Copyright covers the way words or notes or visual images are arranged, not the idea they convey: it protects the form or expression of an idea, not the idea itself.

9 No, it is illegal to install the software on any computer unless you have purchased a licence. In fact the latest version of Microsoft Office will not work unless you register it with Microsoft, and if you attempt to register a copy that has already been registered by someone else you will be found out. Either you or your organisation may be prosecuted.

10 It should be retained for six years, because this is set down in legislation.

11 The regulations cover matters such as the height of your chair and your desk, the way you arrange documents on the desk, the way you key things in and use the mouse, how you set up the software, and the importance of breaks.

CHAPTER 9 Computerised accounting systems

1 A field is a box on screen in which you enter data or select from a list (similar to a spreadsheet cell)

2 A default is the entry that the accounting package knows will normally be made in a particular field, for example today's date or the nominal code that a purchase from a certain supplier would normally be posted to.

3 It is probably not essential to save your work because all your entries are saved as you go along. It is essential to back up your work, however, because the program may become damaged or you may make incorrect entries next time you use it.

4 When a backup is restored all the data currently held in the program is overwritten with the data from the backup.

5 It will not be possible to change the financial year once any data has been posted to the program. At the year end it is necessary to go through a special procedure in order to move into the next financial year.

6 Details such as company name and address will appear on any documents generated by the program, such as invoices and statements, and these will be sent to customers, so you will look very foolish if you can't even spell your own organisation's details properly.

7 The chart of accounts is a sort of template setting out the structure of the main ledger – which accounts are classed as fixed assets, which are current assets, which are current liabilities which are expenses in the profit and loss account, and so on.

8 Sales, Purchase, Direct Expenses, Overheads.

9 You must set up an account for the supplier in the purchase ledger before you can post an invoice received from the supplier.

10 You can either set a default main ledger account when you set up the supplier account, or you can choose the main ledger account at the time that you post the invoice.

11 This is false. The system will not allow you to post a journal that does not balance.

12 Obviously it is good practice to use the correct date for transactions in any system, but in an accounting package dates govern matters such as debtor ageing, monthly reports, and in particular the way the VAT liability is calculated.

13 It is usually better to post the invoice lines individually. It is essential to do so if the individual expenses need to be posted to different main ledger codes.

14 This is false. Receipts from customers need to be allocated to outstanding invoices.

SKILLS BASED ASSESSMENT 3

UNIT 21
WORKING WITH COMPUTERS

The performance criteria tested in this practice simulation are:

Element 21.1 Use computer systems and software

Performance criteria

- Perform **initial visual safety checks** and power up the **computer system**

- Use **passwords** to gain access to the **computer system** where limitations on access to data is required

- Access, save and print data files and exit from relevant software

- Use appropriate file names and save work

- Back up work carried out on a **computer system** to suitable storage media at regular intervals

- Close down the computer without damaging the **computer system**

- Seek immediate assistance when **difficulties** occur

Element 21.2: Maintain the security of data

Performance criteria

- Ensure passwords are kept secret and changed at **appropriate times**

- Ensure computer program and hardware disks are kept securely located

- Identify **potential risks** to data from different **sources** and take steps to resolve or minimise them

- Maintain **security** and **confidentiality** of data at all times

- Understand and implement relevant **legal regulations**

INSTRUCTIONS

You are advised to read the whole of this assessment before commencing in order to familiarise yourself with all of the tasks you will be asked to complete.

You should set out your written answers on the forms provided and attach your computer print-outs with a paperclip. Check your work carefully before handing it in.

Situation

SFE Merchandising is a new business that has been set up by Charlize Veron, one of Southfield Electrical's former marketing staff. Charlize is an expert on store layout and management of stocks and she intends to sell her skills and knowledge, on a consultancy basis, to medium and large retailers to help them to optimise their sales.

Charlize has started her new venture as a sole trader and has taken on some of the risk herself. However, SFE Merchandising is part-financed by Southfield Electrical, and may well be acquired by them if this new venture is a success.

Initial enquiries have been so promising that Charlize has already voluntarily registered for VAT and intends to run the standard VAT accounting scheme, not VAT cash accounting. Some sales will be one-off sales made for cash to clients who do not need to have a credit account: any such sales will be treated as petty cash receipts.

You may assume that all the documents have been checked and authorised.

Charlize rents an office from Habgood Properties who do not have a subsidiary (purchases) ledger account. However, because Charlize spends most of her time working on client's premises she allows another small company to use the office and its equipment (including her computer) two days a week, for which she invoices them every month. This transaction is to be recorded in a Non-trade debtors account and a Rental income account via a journal. (Rent should be treated as exempt from VAT in this case.)

The business commenced trading in January 2004. Charlize has decided to use a computerised accounting package and has asked you to help with this. (The cost of the package itself should be posted to a P & L account, since it will be upgraded every year.)

Tasks to be completed

Part 1 – Operating a computerised accounting system and carrying out computer routines

It is now 31 January 2004 and you are to complete the following tasks.

Task 1

Complete items 1 to 5 on the checklist on page 300. If necessary continue on a separate sheet of paper.

Task 2

Open your accounting package and restore the file SFE_04.003. Your password is Mf49uG4q.

Task 3

Write the appropriate code numbers on the journal slip J001 on page 301. If you think you need to set up any new main ledger accounts then do so now. Then enter the opening balances for the business into the accounting package.

Task 4

A number of invoices and credit notes are shown on pages 301 to 312. In the spaces provided on each document make a note of the customer or supplier code that you intend to use and the main ledger codes. If you think you need to set up any new main ledger accounts then do so now.

Task 5

Identify the main (nominal) ledger accounts needed, creating new ones only if necessary.

Task 6

Set up accounts for each of the suppliers.

Task 7

Enter each supplier invoice and credit note.

Task 8

Set up accounts for each of the customers.

Task 9

Enter each customer invoice and credit note.

Task 10

Back up your work using the file name SFE_04.004 (or the file name suggested by your assessor). If you back up to a floppy disk, label it appropriately.

Task 11

The following items should now be entered.

- A cash receipt shown on page 312.
- Payments to suppliers shown on page 313.
- A standing order payment to Habgood Properties, shown on page 314.
- Receipts from customers, as on the paying in slips on page 314.
- A BACS remittance advice from a customer shown on page 315.
- A petty cash slip, shown on page 315.

Task 12

Refer to the bank statement shown on page 315. If you think you need to set up any new main ledger accounts then do so now. Then reconcile the bank statement, entering any adjustments that you think are necessary.

Task 13

Write the appropriate code numbers on the journal slip J002 on page 316. If you think you need to set up any new main ledger accounts then do so now. Then enter this journal into the accounting package.

Task 14

Print the following items.

- An audit trail
- Customer statements
- Bank reconciliation
- Sales and sales returns day books
- Purchases and purchase returns day books
- Journal day book
- Subsidiary (sales ledger)
- Subsidiary (purchase ledger)
- Main ledger
- Trial balance

Task 15

On counting the petty cash you find that the amount in the tin is £64.68. Complete the petty cash reconciliation statement on page 316.

Task 16

Referring to your print-outs, complete the subsidiary ledger and control account reconciliations on page 316.

Task 17

Back up your work using the file name SFE_04.005 (or the file name suggested by your assessor). If you back up to a floppy disk, label it appropriately.

Task 18

Close down the computer, making any notes that are appropriate at item 6 on the checklist on page 300

Task 19

Charlize is worried that one of her customers will not pay and has asked you how this is done in the computerised accounting package. Write a short note for her on page 316.

Part 2 – Providing information in a word processed format

Task 20

Charlize has a number of questions for you about using computers. Look at the questions on pages 317 to 318 and write your answers using a word-processor. You should use features such as headings, bold, bullet points, tables and so on, as appropriate, following a consistent style throughout the document. Be sure to save your work with an appropriate file name. When you have finished, send your work as an email attachment to your supervisor.

Part 3 – Providing information in a spreadsheet and word processed format

Task 21

When the business started up Charlize was asked by her bank to forecast her income and expenditure for the first three months. It is now early April 2004 and the actual figures are now available. The figures are shown on page 319. Put this information into a spreadsheet and set up formulae to calculate the difference between the forecast and the actual figures. Be sure to save your work with an appropriate file name.

Task 22

Use a word processor to create a brief report for Charlize pointing out any matters that you think are significant in the figures in your spreadsheet. Be sure to save your work with an appropriate file name.

Task 23

Make a copy of your spreadsheet and word processor files as a back up. If you back up to a floppy disk, label it appropriately.

DATA FOR TASKS 1 TO 19

	CHECK LIST	Comments
1	Carry out whatever visual safety checks you think are necessary on the computer and other equipment. If you consider there are hazards around the equipment, how would you improve the situation?	
2	Is your computer stand alone or networked?	
3	Once you are content that it is safe to do so, turn on the computer and enter any password that is needed to access the system.	
4	Make a note of the names of any software packages that you will be using to complete this simulation.	
5	Note down the difficulties you encounter during your work, if any, and how you resolved them or intend to do so.	
6	When you have completed your work explain how you closed down the computer system so as not to cause any damage	

JOURNAL SLIP J001		DATE:	01/01/2004	
To post opening balances as at the start of business				
Details	**Code**	**Debit**	**Credit**	
Loan from Southfield Electrical			2500.00	
Capital			8238.30	
Ford Ka		4999.00		
Car tax		155.00		
Motor insurance		834.30		
Second-hand desk, chair, etc		750.00		
Bank deposit		4000.00		

INVOICE

Dan Industrials
Park Rise
Fenbridge
DR2 7AD
Tel 03033 952060
Fax 03033 514287

VAT Reg 520 6298 62

To: SFE Merchandising
14a, Habgood House
Dagenham Avenue
Benham
DR6 8LV

Invoice number S346219
Date/tax point 3 Jan 2004
Order number
Account number

Quantity	Description	Stock code	Unit amount £	Total £
3	Flatpack office shelving units	SH249	21.99	65.97

		Net total	65.97
		VAT	11.54
		Invoice total	77.51

Subsidiary ledger code ....

Main ledger code(s) ....

INVOICE

Rhymand Stationery Store
7 Market Street
Benham
DR6 2PL
Tel 03033 826374
Fax 03033 826375

VAT Reg 765 9257 72

Your contact is: Bill Smith

To:

SFE Merchandising
14a, Habgood House
Dagenham Avenue
Benham
DR6 8LV

Invoice number   2149
Date/tax point   10 Jan 2004
Order number
Account number

Quantity	Description	Stock code	Unit amount £	Total £
1	Box of 500 business cards	Custom	130.00	130.00

Net total	130.00
VAT	22.75
Invoice total	152.75

Subsidiary ledger code   ....
Main ledger code(s)   ....

INVOICE

The Market Research Society
15 Northburgh Street
London
EC1V 0JR
Tel 020 7490 4911 Fax 020 7490 0608

To:

Ms Charlize Veron
SFE Merchandising
14a, Habgood House
Dagenham Avenue
Benham
DR6 8LV

Invoice number	S56729
Date/tax point	01/01/2004
Membership number	MRSF6521-03

Description	Total
	£
Annual subscription for the year 2004	99.00

Invoice total 99.00

Subsidiary ledger code ....

Main ledger code(s) ....

CREDIT NOTE

Rhymand Stationery Store
7 Market Street
Benham
DR6 2PL
Tel 03033 826374
Fax 03033 826375

VAT Reg 765 9257 72

Your contact is: Bill Smith

To: SFE Merchandising
14a, Habgood House
Dagenham Avenue
Benham
DR6 8LV

Invoice number CN0214
Date/tax point 15 Jan 2004
Order number
Account number

Description	Stock code	Unit amount £	Total £
Misprinted business cards x 150		39.00	39.00

Net total	39.00
VAT	6.83
Total credit	45.83

Subsidiary ledger code ....

Main ledger code(s) ....

Softwac

INVOICE

Hot House
25 Parma Crescent
London SW11 1LT
Tel 020 7652 2221
Fax 020 7652 6508

Website: www.softwac.co.uk

Email: sales@softwac.co.uk

VAT Reg 760 9259 10

To:

SFE Merchandising 14a, Habgood House Dagenham Avenue Benham DR6 8LV

Invoice number   10863
Date/tax point   20-01-04
Order number
Account number   SFEMER01

Qty	Description Stock code	Unit amount £	Total £
1	Desktop PC to your spec	1224.80	1224.80
1	Sage Instant Accounts V.10	98.91	98.91

Net total	1323.71
VAT	231.65
Invoice total	1555.36

Subsidiary ledger code   ....

Main ledger code(s)   ....

INVOICE

SFE Merchandising
14a, Habgood House
Dagenham Avenue
Benham DR6 8LV
Tel 03033 542697 Fax
03033 542697

VAT Reg 524 3764 51

To: Q Q Stores
23 Queens Road
Winnesh
DR2 7PJ

Invoice number 10001
Date/tax point 06/01/2004

Description	Unit amount £	Total £
2 days consultancy, 5 to 6 January 2004	300.00	600.00
	Net total	600.00
	VAT	105.00
	Invoice total	705.00

Subsidiary ledger code ....
Main ledger code(s) ....

INVOICE

SFE Merchandising
14a, Habgood House
Dagenham Avenue
Benham DR6 8LV
Tel 03033 542697 Fax
03033 542697

VAT Reg 524 3764 51

To:

whitehill Superstores
28, whitehill Park
Benham
DR6 5LM

Invoice number   10002
Date/tax point   16/01/2004

Description	Unit amount £	Total £
5 days consultancy, 12 to 16 January 2004	300.00	1500.00

Net total	1500.00
VAT	262.50
Invoice total	1762.50

Subsidiary ledger code   ....

Main ledger code(s)   ....

INVOICE

SFE Merchandising
14a, Habgood House
Dagenham Avenue
Benham DR6 8LV
Tel 03033 542697 Fax
03033 542697

VAT Reg 524 3764 51

To:

Polygon Stores
Grobler Street
Parrish
DR7 4TT

Invoice number   10003
Date/tax point   21/01/2004

Description	Unit amount £	Total £
3 days consultancy, 19 to 21 January 2004	300.00	900.00

Net total	900.00
VAT	157.50
Invoice total	1057.50

Subsidiary ledger code   ....

Main ledger code(s)   ....

INVOICE

SFE Merchandising
14a, Habgood House
Dagenham Avenue
Benham DR6 8LV
Tel 03033 542697 Fax
03033 542697

VAT Reg 524 3764 51

To:

Q Q Stores
23 Queens Road
Winnesh
DR2 7PJ

Invoice number   10004
Date/tax point   23/01/2004

Description	Unit amount £	Total £
1 days consultancy, 23 January 2004	300.00	300.00

Net total	300.00
VAT	52.50
Invoice total	352.50

Subsidiary ledger code ....

Main ledger code(s) ....

INVOICE

SFE Merchandising
14a, Habgood House
Dagenham Avenue
Benham DR6 8LV
Tel 03033 542697 Fax
03033 542697

VAT Reg 524 3764 51

To:
Dagwell Enterprises
Dagwell House
Hopchurch Road
Winnesh
DR2 6LT

Invoice number   10005
Date/tax point   29/01/2004

Description	Unit amount £	Total £
4 days consultancy, 26 to 29 January 2004	300.00	1200.00

Net total	1200.00
VAT	210.00
Invoice total	1410.00

Subsidiary ledger code   ....

Main ledger code(s)   ....

CREDIT NOTE

SFE Merchandising
14a, Habgood House
Dagenham Avenue
Benham DR6 8LV
Tel 03033 542697 Fax
03033 542697

VAT Reg 524 3764 51

To: | Whitehill Superstores
28, whitehill Park
Benham
DR6 5LM

Invoice number   CN001
Date/tax point   19/01/2004

Description	Unit amount £	Total £
Initial consultancy free (0.5 days, 12 January 2004)	300.00	150.00

Net total	150.00
VAT	26.25
Credit total	176.25

Subsidiary ledger code   ....

Main ledger code(s)   ....

CASH SALE

SFE Merchandising
14a, Habgood House
Dagenham Avenue
Benham DR6 8LV
Tel 03033 542697 Fax
03033 542697

VAT Reg 524 3764 51

To: Cash sales
(Whites Bookstores)

Invoice number 10006
Date/tax point 08/01/2004

Description	Unit amount £	Total £
2 hours consultancy, paid for in cash	37.50	75.00
	Net total	75.00
	VAT	13.13
	Invoice total	88.13

Enter via a journal with reference 10006

Date   15 January 2004

Payee

Dan Industrials

£   77.51

000001

Date   18 January 2004

Payee

Rhymand Stationery

£   106.92

000002

Date   24 January 2004

Payee

Softwac

£   1555.36

000003

Standing Order Schedule

Day in month	Payee	£
25	Habgood Properties	200.00

Cheques etc.			Brought forward £					
						£50		
						£20		
						£10		
						£5		
						£2		
						£1		
						50p		
						20p		
						Silver		
			Polygon Stores	1057	50	Bronze		
						Total Cash		
						Cardnet		
							1057	50
						Cheques etc.		
Carried forward £			Carried forward £	1057	50	Total £	1057	50

Date   23/01/2004   500001   FOR SFE MERCHANDISING   06325143

Cheques etc.			Brought forward £					
						£50		
						£20		
						£10		
						£5		
						£2		
						£1		
						50p		
						20p		
						Silver		
			Whitehill Superstores	1568	25	Bronze		
						Total Cash		
						Cardnet		
			QQ Stores	750	00	Cheques etc.	2318	25
Carried forward £			Carried forward £	2318	25	Total £	2318	25

Date   27/01/2004   500002   FOR SFE MERCHANDISING   06325143

DAGWELL ENTERPRISES

Dagwell House
Hopchurch Road
Winnesh
DR2 6LT

BACS remittance advice

The following amount will be remitted to the bank account of

SFE Merchandising

on

31 January 2004

in payment of the following invoice(s)

10005

Amount: £1410.00

PETTY CASH PAYMENT SLIP   **Date:** 9 January 2004   **PCP001**

Description	£
Train fare	23.45

BANK STATEMENT	SFE MERCHANDISING						
			paid out £		paid in £	balance £	
date	details						
2004	Opening balance					0	00
1 JAN	DEPOSIT				4000 00	4000	00
17 JAN		000001	77	51		3922	49
18 JAN	INSURANCE	DD	43	21		3879	28
24 JAN	SUNDRY CREDIT	500001			1057 50	4936	78
25 JAN	STANDING ORDER		200	00		4736	78
26 JAN		000003	1555	36		3181	42
27 JAN	CHARGES JAN 2004						
	SERVICE CHARGE		6	51		3174	91
	TOTAL PAYMENTS/RECEIPTS		1882	59	5057 50		

JOURNAL SLIP J002		DATE:	31/01/2004	
Details		Code	Debit	Credit
Non-trade debtors			80.00	
Rental income				80.00
Being charge for share of office				
space in January 2004				

PETTY CASH RECONCILIATION		
Cash in hand as per print out		
Cash in petty cash tin		
Difference		
Reconciled?	Yes ?	No ?

SALES LEDGER CONTROL ACCOUNT RECONCILIATION		
Total of outstanding sales ledger balances		
Total of sales ledger control account		
Difference		
Reconciled?	Yes ?	No ?

PURCHASE LEDGER CONTROL ACCOUNT RECONCILIATION		
Total of outstanding purchase ledger balances		
Total of purchase ledger control account		
Difference		
Reconciled?	Yes ?	No ?

Note for Charlize concerning customer non-payment

DATA FOR TASK 20

Questions from Charlize about computer issues

1. I have installed some AntiVirus and Internet security software and have been seeing some funny messages on my screen, two of which I've managed to capture by doing a 'print screen'.

   For this one I just clicked on OK

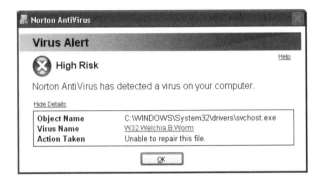

   For this one I left the 'recommended' option selected and clicked on OK.

   Did I do the right thing? Why do these messages appear?

2. All of my customers are large companies. Do you think I need to register under the Data Protection Act?

3. As you know I've agreed to share the office and the computer with another small company, and this helps to keep the cost down, but I'm a bit worried about keeping my data safe and confidential, and I am also wondering whether there are any laws I need to know about such as health and safety. Do you have any advice on this? Just brief details will do.

4. I've received the following email, and I'm very worried about this. However, when I click on the link to fill in my details I just get a message saying the page can't be displayed. What should I do about this?

-----Original Message-----
From: Barclays [mailto:users-billing2@barclays.co.uk]
Sent: 31 January 2004 12:24
To: charlize.veron@sfemerchandising.co.uk |
Subject: official Notice for aII users of Barclays IBank.

Details Confirmation

> **SECURITY ALERT: Please read this important message**
>
> Our new security system will help you to avoid frequently fraud transactions and to keep your investments in safety.
>
> Due to technical update we ask you to confirm your online banking membership details. Please fill the form below.
>
> **Please follow the link below to fill the form "Details Confirmation":**
>
> http://www.personal.barclays.co.uk/goto/pfsolb_login

5. I make a full backup every day, but this takes ages and it is like watching paint dry. Do you have any recommendations about this?

6. Finally, am I right in thinking that once all my invoices and so on are entered into the accounting package I don't need to keep the paper copies?

DATA FOR TASKS 21 TO 23

Forecast for the period January 2004 to March 2004

	£
Sales	27,000
Net rent	360
Travel and motor expenses	500
Subscriptions	99
Other expenses	500

Actual figures for the period January 2004 to March 2004

	£
Sales	21,000
Net rent	360
Travel and motor expenses	99
Subscriptions	823
Other expenses	1,000

SKILLS BASED ASSESSMENT 3

UNIT 21

ANSWERS

ANSWERS TO TASKS 1 – 19

No answer is provided for tasks that are specific to your own work environment or that simply involve creating backup files.

Task 3

You should have entered company details for SFE Merchandising – you can find them on any sales invoice. When preparing to enter the journal you will find that you need to create a new account for Motor Insurance. Use the new nominal account wizard. We suggest the account type 'Overheads' and the category 'Motor Expenses', in which case the account number will be 7301.

Task 4

Obviously, all purchase invoices and credit notes are posted to the Purchases Ledger Control Account (2100) and all sales invoices and credit notes to the Sales Ledger Control Account (1100).

The other codes that we would use are indicated in the following extract from an audit trail (PI = purchase invoice; PC = purchase credit note; SI = sales invoice; SC = sales credit note).

Type	Reference	Date	Subsidiary ledger	Main ledger
PI	S346219	03/01/2004	DANIN001	0040
PI	2149	10/01/2004	RHYMA001	7500
PI	S56729	01/01/2004	MARKE001	8200
PC	CN0214	15/01/2004	RHYMA001	7500
PI	10863	20/01/2004	SOFTW001	0030
PI	10863	20/01/2004	SOFTW001	8202
SI	10001	06/01/2004	QQSTO001	4000
SI	10002	16/01/2004	WHITE001	4000
SI	10003	21/01/2004	POLYG001	4000
SI	10004	23/01/2004	QQSTO001	4000
SI	10005	29/01/2004	DAGWE001	4000
SC	CN001	19/01/2004	WHITE001	4000

Task 5

You should not need to set up any new nominal accounts to post the invoices, but if you did so they should be of the correct type and category.

Task 6, 8

We recommend that you use alphanumeric account codes in the subsidiary ledgers, consisting of the first five letters of the name and the digits 001, for example DANIN001.

Tasks 7, 9

The invoice from the Market Research Society should have the tax code T2, because professional subscriptions are exempt from VAT (see Chapter 9). The invoice from Softwac should be coded to account 0030 for the computer, and account 8202 for the software.

Task 11

Note the following points.

- The cash receipt should be posted as a journal with the invoice number (10006) as the reference: Debit Sales £75.00, Debit Sales Tax Control Account 13.13, Credit Petty Cash £88.13.

- You can use the Bank ... Supplier ... Pay in Full option to post the payments to suppliers. Note that the payment to Rhymand Stationery Store is made net of the credit note.

- The standing order should be posted using the Bank ... Payment option. You are told in the scenario that rent is exempt from VAT, so the tax code is T2. (Note. Just in case you are wondering about this, or have different experience, it is in fact possible for a landlord to make an election to charge VAT on rent, and some landlords do this, but this is well beyond the scope of your current studies.)

- Note that the second payment slip includes receipts from two separate customers, but you should give both receipts the same reference (500002). The payment from Q Q Stores does not exactly match the outstanding invoices, so you should allocate the £750 to invoices in date order.

- Train fares are zero-rated for VAT so the tax code to use is T0.

Task 12

You will need to set up a new nominal ledger account for Bank Charges (Type – 'Overheads', Category – 'Bank Charges and Interest'). There are two items that have not yet passed through the bank account: cheque number 000002 and receipt number 500002. There are two adjustments to post, one for insurance and one for bank charges.

Task 13

You should not have needed to set up any new accounts. The tax code for the journal is T2 (as noted above, rent is VAT exempt in this scenario).

Task 14

You should arrive at the following trial balance if you enter everything correctly.

	Debit	Credit
Office Equipment	1224.80	
Furniture and Fixtures	815.97	
Motor Vehicles	4999.00	
Debtors Control Account	307.50	
Non-Trade Debtors	80.00	
Bank Current Account	6814.24	
Petty Cash	64.68	
Creditors Control Account		99.00
Sales Tax Control Account		774.38
Purchase Tax Control Account	259.11	
Loan from Southfield Electrical		2500.00
Capital		8238.30
Sales		4425.00
Rental Income		80.00
Rent	200.00	
Motor Tax	155.00	
Motor Insurance	834.30	
Travel	23.45	
Office Stationery	91.00	
Bank Charges	6.51	
Subscriptions	99.00	
Insurance	43.21	
Computer Software	98.91	
TOTAL	16116.68	16116.68

Task 15

There should be no difference between the amount in the petty cash account and the amount in the books.

Task 16

Again, there should be no differences.

Task 19

Note for Charlize concerning customer non-payment

Accounting packages generally have special procedures to help with commonly occurring events, such as non-payment by a customer. In Sage there is a 'Write Off, Refund and Returns' wizard, which takes the user step by step by through the process and then posts all the necessary accounting entries.

Task 20

To: **Charlize Veron**
From: **Your Name**
Subject: **Computer issues**
Date: **31 January 2004**

Thank you for your message. I have answered your questions as best I can below, but please feel free to raise any additional queries if you need more information.

AntiVirus and Internet Security alerts

I am very pleased that you have chosen to install this software, and it is clearly working to protect your computer and its data.

In the case of the first message you had no option but to click on OK, but if you look carefully at the message you will note that you are told that it was not possible to repair the virus.

This may be because your anti-virus software is not up to date or there may be another reason.

I suggest that you visit the website of the anti-virus software company and look up the virus named here (W32.Welchia.B.Worm). You are likely to find details of the virus and instructions on what if anything you need to do. These companies usually provide free tools for removing viruses

You did exactly the right thing with the second message. Your Internet Security software includes what is known as a firewall, which prevents unauthorised persons or programs gaining access to your computer via your Internet connection. It does, however, give you the option of allowing third party access, because there may be occasions when you want to permit this.

As you say, if in doubt it is always best to choose the 'recommended' option.

Data Protection Act notification

The Data Protection Act is concerned with what is known as 'personal data', which is data about living individuals. Since your customers are companies, and since you do not have any employees at present, there may well be no need for you to register (or 'notify'), although there is nothing to prevent you from doing so if you wish.

I suggest that you look at the guidance on the relevant government website (http://www.informationcommissioner.gov.uk). This includes an online questionnaire, which will help you decide whether to notify the Information Commissioner about the data that you process.

Even if you do not notify you are still expected to follow the eight data protection principles. These say that data must be:

- fairly and lawfully processed;
- processed for limited purposes;
- adequate, relevant and not excessive;
- accurate;
- not kept for longer than is necessary;
- processed in line with your rights;
- secure; and,
- not transferred to countries without adequate protection.

Sharing your office: data security

The most obvious measures that you can take are the sort of things you would do to keep your own house secure and protect its contents.

- Make sure that the office is kept locked when it is unattended

- Make sure that there are suitable fire precautions

- Stress to the person you share with the importance of behaving in a safety-conscious manner when in the office and using equipment.

Specifically regarding your data, I very strongly recommend that you set up user accounts on your computer. You should have at least one account for yourself and one for the other user. You may need to upgrade your operating system before you can do this (for example from Windows XP Home edition to Windows XP Professional), but it would not be too expensive and it would certainly be worthwhile.

User accounts allow you to restrict what individual users can and cannot do (for instance you can stop the other user from installing any new software) and what files individual users can and cannot access.

You should set a password for your own user account(s) and make sure that all passwords are kept secret. Above all don't write them down on a Post-it note stuck to the computer!

A good password is at least eight characters long and consists of both letters (a mixture of capitals and small letters) and numbers. You should change your password at least every six months, and immediately if you suspect that someone else has discovered it.

For extra security you can also set passwords for some programs (for instance an accounting package) and for individual files. If you do that, make sure you use a different password to the one that you use to access the main system.

Sharing your office: health and safety

Since you are not an employer you are not, in theory, responsible for the health and safety of anyone other than yourself. However, it is very much in your own interests that you follow the good practice set out in legislation such as the Display Screen Regulations 1992.

These regulations cover matters such as desk layout, sitting position, and the importance of regular breaks (stretching your legs), and if you follow the simple guidelines you will find that you both work more efficiently and feel better while you are doing so.

Email from Barclays

This is NOT an email from Barclays bank, in fact, but what is sometimes known as a hoax. It is the most dangerous type of hoax because the perpetrators are attempting to discover your Internet banking details.

You should not click on the link again, and certainly not forward the email to anyone else. The best thing to do with it is to delete it.

I suggest you look at your bank's website, which almost certainly contains further information and advice about these hoaxes. As a general rule banks do not contact their customers by email in any circumstances.

Backups

It sounds as if you are making a full backup of your entire computer system each time, so I can understand why it is taking a long time. It is unlikely that you need to backup the entire system every day, but you should operate a daily routine of backing up any new files that you have created and any files that you have altered during the day.

It is practically impossible for a small business to have a backup system that guarantees that there will never be any loss of data, but a regime such as the following will keep any loss of data to a minimum.

You do not say which backup tool you are using, but it is usually possible to configure these so that (for example) they only backup data that has changed since the last backup, or they only backup specific folders and sub-folders.

- I recommend that you save all files that you wish to keep safe in sub-folders within the Windows folder called My Documents. Transfer any that you may have saved elsewhere to this location – you can make as many sub-folders as you wish.

- As soon as possible, once you have everything in one place, you should make a separate copy of your My Documents folder and its sub-folders on a removable disk such as a CD-R. Be sure to label the CD-R in a way that makes it easy to identify if it is needed: the date is usually enough. This disk should be stored away from the office, in case of fire or theft.

- You should then schedule your backup software to do a daily backup of your My Documents folder. I would be happy to help you with this if you wish. The computer can do backups automatically, overnight: there is no need for you to sit and watch, so long as you leave the computer on.

- On a weekly or monthly basis (depending on how much new work you create each day), you should make another copy of your latest backup on a new removable disk. Again, these disks should be properly labelled and stored away from the office, in case of fire or theft.

- Particular care should be taken with accounting data, since this is vital to the smooth-running of your business. Most accounting packages encourage you to take a back-up when you attempt to close the program down, and I recommend that you take this option whenever you have made new entries.

Finally, I recommend that you use Auto-recover facilities in any programs that offer them – this ensures that a temporary backup is saved every few minutes while you are working on a document, and helps to guard against power failure or unexpected problems.

Document retention

I am afraid that company law and tax law requires you to keep most accounting records for a period of at least six years.

It may not be necessary to keep a paper copy of accounting ledgers, so long as you have backup files that would allow them to be recreated and printed out again if necessary, but you should certainly keep suppliers' invoices, bank statements and so on for at least the minimum period.

Task 21

Here is our spreadsheet.

	A	B	C	D	E
1		Budget	Actual	Variance	
2		£	£	£	
3	Sales	27,000	21,000	-6,000	Adverse
4					
5	Net rent	360	360	0	
6	Travel and motor expenses	500	823	323	Adverse
7	Subscriptions	99	99	0	
8	Other expenses	500	1,000	500	Adverse
9		1,459	2,282		
10					
11	Net profit	25,541	18,718	-6,823	Adverse

Here are the formulae, just in case it is not obvious

	A	B	C	D	E
1		Budget	Actual	Variance	
2		£	£	£	
3	Sales	27000	21000	=C3-B3	Adverse
4					
5	Net rent	360	360	=C5-B5	
6	Travel and motor expenses	500	823	=C6-B6	Adverse
7	Subscriptions	99	99	=C7-B7	
8	Other expenses	500	1000	=C8-B8	Adverse
9		=SUM(B5:B8)	=SUM(C5:C8)		✚
10					
11	Net profit	=B3-B9	=C3-C9	=C11-B11	Adverse

Task 22

Here is the report that we would have written.

To: Charlize Veron
From: Your Name
Subject: Computer issues
Date: 2 April 2004

Based on the figures you provided here is a comparison of your budgeted and actual income and expenditure for the first three months of your business's operation.

	Budget	Actual	Variance	
	£	£	£	
Sales	27,000	21,000	–6,000	Adverse
Net rent	360	360	0	
Travel and motor expenses	500	823	323	Adverse
Subscriptions	99	99	0	
Other expenses	500	1,000	500	Adverse
	1,459	2,282		
Net profit	25,541	18,718	–6,823	Adverse

This apparently shows that you have made nearly £7,000 less than you anticipated, but please don't be downhearted about this. A net profit of nearly £19,000 is very impressive for the first three months of any business.

The following matters also need to be taken into consideration.

■ Your budgeted sales were clearly over-optimistic, but that is probably because you did not take into account the amount of time you would need to spend on winning new customers and on general administration.

■ It is possible that travel and motor expenses include some large amounts that have been paid in advance (for example road tax and insurance) and cover the whole year, not just three months.

■ It is difficult to comment on the reasons for the £500 extra expenditure on 'Other expenses' without knowing exactly what these are. Again I suspect that there are at least some amounts that should be spread over a longer period than 3 months, for example stocks of business stationery.

I suggest that I prepare a further report after my next visit so that I can look into these matters in more detail and help you prepare more realistic figures for the remainder of the year.

INDEX